Leading the Learning School

Raising Standards of Achievement by Improving the Quality of Learning and Teaching

Colin Weatherley

Published by Network Educational Press Ltd.
PO Box 635
Stafford
ST16 1BF

First Published 2000
© Colin Weatherley 2000

ISBN 1 85539 070 1

Every effort has been made to contact copyright holders and the publishers
apologise for any omissions which they will be pleased to rectify at the
earliest opportunity.

Extracts from the West Lothian Headteacher Conference included by
permission of the West Lothian Council Education Services.

Series Editor: Prof Tim Brighouse
Project Managers: Chris Griffin & Peter Wrapson
Design & layout: Neil Hawkins, Network Educational Press Ltd.
Illustrations by Barking Dog

Printed in Great Britain by
MPG Books Ltd., Bodmin, Cornwall

Foreword

A teacher's task is much more ambitious than it used to be and demands a focus on the subtleties of teaching and learning and on the emerging knowledge of school improvement.

This is what this series is about.

Teaching can be a very lonely activity. The time-honoured practice of a single teacher working alone in the classroom is still the norm; yet to operate alone is, in the end, to become isolated and impoverished. This series addresses two issues – the need to focus on practical and useful ideas connected with teaching and learning and the wish thereby to provide some sort of an antidote to the loneliness of the long-distance teacher who is daily berated by an anxious society.

Teachers flourish best when, in key stage teams or departments (or more rarely whole schools), their talk is predominantly about teaching and learning and where, unconnected with appraisal, they are privileged to observe each other teach; to plan and review their work together; and to practise the habit of learning from each other new teaching techniques. But how does this state of affairs arise? Is it to do with the way staffrooms are physically organized so that the walls bear testimony to interesting articles and in the corner there is a dedicated computer tuned to 'conferences' about SEN, school improvement, the teaching of English etc., and whether, in consequence, the teacher leaning over the shoulder of the enthusiastic IT colleague sees the promise of interesting practice elsewhere? Has the primary school cracked it when it organizes successive staff meetings in different classrooms and invites the 'host' teacher to start the meeting with a 15 minute exposition of their classroom organization and management? Or is it the same staff sharing, on a rota basis, a slot on successive staff meeting agenda when each in turn reviews a new book they have used with their class? And what of the whole school which now uses 'active' and 'passive' concerts of carefully chosen music as part of their accelerated learning techniques?

It is of course well understood that even excellent teachers feel threatened when first they are observed. Hence the epidemic of trauma associated with OFSTED. The constant observation of the teacher in training seems like that of the learner driver. Once you have passed your test and can drive unaccompanied, you do. You often make lots of mistakes and sometimes get into bad habits. Woe betide, however, the back seat driver who tells you so. In the same way, the new teacher quickly loses the habit of observing others and being observed. So how do we get a confident, mutual observation debate going? One school I know found a simple and therefore brilliant solution. The Head of the History Department asked that a young colleague plan lessons for her – the Head of Department – to teach. This lesson she then taught, and was observed by the young colleague. There was subsequent discussion, in which the young teacher asked,

> *"Why did you divert the question and answer session I had planned?"*

and was answered by,

> *"Because I could see that I needed to arrest the attention of the group by the window with some 'hands-on' role play, etc."*

This lasted an hour and led to a once-a-term repeat discussion which, in the end, was adopted by the whole school. The whole school subsequently changed the pattern of its meetings to consolidate extended debate about teaching and learning. The two teachers claimed that, because one planned and the other taught, both were implicated but neither alone was responsible or felt 'got at'.

So there are practices which are both practical and more likely to make teaching a rewarding and successful activity. They can, as it were, increase the likelihood of a teacher surprising the pupils into understanding or doing something they did not think they could do rather than simply entertaining them or worse still occupying them. There are ways of helping teachers judge the best method of getting pupil expectation just ahead of self-esteem.

This series focuses on straightforward interventions which individual schools and teachers use to make life more rewarding for themselves and those they teach. Teachers deserve nothing less, for they are the architects of tomorrow's society, and society's ambition for what they achieve increases as each year passes.

Professor Tim Brighouse

Acknowledgements

I should like to express particular thanks to the following people:

Chris Dickinson, whose inspirational presentation at the 1998 West Lothian Headteachers' Conference stimulated me to write this book.

Bruce Bonney, Jack Drury, Pete Fox, Rick Gordon and Tom Julius of the *Critical Skills Programme* Leadership Community, USA, which have created such an immensely powerful learning, teaching and management programme.

Professors Sally Brown, John MacBeath and Mary Simpson, who have been a source of inspiration to me over many years.

Chris Griffin and Peter Wrapson, who have given unstintingly of their editorial expertise and energy.

Dorothy Weatherley, who first suggested that I should write a book (or words to that effect!) and then showed great fortitude and good humour in living with the consequences.

Colin Weatherley
November, 2000

Contents

LEADING THE LEARNING SCHOOL
THE BIG PICTURE

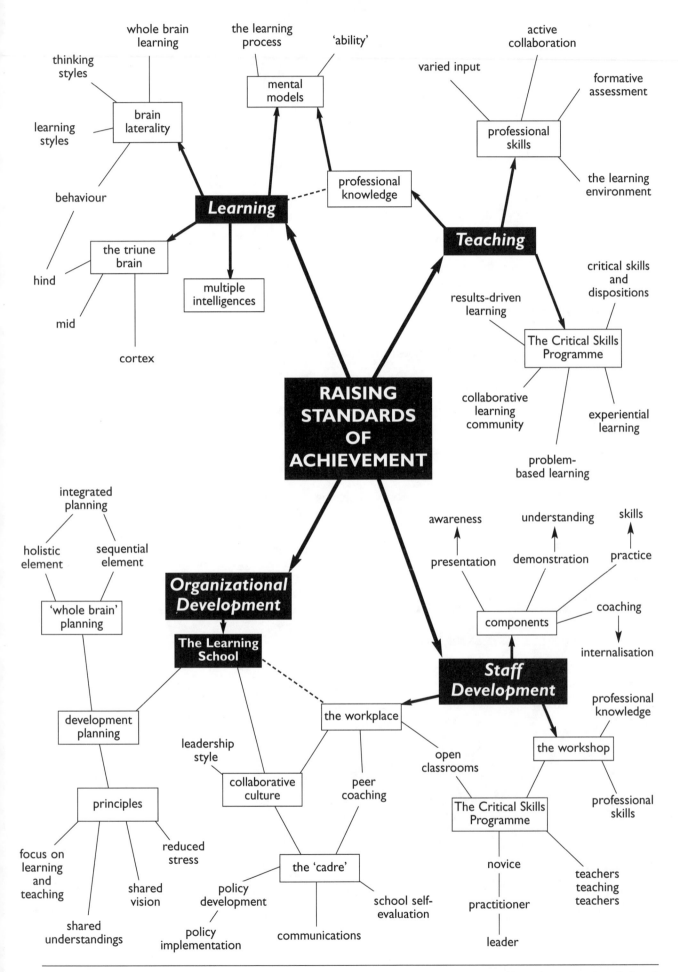

Introduction

> **This introduction describes the purpose, theme and format of the book.**
>
> ➡ **The purpose - to provide a practical guide to effective school management based on up-to-date knowledge about learning.**
>
> ➡ **The theme - that there is now ample, authoritative research evidence to show that effective programmes to raise standards of achievement must:**
>
> - **focus continually on improving the quality of learning and teaching;**
>
> - **rigorously apply key principles of learning to the processes of teaching, staff development and organizational development;**
>
> - **comprehensively address all of these issues.**
>
> ➡ **The format - is also based on key principles of learning. It allows the reader to glean relevant information quickly and easily, without having to read from cover to cover in a logical sequence.**

Each of the four sections starts with a visual diagram as well as a text summary of the main issues to be dealt with in that section. There is also a summary of the previous and succeeding sections so that each section is placed in context and made as free-standing as possible. This inevitably leads to some repetition but makes the book more useful as a practical guide.

The diagram opposite is a composite visual outline of the main issues that the book deals with as a whole. These are also summarised on pages 11-13.

One of the most important conclusions of modern brain research is that the two halves of our brain process information in quite different ways. One - usually the *left hemisphere* - processes language in a logical, critical, sequential fashion. The other - usually the *right hemisphere* - is more concerned with relationships, creativity and the holistic 'big picture'. Most of us have a preference for thinking with one or the other hemisphere, but for maximum effectiveness we should use both hemispheres in an integrated way. This is often referred to as *'whole brain' learning*.

The combination of visual (holistic) and text (sequential) summaries at the beginning of each of the main sections caters for different thinking preferences and hopefully will encourage whole brain thinking and learning. The use of sketches throughout the book is also designed to appeal to the right side of the brain.

The main stimulus to write this book came from a two-day conference for some 150 headteachers and other senior educationists in West Lothian, Scotland, in May 1998. The conference was titled **Raising Standards by Improving the Quality of Learning and Teaching** and the four speakers were:

- Professor David Perkins - Co-Director of Harvard University's *Teaching for Understanding Project*;

- Maggie Farrar - Principal of The City of Birmingham's *University of the First Age*;

- Professor John MacBeath - Co-Director of the Strathclyde University/London Institute of Education *Improving School Effectiveness Project* (Professor MacBeath now holds the chair of Educational Leadership at Cambridge University);

- Chris Dickinson - author of the best-selling *Effective Learning Activities* in the Network Press *School Effectiveness Series*.

The conference made a deep impression on all who attended. Most of the issues which it covered are dealt with in some depth in *Sections One - Four*. However, it is also worth giving a flavour at this point of the collective impact that the speakers made, through a selection of quotes from discussion group reporters in the final plenary session (emphases added).

> **'RAISING STANDARDS BY IMPROVING THE QUALITY OF LEARNING AND TEACHING'**
>
> **Quotation 1**. 'We have been made aware that many of our current actions and decisions are based on *outdated mental models*...a greater understanding of *brain functioning* should help our staff to improve their teaching approaches.'
>
> **Quotation 2**. 'We need to keep more up-to-date with current knowledge about learning... We need to design *more appropriate learning tasks* and to provide a rich curriculum which caters for *different learning needs and preferences.*'
>
> **Quotation 3**. 'We need to promote a culture which enables us to focus our management energies more effectively onto *supporting classroom learning.*'
>
> **Quotation 4**. 'We were struck by the potential effectiveness of the *staff development model* you described... Teachers need to see each other teach more often and to engage in *peer coaching* so that staff development becomes part of the normal school day. There are significant organizational implications here, for schools and the authority as a whole.'
>
> **Quotation 5**. 'The organization of the school should promote *collaboration* and the *sharing of ideas.*'

It is clear from these comments that the conference speakers had convinced this large group of senior education managers that effective programmes to raise standards of achievement in our schools will need to address all of the following issues:

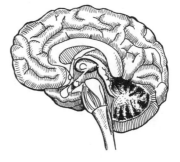

- **improving teachers' professional knowledge** - especially in relation to *brain functioning and the learning process;*

- **improving teachers' professional skills** - by enabling them to use this knowledge to design *more effective learning activities* and *improve their classroom practice;*

- **promoting effective staff development programmes** - which enable teachers to improve their classroom practice by internalising new knowledge through *peer coaching* and other means of *in-school support;*

- **re-examining organizational issues** - so as to promote 'learning schools' where the emphasis is on *collaboration* and *self-evaluation* and the permanent, overarching management priority is to improve *learning and teaching.*

These, then, are the main issues that the book addresses. But two further points require emphasis.

1. These issues are closely interdependent

For example, in-service training to improve teachers' professional knowledge will be of little benefit if these same teachers are not then given time and opportunity to *internalise* this knowledge so that it impacts permanently and positively on their classroom practice and other professional skills.

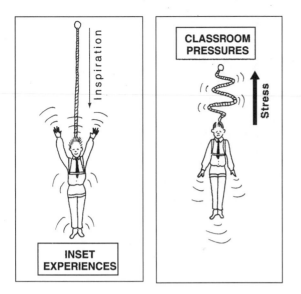

There are too many cases where an enthusiastic response to an in-service course has produced an initial change in practice, followed by a fairly rapid retreat towards the previous status quo as the everyday pressures of the classroom have kicked in. This has been called 'the bungee rope syndrome'!

Teachers, therefore, need plenty of in-school support from colleagues to resist the bungee rope effect. This is likely to require some fundamental changes to the organizational structures and processes of the school. And this in turn has significant implications for the relationship between individual schools and their education authority.

2. Principles are indivisible

The contention throughout the book is that effective programmes to raise standards of achievement in schools must be based on the application of key principles of learning to management procedures *at all levels*, from classroom to whole-school management. In other words - ***education should be a learning service in every sense and at every level.***

Because of this emphasis on applying the same principles of learning at all levels of management, there is a good deal of deliberate overlap between the sections. In particular, a number of significant quotes from the literature on learning and school improvement are used repeatedly to emphasise the 'indivisibility of principles' principle.

One of the most persuasive definitions of a learning school is that given by Peter Holly and Geoff Southworth in **The Developing School** (*1989*). The content and format of this book closely reflect this description, as follows:

> 'In the Learning School:
>
> ● the focus is on children and their learning; (*Section One*)
>
> ● individual teachers are encouraged to be continuing learners themselves; (*Sections One and Two*)
>
> ● the group of teachers (and sometimes others) who constitute the 'staff' is encouraged to collaborate by learning with and from each other; (*Section Three*)
>
> ● the school (i.e. all those people who constitute the 'school') learns its way forward. The school as an organization is a 'learning system'; (*Section Four*)
>
> ● the headteacher is the leading learner.' (*Sections One - Four inclusive!*)

Adapted from **The Developing School***, Holly, P & Southworth, G (Falmer Press, 1989)*

Summary

Section One: Learning consists of a single chapter -

Chapter 1: Key Principles of Learning. It outlines some important recent discoveries about the brain and learning and identifies 13 key principles to guide the design and practice of learning and teaching.

The section looks at the issues of *whole brain learning; styles of thinking and learning*; and *multiple intelligences*, as well as the concept of *the triune brain* and its implications for the kinds of classroom and whole-school environments which will best motivate children and promote learning for understanding.

It concludes with an analysis of two widely held 'outdated mental models' (see 'Quotation 1' on page 8), which can have harmful effects on classroom relationships and undermine the effectiveness of teachers' practice. These are:

- the concept of *ability* - as used, for example, in the term 'mixed ability';

- the nature of *the learning process.*

Section Two: Teaching contains two chapters.

Chapter 2: Key Principles of Teaching - looks at the general implications of the principles of learning identified in Chapter 1 for the design of learning activities and the improvement of classroom practice. Four main issues are addressed:

- *managing the learning environment* - providing challenge with support; optimising levels of stress; raising self-esteem; engaging positive emotions and attention;

- *providing varied and stimulating input* - catering for different styles of thinking and learning, and multiple intelligences;

- *designing active, collaborative learning experiences* - to develop neural networks; encourage 'understanding through performance'; promote meaning and memory;

- *using formative assessment* - to consolidate and differentiate new neural links through timely and accurate feedback; review and reflection; self-, peer- and teacher-assessment.

Chapter 3: The Critical Skills Programme - describes an outstanding teaching programme which addresses all of the above issues in a practical and highly effective way. 'Critical Skills' developed out of a partnership between educationists and business leaders in New Hampshire, USA in 1981. It has a firm base in up-to-date learning theory, a heavy emphasis on practical 'tools' for classroom use, and a strong commitment to involve practising teachers in training other teachers.

Section Three: Staff Development again contains a single chapter -

Chapter 4: Promoting Effective Teaching. The theme here is that the same learning principles which should guide the design and teaching of learning activities for *pupils* should also underpin the design and provision of staff development activities for *teachers*. In other words, if teachers are to deepen their knowledge of *learning* and internalise this knowledge to improve their *teaching*, their own professional development experiences must firmly address the teaching issues covered in Chapter 2.

Bruce Joyce and Beverly Showers are the leading international authorities in this field. They have analysed effective and ineffective staff development programmes over many years in terms of their components and their impact. From their research they have produced an insightful and potentially highly effective model which the West Lothian headteachers referred to in 'Quotation 4' on page 8. Key aspects of this model are described in both Chapters 4 and 5.

Joyce and Showers have incorporated two important concepts into their model. These are:

i) the distinction between *workshop* (INSET) and *workplace* (the classroom);

ii) *peer coaching*, which enables colleagues to provide critical support for each other through the demanding transition from workshop to workplace. The implications of these concepts are discussed.

Section Four: Organizational Development - contains two chapters, each dealing with a different aspect of this crucial but complex issue. As Chris Dickinson pointed out at the aforementioned West Lothian conference:

> 'We frequently ask teachers to do new things in old contexts - that is, we attend to curriculum and staff development aspects without addressing key aspects of organizational development. It's a bit like asking someone to bake a cake on a spit!'

The central argument in both chapters is that a learning school must be consciously managed according to the principles of learning identified in Chapter 1. This argument is then taken forward by means of an analogy between a *learning organization* and a *learning organism*.

Chapter 5: Creating a Collaborative Culture - outlines the crucial importance of such a culture in promoting improvements in learning and teaching throughout a school. It describes how collaboration can be promoted by applying the following principles of learning to staff management:

● using *the triune brain* model to help make stress more controllable;

● promoting understanding through *action and reflection*;

- creating communication systems that value the full range of *multiple intelligences* and cater for *different styles of learning and thinking;*

There is also a particular focus on the kinds of organizational structures and processes that will facilitate *self-evaluation; effective communications;* and *collaborative policy development and implementation.* These are exemplified in a case study showing how *Critical Skills Programme* materials and methods (Chapter 3) can be applied very effectively to create a collaborative school culture.

Again, the work of Joyce and Showers is a fruitful source of relevant and helpful ideas - most notably their concept of *the cadre,* a small cross-hierarchical working group which epitomises the collaborative approach and provides the focus for key developmental aspects of school management. The chapter finishes with a case study illustrating the application of this model in a primary school.

Chapter 6: Development Planning for Learning Schools - evaluates the effectiveness of the current model of this key management tool, in light of the principles of learning identified in Chapter 1. The work of important international figures in educational and business management - notably Michael Fullan and Peter Senge - is also examined in some depth and an alternative planning model proposed. The chapter deals with two main issues:

- putting *'learning and teaching at the heart of the plan'* - giving practical meaning to this oft-expressed aspiration by re-ordering the key development areas so that learning and teaching are the permanent, overarching priorities;

- using a *whole brain approach to development planning* - integrating a holistic, creative element with the current logical, sequential approach.

Appendix 1: **A Selection of Learning Materials from the Critical Skills Programme** - includes examples of the different kinds of 'Challenges' which form the core of the *Critical Skills Programme* and various teaching 'tools' which are used to promote the development of the 'critical skills and fundamental dispositions'.

Appendix 2: **Two Worked Examples of Whole Brain Development Planning** - consists of two worked examples - one primary, one secondary - illustrating how the whole brain model of planning can function effectively in practice.

Appendix 3: **References, Recommended Reading and Useful Addresses** - contains a list of reference books, videos, teaching programmes and relevant addresses, with notes on their potential use and value.

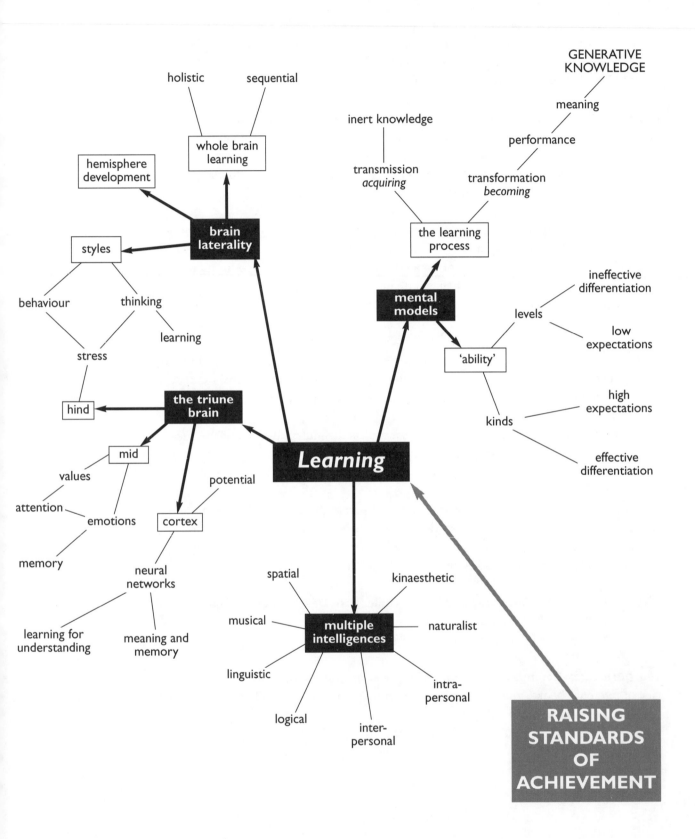

Section One: Learning

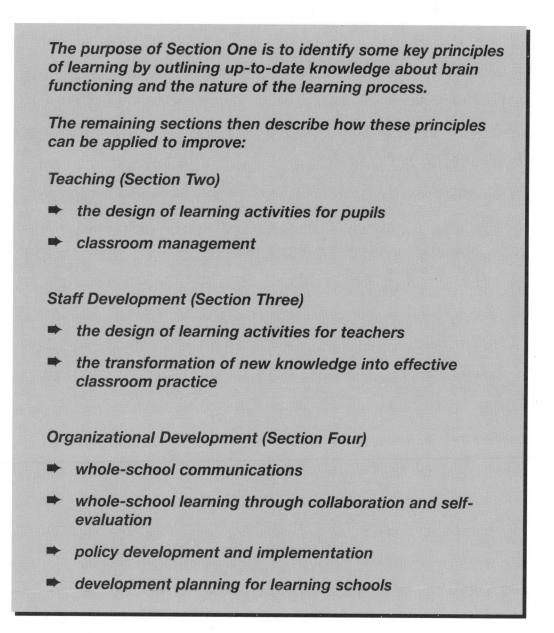

The purpose of Section One is to identify some key principles of learning by outlining up-to-date knowledge about brain functioning and the nature of the learning process.

The remaining sections then describe how these principles can be applied to improve:

Teaching (Section Two)

➡ the design of learning activities for pupils

➡ classroom management

Staff Development (Section Three)

➡ the design of learning activities for teachers

➡ the transformation of new knowledge into effective classroom practice

Organizational Development (Section Four)

➡ whole-school communications

➡ whole-school learning through collaboration and self-evaluation

➡ policy development and implementation

➡ development planning for learning schools

Section One consists of one chapter -

Chapter 1: Key Principles of Learning

The main issues* addressed in Chapter 1 are (see also the visual layout opposite):

1. The Triune Brain

- *the hind brain*: primitive behaviours and the inhibition of thinking;
- *the mid brain*: emotions and memory; values and attention;
- *the cortex*: underused potential; neural networks; learning for understanding; meaning and memory.

* A much more comprehensive treatment of these issues is included in Alistair Smith's **Accelerated Learning in Practice** (Network Educational Press, 1998).

2. Brain Laterality

- right/left hemisphere differences; whole brain learning; styles of thinking and learning; behaviour and gender differences; hemisphere development.

3. The Theory of Multiple Intelligences

- implications for the design of classroom activities and the concept of 'mixed ability'.

4. Misleading Mental Models

- *ability*: levels versus kinds - implications for expectations, 'ethos of achievement', differentiation, selection versus 'mixed ability';
- *the learning process*: transmission versus transformation - the construction of personal meaning; understanding through performance; the design and use of effective learning activities.

Chapter 1: Key Principles of Learning

> 'There's an explosion in brain research that is sending shock waves throughout learning, teaching and education... Many now realise that we never had a coherent foundation for learning; it was merely a model for teaching and controlling the learners.'

Completing the Puzzle: A Brain-Based Approach to Learning, *Jensen, E (The Brain Store, 1996)*

> 'We have been made aware that many of our current actions and decisions are based on outdated mental models.'
>
> 'A greater understanding of brain functioning should help our staff to improve their teaching approaches.'
>
> 'We need to keep more up-to-date with knowledge about learning.'

West Lothian Headteachers discussion groups (1998)

It has been authoritatively estimated that about 90% of our knowledge about the brain and learning has been discovered in the last decade*. This is hardly surprising when you consider that almost 90% of the neuroscientists who ever lived are alive today!

* In July 1989 President Bush officially proclaimed the 1990s the 'Decade of the Brain'.

The consequent 'explosion' in our knowledge about the brain to which Eric Jensen refers is of enormous significance for educators at all levels. And yet, as the comments from the West Lothian Headteachers indicate, it seems that a surprisingly small proportion of teachers are even aware of this ongoing revolution in our knowledge of the brain, let alone incorporating it into their practice.

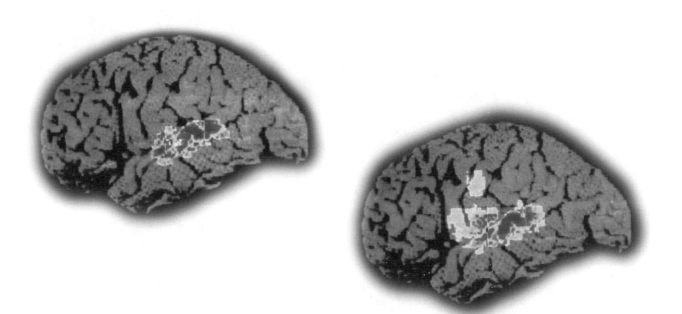

Scans of the brain showing reaction of the cortex to different stimulus conditions.

Robert Sylwester, Professor of Education at the University of Oregon, USA, has recently described the challenge which faces us in the following way:

> '(Brain) monitoring technology has evolved rapidly during the current computer age, as have the research fields that study the brain - with greater wonders yet to come. Our brain is at the edge of understanding itself!...(but)...Educators have never had the scientist's freedom to patiently wait for the research technology to catch up with their curiosity. Every year a new batch of students arrives at the school door, whether we understand how their brains develop or not. We have had to find a way to bypass students' brains in order to carry out our professional assignment...
>
> 'Our solution has been to focus on the visible, measurable, pliable manifestations of cognition, rather than on cognitive mechanisms and processes...(but)...the problem with partial knowledge that focuses only on outward behaviour is that it can lead to inappropriate, generalised conclusions...
>
> 'The education profession is now approaching a crossroads. We can continue to focus our energies on the careful observation of external behaviour...or we can join the search for a scientific understanding of the brain mechanisms, processes, and malfunctions that affect the successful completion of complex learning tasks... *Knowing why* generally leads to *knowing how to*.'

A Celebration of Neurons: An Educator's Guide to the Human Brain, *Sylwester, R (ASCD, 1995)*

The issues to be addressed in parts 1-4 of this chapter, then, relate to Sylwester's 'search for a scientific understanding'. They are:

1. Paul MacLean's concept of **the triune brain;**

2. Roger Sperry's work on **brain laterality;**

3. Howard Gardner's theory of **multiple intelligences;**

4. **misleading mental models** which impede efforts to raise standards of achievement.

Note that the principles derived from examining these issues do not constitute a comprehensive list of 'principles of learning'. They are suggested as 'key principles' only in the sense that *standards of achievement in our schools are unlikely to be raised significantly unless these principles are applied clearly and consistently to the management of education at all levels.*

1. The Triune Brain

Dr. Paul MacLean originally proposed this model of the brain in 1949, when he was Director of the Laboratory of Brain and Behaviour at the U.S. Institute of Mental Health. More recent research has shown that the model is a considerable over-simplification in that the behaviours he associated with the three separate parts are actually more widely distributed throughout the whole brain. Nevertheless, the functional distinctions which he made remain useful in understanding the causes of different kinds of learner behaviour.

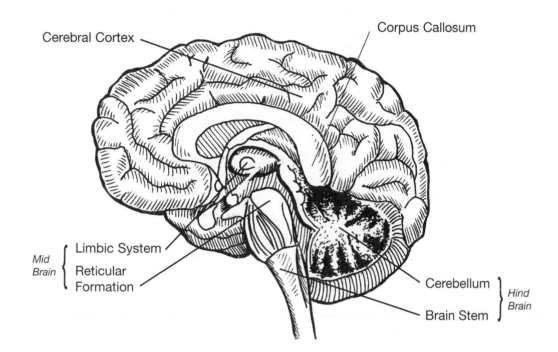

Maclean suggested that the brain is actually three brains in one:

(i)   The hind or reptilian brain

(ii)   The mid brain or limbic system

(iii) The cerebral cortex

(i) The hind or reptilian brain - includes the brain stem and cerebellum and is responsible for primitive, instinctive, survival-orientated behaviours* such as:

-   *territoriality* (e.g. defending possessions);

-   *mating rituals* (e.g. flirting);

-   *ritualistic display* (e.g. attention-seeking);

-   *hierarchical behaviour* (e.g. gangs);

-   repetitive, predictable *daily routines.*

* For a very clear account of the significance of the reptilian brain and limbic system to classroom behaviour, see **Best Behaviour** *(Network Educational Press, 1998) by Peter Relf et. al.*

The key point here is that, under threat, blood drains into the hind brain to support survival behaviours. This effectively 'switches off' the mid brain and cortex which are largely responsible for thinking and memory. In other words *a learner under threat is unable to think and learn effectively.* As Eric Jensen puts it:

'Survival always overrides pattern-detection and problem-solving. This fact has tremendous implications for learning. Threat and induced learner helplessness have got to be reduced from the learning environment to achieve maximum potency... It's not stress that's bad, it's *uncontrollable* stress that's bad...

'Research now tells us that threatening learners may foster more of the same behaviour that we are trying to avoid... A threat is any stimulus that causes... defensiveness or a sense of helplessness in the learner. An example of a subtle threat...is when an assignment is given, and the learner lacks the resources to carry it out... Threats adversely affect one's ability to plan...and to stay engaged at a task...'

Jensen, E (op. cit.)

Therefore we can identify a *first key principle of learning*:

The learning environment should minimise threat and uncontrollable stress.

(ii) The mid brain or limbic system - consists of several interconnected almond to walnut sized structures and is largely responsible for:

- social bonding;
- sexuality;
- emotions;
- expressiveness;
- values (i.e. what we value and what we feel is true);
- memory.

There are therefore strong links between emotions (both felt and expressed) and memory. We are more likely to remember emotionally-laden events. As Robert Sylwester observes (emphases added):

'Memories formed during a specific emotional state tend to be easily recalled during events that provoke similar emotional states. Thus, family arguments and happy occasions tend to spark the recall of similar arguments and happy times. Similarly, *classroom simulations and role-playing activities enhance learning* because they tie curricular memories to the kinds of real-life emotional contexts in which they will later be used.'

Sylwester, R (op. cit.)

At the boundary between the hind and mid brains lies the *reticular formation*, which also plays a crucial role in learning by *controlling our attention*. It does this by filtering out unwanted (i.e. *un-valued*) messages from the millions of stimuli that bombard our central nervous system every second, so that the cortex can focus on processing information that we value. And since we tend to value information and experiences which have positive emotional impact on our self-image and self-esteem, this clearly has significant implications for the design of learning activities and for classroom management.

Sylwester goes on to make a further important point about the crucial role of emotion in learning:

> 'By separating emotion from logic and reasoning in the classroom we've simplified... management and assessment, but we've also then separated two sides of one coin - and lost something important in the process. It's impossible to separate emotion from the important activities of life. Don't even try.'

Sylwester, R (op. cit.)

Therefore we can identify *two further key principles of learning*:

The learning environment should -

- *promote positive self-image and high self-esteem;*

- *engage positive emotions.*

(iii) The cerebral cortex - is the main area of the brain concerned with processing and storing information - i.e. with *thinking* and *remembering* - though, as we've already seen, it is very much integrated with, and in some cases controlled by, the other two 'brains'.

A key feature of the cortex is that it is physically divided into two halves or 'hemispheres' which process information in different ways. This feature - *brain laterality* - is dealt with in the next part of the chapter. The remainder of this section deals with two other issues of great significance to classroom learning and teaching. These are:

- the *potential power* of the human brain

- how *thinking and learning* take place

Brain potential. The key functional unit of the cortex is the *neuron* (see overleaf). There are approximately *100 billion neurons* in the whole cortex, each of which is capable of operating at a greater level of complexity than the most powerful microprocessor yet devised, and each of which is capable of making up to 20,000 connections with any one of the others!

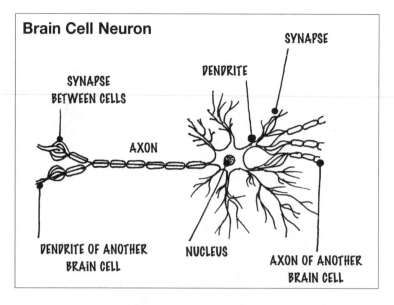

Brain Cell Neuron

SYNAPSE

DENDRITE

SYNAPSE
BETWEEN CELLS

AXON

DENDRITE OF ANOTHER
BRAIN CELL

NUCLEUS

AXON OF ANOTHER
BRAIN CELL

Adapted from **Accelerated Learning in Practice**, *Smith A (Network Educational Press, 1998)*

As Professor Susan Greenfield explains in her landmark book **The Human Brain** (*1997*):

'To get an idea of just how big a hundred billion is, the Amazon rain forest offers an appropriate analogy. The Amazon rain forest stretches for 2,700,000 square miles and it contains about a hundred billion trees. There are about as many trees as neurons in the brain. But the metaphor need not stop there: if we now consider the huge number of connections between neurons, then we could say that there are about as many as leaves on the trees in the Amazon jungle. It is virtually impossible to imagine on a global scale the fervour of chemical and electrical activity, even if only 10 per cent of our hundred billion neurons were signalling at any one moment...'

The Human Brain, *Greenfield, S (Weidenfeld & Nicolson, 1997)*

Greenfield goes on to explain that:

> 'The brain is built up from single neurons in increasingly complex circuits. These connections are not like a row of people just holding hands... Between ten thousand and one hundred thousand neurons make contact with any particular neuron. In turn, any particular neuron will become one of many thousands of inputs for the next cell in the network.
>
> 'If we took a piece of the brain the size of a match head alone, there could be up to a billion connections on that surface... If you counted the connections between neurons in the cortex at a rate of one connection a second, it would take thirty-two million years!' *

Greenfield, S (op. cit.)

And Tony Buzan refers to the work of Professor Anokhin of Moscow University, whose conclusion after 60 years of investigation into the nature of brain cells was that:

> 'No human yet exists who even approached (using) the full potential of his brain. This is why we don't accept any pessimistic estimates of the limits of the human brain. It is unlimited!'

The Mind Map Book: Radiant Thinking, *Buzan, B & Buzan, T (BBC, 1995)*

* Another way of illustrating the immensity of the potential number of neural links is by pointing out that it is '1' followed by a string of '0's the length of which would stretch from the Earth to the planet Mercury - approximately!

Yet sentences like the following continue to feature in school mission statements the length and breadth of the country:

'Our aim is to help all our pupils to achieve their full potential.'

Given what we already know about the brain's potential processing and storage power, it is no mere semantic quibble to note that such statements show little awareness of the true potential of the brain. For it is now abundantly clear that 'achievement of full potential' is a hugely unrealistic ambition! And, more significantly, that *differences in levels of achievement between individual pupils pale into insignificance in comparison to the improved standards that all pupils could achieve if we focused more of our efforts on ways of promoting brain-based learning.*

Greenfield's and Anokhin's observations also challenge the common conception of the term 'ability' and so have significant implications for the ways in which teachers interact with their pupils. This issue is addressed in some depth at the end of this chapter (see pages 40/41), and in Chapter 2 (pages 52-57).

Thinking and learning. It is now generally recognised that learning occurs when neurons form new connections, and that these connections are formed when we have to think, to solve problems, to perform. As David Perkins puts it:

> 'Learning is a consequence of thinking... As we think about and with the content that we are learning, we truly learn it.'

Smart Schools, *Perkins, D (The Free Press, 1992)*

Perkins suggests that the pre-eminent goal of education must be the development of 'generative knowledge' which he defines as:

> 'Knowledge that does not just sit there but functions richly in people's lives to help them understand and deal with the world.'

Perkins, D (op. cit.)

And generative knowledge is developed through *active performance; review and reflection*; and *timely, accurate feedback.*

Active performance - involves activities such as tackling complex, open-ended problems, preparing presentations, and role-playing, all of which require learners to collaborate and to 'think about and with the content that (they) are learning'. The old saying that 'we forget 90% of what we hear but we remember 90% of what we teach' does indeed have a solid basis in theory. Recent discoveries about the brain shed further light on the reasons why these kinds of active performance are so essential to effective learning.

It is now thought that the billions of neurons in the cortex are pre-programmed at birth into millions of relatively small neural networks, each of which is responsible for a minimal area of perception such as seeing a vertical line. Thinking causes new links to be formed between these networks as the brain combines them in new ways to solve novel problems. Thinking also causes repeated electrical and chemical impulses to flow along existing neural links.

Each time an impulse flows along an axon the cells which surround it are stimulated to produce more *myelin*, a fatty material which insulates the axon rather like the plastic covering on an electrical cable. And the more myelin is laid down, the more robust and easily activated is the link.

Links which are not regularly activated do not build up a sufficiently thick myelin sheath and degenerate - the memory fades. In other words it's a '**use it or lose it**' brain.

So thinking, learning and intelligence are closely related to the nature, number and robustness of neural links in the cortex.

But there's more to effective teaching than simply providing opportunities for active learning. Learners also need regular opportunities to *review and reflect* on their learning; and regular *feedback* on how their learning is progressing.

Review and reflection. The importance of these elements is best understood through a sporting analogy. Effective sports training must include regular periods of rest so that the muscles, sinews and circulatory system have a chance to recover and develop appropriately in response to the period of exercise. Failure to provide regular rest - 'overtraining' - leads to muscle fatigue and deteriorating performance.

Similarly, *reviewing* previous work gives an opportunity for newly developed neural links to myelinate; and the *reflection* process - sometimes referred to as 'metacognition' - stimulates the formation of new connections between existing neural networks. This process almost certainly underlies Piaget's concept of accommodation of existing schemata to new information and ideas.

Professor Neville Bennett of Exeter University summarises the situation in this way:

> 'Current conceptions of learning perceive children as intellectually active learners already holding ideas, or schemata, which they use to make sense of their everyday experiences.
>
> 'These schemata are partial and incomplete.* Learning in classrooms thus involves the extension, elaboration or modification of schemata.'

It is doubtful if schemata can ever be called complete since we are always learning by extending, elaborating or modifying our schemata.

Managing Learning in the Primary Classroom, *Bennett, N (Trentham Books, 1992)*

The sporting analogy may be taken a stage further. Just as scientific research is being applied with increasing sophistication and effectiveness to sports training, so is it providing increasingly relevant information on learning. For example, in a recent article entitled **How Julie's Brain Learns**, Eric Jensen makes the following challenging observation (emphases added):

> '(Most teachers have) strong models of so-called good teaching, including the traditional stand-and-deliver model, in which the goal is to get and keep students' attention. But the process of learning is complex... The physiological state in which we learn mediates how much we comprehend...
>
> 'Too much attention to *anything* may be counteradaptive. An excessively focused brain may be more susceptible to predators*...when teachers insist on holding on to students' attention, they miss the fact that much learning comes through indirect acquisition such as peer discussion... By making excessive attention demands on students, teachers can create resentful learners.
>
> 'Ultimately, brain-compatible teachers may engage learners attention only 20 to 40 percent of the time and still do a great job. *Teachers need to keep attention demands to short bursts of no longer than the age of their learners in minutes.*'

See page 28.

How Julie's Brain Learns, *Jensen, E (Educational Leadership, November 1998)*

Feedback. The impact of the reflection process is greatly enhanced by timely and accurate feedback - or formative assessment - whether from the teacher or from discussions with fellow students. In Bennett's terms, this encourages learners to elaborate and modify their developing schemata. Or as Eric Jensen again puts it:

> 'Timely and accurate feedback helps neurons learn first to fire together, then to wire together as a network. When we activate the right neurons, we get a smarter organism. Superior learners learn by systematic trial and error. Eventually, they will get the right answer, but more important, they eliminate the wrong answers. In some ways, the worst thing that can happen is for a student to get the right answer immediately. Teachers need to orchestrate circumstances that allow more trial and error. This might include research, discussions, team problem-solving, and projects that have built-in opportunities for self-correction.'

Jensen, E (op. cit.)

Unfortunately, such feedback is notably rare in most classrooms. For example, in a recent major review of research into classroom assessment, Black and Wiliam of King's College London found that:

> 'All of these studies show that innovations which include strengthening the practice of formative assessment produce significant, and often substantial, learning gains... Many of them show that improved formative assessment helps...low attainers more than the rest...(but)...
>
> 'There is a wealth of research evidence that the everyday practice of assessment in classrooms is beset with problems and short-comings... The giving of marks and the grading functions are over-emphasised, while the giving of useful advice* and the learning function are under-emphasised... The collection of marks to fill up records is given greater priority than the analysis of pupils' work to discern learning needs.'

*Jensen's 'timely and accurate feedback'.

Inside the Black Box, *Black, P & Wiliam, D (King's College London 1998)*

As Eric Jensen has pointed out, effective learning involves taking risks and learning from our failures as well as successes. It is only by correcting mistakes that we refine our schemata so that they become more accurate and powerful representations of the world. But students will be unwilling to make mistakes if they feel insecure about their learning. This reinforces the need for a classroom culture which promotes a positive self-image and high self-esteem, and for pupils to be clear and confident about what they are to learn.* Indeed, Black and Wiliam go on to state that:

* See Jensen's quotation from **Completing the Puzzle** on page 20.

> 'What is needed is a culture of success, backed by a belief that all can achieve... Many of the successful innovations have developed self- and peer-assessment by pupils...(but)...pupils can only assess themselves when they have a sufficiently clear picture of the targets that their learning is meant to attain. Surprisingly, and sadly, many pupils do not have such a picture, and appear to have become accustomed to receiving classroom teaching as an arbitrary sequence of exercises with no overarching rationale... Self-assessment by pupils, far from being a luxury, is in fact an essential component of formative assessment.'

Black, P & Wiliam, D (op. cit.)

Leading the Learning School

Finally, an important consequence of the way that neural connections develop in the cortex (see Greenfield's observations on page 23) is that the brain is a 'parallel processor', able to process many hundreds of pieces of information simultaneously. Much of this information is processed unconsciously, and much is perceived through peripheral rather than focused vision.

Consequently, the environment in which we learn can be a source of significant peripheral messages which affect our ability to learn effectively. Positive, reinforcing visual messages on classroom walls can promote positive self-image and high self-esteem by impacting on the mid-brain centres responsible for emotions and values (see page 20/21).

Therefore we can derive *three more key principles of learning* from our current knowledge of how the cortex functions. These are:

Learning activities should -

- *encourage learners to perform their understandings;*
- *provide regular opportunities for review and reflection;*
- *include timely and accurate feedback.*

2. Brain Laterality

The Triune Brain model essentially describes aspects of brain functioning that we all have in common. By contrast, in parts 2 and 3, we consider ways in which individual brains differ. In this part we look first at the ways in which preferences for using different parts of the brain lead to different preferred styles of thinking and learning and the significant consequences this has for the design of effective learning activities.

The cortex of the brain is divided into right and left hemispheres. Roger Sperry's Nobel Prize-winning 'split brain' research in the early 1960s showed that these have distinctly different functions, as shown in the diagram below.

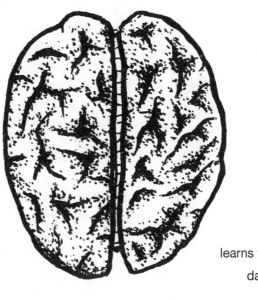

Left Brain	Right Brain
language	forms and patterns
logic	spatial manipulation
mathematical formulae	rhythm
number	musical appreciation
sequence	images and pictures
linearity	dimension
analysis	imagination
words of a song	tune of song
learning from the part to the whole	learns the whole first then parts
phonetic reading system	daydreaming and visioning
unrelated factual information	whole language reader
	relationships in learning

The hemispheres are linked by the *corpus callosum* which contains about 300 million axons - generally more in females than in males. These allow the two hemispheres to communicate and collaborate on complex thinking and action.

Because hemisphere specialisation is reversed in a small percentage of the population, many neurologists prefer to label them by function rather than position, i.e. 'gestalt' (generally right) and 'logic' (generally left) but they will be referred to here by their more common names of 'right' and 'left'.

The right hemisphere matures earlier in life than the left. It is more sensitive to longer wavelengths of light and sound, and controls gross motor movements. It is through this hemisphere that we see the 'big picture', perceive relationships and patterns, synthesise ideas, carry out creative thinking, and experience musical pitch and tone.

The left hemisphere is more sensitive to shorter wavelengths and controls fine motor movements. It is responsible for perceiving fine detail, for logical, sequential processing (e.g. the mechanics of language and number), and for critical, analytical thinking.

This specialization is of great biological significance. As Robert Ornstein explains:

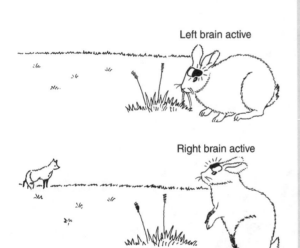

Left brain active

Right brain active

'Studies (on other mammals)...provide striking evidence on the depth of the division of the hemispheres. (This) is based on a way of approaching the outside world that evolution worked out long before it thought of us... Each of these ways of organizing reality must have had immediate advantages...well before human beings appeared on the planet... Our two sides of the brain are very profoundly different, and this difference runs deep... And the benefit seems pretty clear.

'Having an overall picture (from the right hemisphere) would serve very well for an animal getting around in the world. We quickly have to recognize situations that are safe or that have difficulties, and we need to recognize facial expressions, body movements, frame of mind, and others'...intentions toward us...

'At the same time, rapid and precise actions need a simplicity of attention. An animal can't spend its life forever searching the horizon. A physical reaction needs to be made next, ...a sequence of precise, rapid-fire decisions, and this decision-making seems best done by the left hemisphere. Similarly, in speech, one particular word has to follow the one before; we can't say everything at once.'

The Right Mind, *Ornstein, R (Harcourt, Brace and Co., 1997)*

Leading the Learning School

There are two key points here.

(i) Most people show a bias towards using one or other hemisphere - though the degree of bias varies considerably. This, in turn, influences our learning and thinking preferences - our so-called *styles of thinking and learning*.

(ii) Effective thinking and problem-solving requires *'whole brain' learning* which integrates the specialist functions of both hemispheres.

(i) Styles of thinking and learning. There are two main ways of categorising thinking and learning styles, relating to how we *process* and how we *perceive* information. The key issue here is that learners with a strong bias towards one style are greatly disadvantaged if their learning experiences continually favour a different style.

Processing information.
Processing preferences are largely determined by a bias towards using one or the other hemisphere. People with a *strong right brain bias* need to see the 'big picture', to know the full context of what's coming before they can make sense of sequentially presented material, however logical the sequence. They find jigsaw puzzles difficult to do without the picture on the front of the box!

By contrast, those with a *strong left brain bias* are less interested in the overall context but severely hampered by a presentation which is not ordered into a clear, logical sequence. When doing a jigsaw puzzle they will be more interested in finding visual and spatial links between individual pieces than with seeing where they fit into the overall picture.

Individual learners differ in their degree of bias towards each style of processing. Most of us have only a moderate bias and so we are able to cope with a teaching approach based on a style different from our own. But some learners have such a significant bias that they are severely disadvantaged in these circumstances.

It is important to note that their difficulty is not through lack of ability to process the information effectively, but because that information is continually presented in an inappropriate way. This clearly raises significant issues for classroom practice (see Chapter 2).

Perceiving information.
Our brain perceives the world through three main modalities: *auditory; visual;* and *kinaesthetic*. These modalities are not confined to specific hemispheres in the same way as the processing functions but they are confined to specific areas of the cortex, and since they also greatly influence how we learn it makes sense to consider them at this point.

Essentially, auditory learners learn from what they hear, visual learners from what they see, and kinaesthetic learners from movement and what they touch. We all learn in all three modalities but again, most people prefer one to the other two. And again, the degree of preference varies considerably. In **Quantum Learning** (*1992*) Bobbi Deporter quotes Michael Grinder, a noted authority on learning and teaching styles:

> 'In every group of thirty students about six prefer one of the modalities over the other two so strongly that they struggle to understand the instructions most of the time, unless special care is taken to present them in their preferred mode. For these people, knowing their best modality can mean the difference between success and failure...'

Quantum Learning, *Deporter, B & Hernacki, M (Judy Piatkus (Publishers) Ltd., 1992)*

Here are a few of the characteristics that Deporter lists for each of these types of learner:

Auditory Learners (34% of the population)

- are talkative, love discussion, and go into lengthy descriptions
- talk to themselves while working
- are easily distracted by noise
- learn by listening and remember what was discussed rather than what was seen

Visual Learners (29% of the population)

- are neat and orderly
- are appearance-orientated in both dress and presentation
- usually are not distracted by noise
- doodle during conversations and meetings

Kinaesthetic Learners (37% of the population)

- touch people to get their attention
- are physically orientated and move a lot
- gesture a lot
- can't sit still for long periods of time

This is only a small selection of the characteristics listed by Deporter. Even so, their implications for classroom management should be immediately obvious! Again, these are considered further in *Chapter 2*.

Meantime, it is also worth noting that some of these learning preferences are more likely to occur in one sex than the other. Three examples are outlined in the next section to emphasise their significance for the design of effective learning activities and classroom management. Jon Pickering's book **Raising Boys' Achievement** (*Network Educational Press, 1997*) provides a much more comprehensive treatment of this issue.

Some gender differences in learning and behaviour.

- Boys are more likely to be kinaesthetic learners. Girls are more likely to have a visual preference.

This is one reason why many more boys than girls find it difficult to obey classroom rules like the following, which are mostly taken from a set recommended in a widely used commercial behaviour management programme.

- Keep your eyes on the teacher or on your paper.
- No talking when the teacher is talking.
- Raise your hand and wait to be called upon to ask or answer a question.
- Ask for permission before you leave your seat.
- No swinging on your chair.

- Boys are more likely than girls to be right brain dominant.

Most school work favours left brain thinking. Material is typically presented in a logical, sequential way without the benefit of an integrating 'big picture' (see, for example, the quotation from Black and William at the foot of page 26). An example of this is the common technique of uncovering one line of information at a time on an overhead transparency. This can be extremely frustrating to strongly right-brained learners!

So logical, sequentially presented work which lacks an integrating 'big picture' can be another significant cause of boys' behaviour problems. On the other hand, boys are more likely to enjoy activities such as map reading, which involve working on the 'big picture'.

● The corpus callosum is generally better developed in girls than boys.

One consequence of this is that girls are generally better able to articulate their feelings by linking language (left brain) with emotions (right brain). By contrast, boys are more likely to resort to physical ways of expressing their feelings. Again, this has obvious consequences for classroom behaviour!

Brain hemisphere development.

Robert Ornstein describes how the right hemisphere matures at an earlier age than the left to aid survival:

> 'The right hemisphere...becomes responsive to the effects of the outside world at the time...when spatial abilities, such as finding the mother and control of large limb movements, are getting wired up. These are obviously so necessary for survival. And the left hemisphere begins to become more and more mature... when the baby is exposed to spoken language, and learning the more refined movements of infancy.'

Ornstein, R (op. cit.)

In her best-selling book **Smart Moves** (*Great Ocean, 1995*), neurophysiologist and special needs teacher Carla Hannaford points out that the right hemisphere normally reaches full maturity between 4.5 and 7 years of age but the left not until 7 to 9 years. Therefore, for many children under the age of 7, learning activities which involve a high level of linear, logical processing and fine motor control are likely to be frustrating and counter-productive.

On this basis Hannaford criticises the British early years curriculum:

> 'Under normal circumstances children at the age when they enter kindergarten already have wonderful imaginations and a very large vocabulary. The British curriculum, ...however, begins alphabet and number recognition immediately, with reading following in quick order. This might not be a problem if we involved image, emotion and movement, and built on the student's imagination and vocabulary. Strangely, we do just the opposite. We teach children to 'sit still', learn letters and numbers in a linear fashion (that includes printing, a very linear, left hemisphere process), and read books with simplistic vocabulary, no emotion and few images.'

Smart Moves, *Hannaford, C (Great Ocean, 1995)*

She contrasts this situation unfavourably with the Danish school system which:

> '...respecting natural brain development patterns, does not start children in (primary) school until six or seven years of age. They teach reading and writing from a holistic, gestalt processing format and then move to the details later, around age eight, when the left hemisphere is ready to handle it. Reading is not taught until age eight - and Denmark boasts 100% literacy.'

Hannaford, C (op. cit.)

Not all literacy experts would agree with Hannaford and the issue is in any case complex and not yet fully understood. Nevertheless, there is clearly a concern that current political pressures to raise early literacy standards could lead to many children undertaking activities for which their brains are not ready, with potentially harmful effects on their intellectual development and self-esteem. After all, we do not expect babies to stand and walk before they have gone through the earlier developmental stages of sitting and crawling, which they do at widely differing rates. Yet most late walkers nevertheless develop into perfectly competent, physically well co-ordinated adults.

(ii) 'Whole brain' learning. The most effective thinking and learning involves the integrated use of both sides of the brain - for example:

- *emotional* as well as *logical* reasoning;
- *creative* as well as *critical* thinking;
- *synthesis* as well as *analysis* of information;
- searching for *patterns and relationships* as well as sequencing *decisions and actions*.

Therefore, learning experiences should actively encourage *all* learners, including those with strong biases, to use *both* hemispheres to process information. For example, covering an overhead transparency in the manner described on page 31 not only frustrates right brain thinkers but also fails to encourage left brain thinkers to look for patterns and relationships.

The answer is to design learning experiences which stimulate both halves of the brain. In the above example this would involve showing the whole of the transparency first, to explain the main features and their interrelationships, before focusing on the individual elements.

In the Scottish Office Quality, Standards and Audit Division's booklet **How good is our school?: Self-evaluation using performance indicators** (*HMSO 1996*), Performance Indicator 3.1: 'Quality of the teaching process' puts it this way:

> 'The purposes of activities are shared with pupils and care is taken to explain work to them within the context of what they already know and can do.'

A very good example of whole brain presentation of information in everyday life is TV weather forecasting, which starts with the general situation (the 'big picture') before moving into the details.

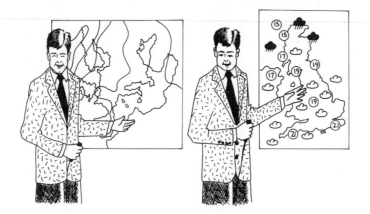

It is also worth noting that whole brain learning can be the property of a group as well as an individual. Human beings have achieved success on this planet, not by being bigger, stronger or faster than other animals, but by learning to combine different thinking styles and intelligence strengths (see *part 3*) in co-operative group action. As David Kolb puts it:

'If there are evolutionary pressures toward "the survival of the fittest" in the human species, these apply not to individuals but to the human community as a whole. Survival depends not on the evolution of a race of identical supermen but on the emergence of a co-operative human community that cherishes and utilizes individual uniqueness.'

Experiential Learning: Experience as the Source of Learning and Development,
Kolb, D © 1984 (Reprinted by permission of Practice-Hall, Inc., Upper Saddle River, NJ)

Activities which encourage co-operative, collaborative group work and active, complex problem solving increase pupils' awareness of the value of different ways of thinking. Again, this raises significant issues for classroom practice which are further reinforced by Howard Gardner's *Theory of Multiple Intelligences*.

Leading the Learning School

3. The Theory of Multiple Intelligences

Howard Gardner first proposed this theory in his landmark book **Frames of Mind** (*Fontana, 1983*). It has since become widely accepted and has spawned many books describing its application to education.

Gardner suggests that the human brain is designed to process eight distinctly different forms of intelligence which, though closely interrelated, are located in different parts of the brain. For Gardner, an intelligence:

> ' ...entails the ability to solve problems or fashion products that are of consequence in a particular cultural setting... The problems...range from creating an end to a story...to repairing a quilt. Products range from scientific theories to musical composition to successful political campaigns.'

Frames of Mind (Second Edition), *Gardner, H (HarperCollins Publishers Ltd., 1993)*

The eight intelligences are described briefly here because of their significance for classroom practice (*Section Two*), staff development (*Section Three*) and school management (*Section Four*). Alistair Smith's books **Accelerated Learning in the Classroom** (*Network Educational Press, 1996*) and **Accelerated Learning in Practice** (*Network Educational Press, 1998*) provide much more comprehensive accounts from which the following summary is largely derived.

Linguistic Intelligence - clarity with language, sensitivity to sounds, to the meaning and order of words, and the different functions of language. Learners with high linguistic intelligence enjoy listening to stories and expressing their ideas orally and on paper.

Musical - recognition of tonal patterns, sensitivity to rhythm and beats. Learners with high musical intelligence enjoy the rhythms and rhymes of songs and raps. They may learn well by recording their own learning to music. Constructing raps and jingles helps to develop this intelligence.

Logical-Mathematical Intelligence - understanding the world through a grasp of the actions that can be performed on objects. Learners with high logical-mathematical intelligence enjoy discerning patterns and relationships, and solving non-verbal problems involving sequence, logic and order (Jean Piaget's model of cognitive development is generally regarded as a description of this intelligence).

$$-4x + 2y = 10$$
$$y = 4 - x$$

Visual and Spatial Intelligence - ability to perceive the world accurately and to be able to recreate aspects of our visual experience. Learners with high visual/spatial intelligence tend to be highly creative. Peripheral messages placed at - or higher than - eye level stimulate the use and development of this intelligence.

Bodily-Kinaesthetic Intelligence - deals with physical movement and the knowledge of how the body operates. Learners with high bodily-kinaesthetic intelligence enjoy role-play and mime, field trips and group games, all of which also stimulate its development.

Naturalist Intelligence - ability to recognise and classify animals, plants and minerals. Learners with high naturalist intelligence enjoy the natural environment and are sensitive to its interrelatedness. Activities which emphasise the importance of caring for the class and school environment stimulate the development of this intelligence.

Interpersonal Intelligence - ability to notice and make distinctions between the moods and temperaments, motivations and intentions of other people. Learners with high interpersonal intelligence enjoy discussion and interviewing people. Collaborative group activities help to develop this intelligence.

Intrapersonal Intelligence - involves a well-developed sense of self, the ability to access one's own feelings and emotions and to use them as a means of understanding and guiding one's behaviour. Learners with high intrapersonal intelligence enjoy introspection, philosophical discussion and expressing their feelings. This intelligence is developed by activities which encourage regular reflection on learning and behaviour.

Three conclusions from Gardner's work are of particular relevance to school and classroom management. These are:

(i)   Each of the eight intelligences can *develop* throughout life, given appropriate learning experiences.

(ii)   Every learner has a different combination of strengths and weaknesses amongst the intelligences. This is significant for the key issues of *differentiation* and *'mixed ability'* teaching.

(iii)   Understanding develops through *active performance* which is best done initially through the strongest intelligence(s).

(i) Developing the intelligences. The notion that intelligence/ability is something we are born with and can do little to alter - that 'we are what we are' - is still deeply ingrained in Western society. It was most clearly defined in 1920 by H. H. Goddard:

> 'Stated in its boldest form, our thesis is that the chief determiner of human conduct is a unitary mental process which we call intelligence: that this process is conditioned by a nervous mechanism which is inborn: that the degree of efficiency to be attained by that nervous mechanism, and the consequent grade of intellectual or mental level for each individual is determined by the kind of chromosomes that come together with the union of the germ cells: that it is but little affected by any later influence except such serious accidents as may destroy part of the mechanism.'

Quoted in **The Mismeasure of Man (Revised Edition)**, *Gould, S (Penguin Books Ltd., 1995)*

By contrast, in **Outsmarting IQ** (*The Free Press, 1995*) Howard Gardner's colleague David Perkins advances a powerful case for the notion of 'learnable intelligence'. According to Perkins, most, if not all, of the intelligences have three components, two of which are undoubtedly 'learnable'. The three components are:

> ● *Neural intelligence*: 'The contribution of the efficiency and precision of the neurological system to intelligent behaviour.'*
>
> ● *Experiential intelligence*: 'The contribution of context-specific knowledge to intelligent behaviour. This contribution is learned, the result of extensive experience thinking and acting in particular situations over long periods of time.'
>
> ● *Reflective intelligence*: 'The contribution to intelligent behaviour of strategies for various intellectually challenging tasks, attitudes conducive to persistence, systematicity, and imagination in the use of one's mind, and habits of self-monitoring and management. Reflective intelligence is in effect a control system for the resources afforded by neural and experiential intelligence, bent on deploying them wisely. Reflective intelligence can be advanced considerably by learning.'

* Equivalent to Goddard's unitary mental process.

Adapted from **Outsmarting IQ**, *Perkins, D (The Free Press 1995)*

The section on *'Thinking and Learning'* (pages 23-27) describes ways in which experiential and reflective intelligence can be 'advanced considerably by learning'. These are considered in greater depth in *Section Two*.

(ii) Differentiation and 'mixed ability' teaching. A common but relatively ineffective approach to mixed ability teaching is to design learning materials at three levels of complexity – for 'able', 'average' and 'less able' pupils - the so-called 'Motorway Model of Differentiation'! This approach is based on a *simple, quantitative* model of ability but the research described on pages 27-37 shows that many of the differences in abilities and learning preferences between individual learners are *complex* and *qualitative*.

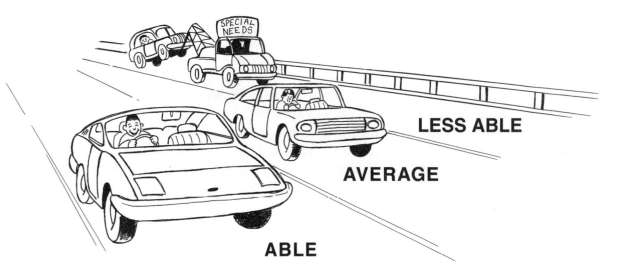

The negative impact of this simplistic model of ability is considered in more depth in part 4 of this chapter. Meantime, it is worth pointing out that a radically different model underpins much of the Japanese education system - generally considered to be significantly more effective than our own.

For example, James Stigler and James Hiebert of the Third International Mathematics and Science Study (TIMSS) have contrasted Japanese and U.S. teachers' beliefs about differences between learners in the following way:

> 'Many U.S. teachers believe that individual differences are an obstacle to effective teaching. As the range of differences increases, the difficulties of teaching increase... This is an obvious reason for tracking students into separate classes by ability...
>
> 'Japanese teachers view individual differences...as a resource for both students and teachers. Individual differences are beneficial for the class because they produce a range of ideas and solution methods that provide the material for students' discussion and reflection... In addition, tailoring instruction to specific students is seen as unfairly limiting and as prejudging what students are capable of learning... It is expected that different students will understand different methods and...the different methods that are shared allow each student to learn some things.'

The Teaching Gap, *Stigler, J & Hiebert, J (The Free Press, 1999)*

Leading the Learning School

Stigler and Hiebert's observations on U.S. teachers' beliefs probably apply with equal force to the U.K., as discussed in part 4.

(iii) Understanding through performance. The section on *'Thinking and Learning'* also describes the important part played by active performance in developing memory and understanding through strong, interconnected neural links. But in most classrooms 'performance' still overwhelmingly means writing words and mathematical symbols on paper. This is fine for those with well developed linguistic and/or logical-mathematical intelligences. It is much less so for those whose strengths are in other intelligences.

For sure, literacy and numeracy skills are so important in our modern society that we need to do all we can to help pupils develop them. But if we only allow pupils to develop and demonstrate their understandings through written work, we will undoubtedly penalise many of them unnecessarily and unfairly. And we will compound the problem further if we then label these penalised pupils 'average' or 'less able' simply because their strengths lie in other intelligences.

Fortunately many examples of good practice have been developed which do encourage learners to use the full range of intelligences. Many of these are described in Chapter 3. As Robert Sylwester observes:

> 'Imaginative teachers have always used multiple approaches to the curriculum in order to open as many cognitive doors as possible. They presented information to students via one intelligence and then challenged them to paraphrase it using another. They developed open-ended projects that encouraged students to explore multiple approaches to the problem. They encouraged students with different interests and abilities to work together. It has always been done. Gardner's focus on the complexity of intelligence has provided welcome scientific support for those who have long believed that our society subscribes to too narrow a view of intelligence.'

Sylwester, R (op. cit.)

From research on brain laterality and the theory of multiple intelligences, therefore, we can derive *four more key principles of learning*. These are:

Learning activities should -

- *encourage the use of whole brain learning;*
- *cater for different thinking and learning styles;*
- *provide ample opportunities for learners to use and develop the full range of multiple intelligences.*

The learning environment should -

- *recognise that individual learners have legitimately different behavioural needs.*

How these and the other key principles might best be applied in the classroom is considered in some depth in Chapters 2 and 3.   Meantime, we need to consider finally in this chapter the impact that this new knowledge about the brain ought to have on current conceptions about learning. In particular, we need to consider how more accurate mental models of ability and the learning process should enable teachers to interact more effectively with their pupils.

4. Misleading Mental Models

In his excellent best-selling book **The 7 Habits of Highly Effective People** (*Simon & Schuster Inc., 1989*) Stephen Covey graphically illustrates the problems caused when we operate with inaccurate and misleading mental models by comparing them to road maps. For example, if you were looking for a hotel in Birmingham but were using a map of Manchester that was labelled Birmingham, you would end up lost and unable to find your hotel. This would not be due to a lack of motivation or effort but because you had an inaccurate and misleading map.

The ways in which we think and act are largely determined by the multitude of mental models – or 'maps' – which we construct from our experiences. If any of these are inaccurate or misleading our behaviour will be correspondingly inappropriate. As one of the West Lothian discussion groups put it:*
'We have been made aware that many of our current actions and decisions are based on outdated mental models.'

* See 'Quotation 1' on page 8.

Unfortunately, the way many teachers think and act in the classroom continues to be influenced by two outdated and misleadingly inaccurate mental models. These relate to:

(i) The concept of *ability*.

(ii) The nature of the *learning process*.

(i) Ability. The notion of ability as a single, unchangeable attribute seems still to be almost as widespread in the education profession as in society at large (see Goddard's definition on page 37).

Actions that are based on this mental model focus on identifying the notional *quantity* of ability possessed by individual pupils and on providing different *levels* of work to suit different levels of ability. And the term 'mixed ability' is taken to mean simple, quantitative differences as opposed to the complex, qualitative differences that we now know to exist in all classrooms.

Leading the Learning School

By contrast, the research described in this chapter shows overwhelmingly that we need to start thinking about *kinds of abilities* rather than *levels of ability*. Or as Eric Jensen characteristically puts it:

> 'It's now time for educators and parents to quit asking the old question, How smart are you? ... The new question is, How are you smart?'

SuperTeaching, *Jensen, E (The Brain Store, 1995)*

The simplistic, quantitative model of ability has a particularly pernicious impact on teachers' and pupils' levels of expectation. This is dramatically illustrated by the following comment from a classroom teacher at a seminar on achievement:

> 'Quite recently I was challenged by some of my colleagues for using bridging materials with a Standard Grade Foundation class to help them achieve General grades. My colleagues seemed to think that I was somehow cheating by enabling my students to achieve grades that were not appropriate to their 'ability level'.

Raising Achievement: mixed ability or setting? *West Lothian Education Seminar No.3, 1997*

And as Henry Ford once observed:

> 'Whether you think you can or you think you can't, you're probably right!'

(ii) The learning process. The evidence reviewed in the section on *'Thinking and Learning'* indicates that learning for understanding involves the active construction of personal meaning from experience. Yet there is still a widespread conception that learning simply involves the acquisition of pre-formed ideas. These two contrasting mental models are based on constructivist and behaviourist principles of psychology respectively. They have also been called the transformation and transmission models of learning, which Douglas Barnes contrasts in the following way:

> '...many teachers see knowledge as the possession of trained adults...(but) even when a trained adult has formulated...a series of statements...these...remain no more than marks upon paper until learners have worked upon it themselves, and related it to what they already know.'

From Communication to Curriculum, *Barnes, D © (Bonyton-Cook, 1992)*

Professor Sally Brown of Stirling University reinforces this point:

> 'Teaching and learning are not to be construed as a process of delivering knowledge into the empty mind of a learner. On the contrary, pupils construct their own schemes of ideas (schemata) to make sense of their experience and, no matter how misguided those ideas appear to be, they will not be overturned by simply imparting the 'correct' information...
>
> 'This constructivist approach, therefore, conceives of learning as a complex and active process...and of the notion of delivering a curriculum as contrary to the reality of pupils' minds.'

Raising Standards, *Scottish Council for Research in Education Fellowship Lecture (1992)*

Yet the widespread use of verbs such as 'deliver', 'acquire', 'impart' and 'instil' reveals that the transmission model of learning still dominates thinking in educational circles, almost as much as in wider society. It seems as though teachers are expected to behave like postmen, delivering packages of pre-formed knowledge into the minds of pupils who are meant to passively acquire, miraculously understand and then effectively use it!

As David Kolb has observed:

> '...behaviourist theories of learning... are based on the idea that there are elements of consciousness that always remain the same... It is the notion of constant, fixed elements of thought that has had such a profound effect on prevailing approaches to learning and education, resulting in a tendency to define learning in terms of its outcomes, whether these be knowledge in an accumulated storehouse of facts or habits representing behavioural responses to specific stimulus conditions. If ideas are seen to be fixed and immutable, then it seems possible to measure how much someone has learned by the amount of these fixed ideas the person has accumulated.'

Experiential Learning: Experience as the Source of Learning and Development,
Kolb, D © 1984 (Reprinted by permission of Practice-Hall, Inc., Upper Saddle River, NJ)

The typical classroom exchange in which pupils demonstrate their understanding by giving correct answers to the teacher's closed questions, as here described by Douglas Barnes, is a striking example of this mental model in operation*:

*See also the extract from **Using Discussion in the Classroom** on page 53!

> 'Whereas on each occasion the teacher speaks several sentences, each pupil contributes no more than a word or phrase. It is the teacher who is using language to shape meanings, not the pupils, who are given only slots to fill in with single words. If they are to understand it must be through his eyes...
>
> 'Both the traditional teacher-dominated lesson and the mode of working implied by worksheets are based upon an implicit distrust of children's ability to learn.'

Barnes, D (op. cit.)

Yet, as we have seen, understanding and memory will only develop if learners are given plenty of opportunities for active learning or, as David Perkins puts it, to perform their understandings.

Transmission model worksheets are often used on educational visits, e.g. to zoos, where pupils might be invited to find various animals and then answer questions such as 'Where does the animal live?' or 'What does it eat?' by copying information from the notice boards.*

* See also the examples shown on pages 52 and 54.

Clearly, little or no mental processing is involved in this 'activity' , so pupils are unable to make strong neural links or extend and elaborate their developing schemata by connecting new links to existing networks. As a result, they are unable to develop real understanding or memory.

By contrast, a transformation approach might ask the pupils to work in groups to prepare an illustrated guide to the zoo for a visit by younger pupils. Not only would this require pupils to perform their understandings and so build strong, interconnected neural links; it would also give them the opportunity to use more than just their linguistic intelligence, especially if they were encouraged to think of imaginative ways of presenting their information to younger children, e.g. by creating mobiles of the animals.

The 'Motorway Model' of differentiation described on page 38 combines both of these outdated mental models to produce a strikingly inappropriate solution to a pedagogical problem. Not only does it assume that different pupils have different amounts of a single 'ability'; it also assumes that more able pupils should be allowed to cover curriculum content at maximum speed, unencumbered by their less able brethren. This epitomises the transmission model of learning in which no account is taken of the need to reinforce and differentiate neural links once they have formed.

If we consider Gardner's multiple intelligences together with the three components of Perkins' model of an intelligence, it seems reasonable to conclude that able pupils have relatively high neural components in the linguistic and/or mathematical intelligences that are so prized in most school work. These will enable them to form new neural connections, i.e. to 'learn' new information relatively quickly. But unless they are given sufficient opportunities to perform, and time to review and reflect on this new learning, these new connections will be unable to myelinate properly and so they will soon fade - a common enough phenomenon after 'swotting' for examinations!

In other words, Perkins' other two components - the 'learnable' intelligences - will only develop if pupils (all pupils) are given plenty of opportunities to perform, review and reflect on their learning. Galloping through a course in the fast lane may allow more able pupils to score high marks in examinations but it is also a sure recipe for insecure understanding (see the case of Peter described below).

By contrast, working collaboratively with other pupils provides many opportunities and challenges for all of them to explain - i.e. perform - their developing understandings to each other and so encourage the myelination process.*

*A striking example of the effectiveness of this kind of collaboration is described by Douglas Barnes (op. cit. page 37).

From this review of mental models, therefore, we can derive *three final key principles of learning*. These are:

Teachers' interactions with their pupils should be based on the following understandings -

- *differences between pupils' abilities are complex and qualitative rather than simple and quantitative;*

- *there are no practical limits to the development of individual pupils' abilities;*

- *learning for understanding is achieved through the performance of challenging, open-ended tasks rather than by giving correct answers to closed questions.*

Epilogue: A Tale of Two Pupils

Finally, let us consider the notional example of two very differentially able boys, Peter and Paul - though they could equally well be two girls, or a boy and a girl.

Peter has strong linguistic and logical-mathematical intelligences. He enjoys listening to most of his teachers and conveying ideas in writing. Peter is a predominantly visual learner. He is content to sit quietly for lengthy periods and always produces neat work. He prefers individual working to group discussion.

Peter has a moderate left brain bias to his thinking. He copes easily with work presented logically and sequentially without the benefit of a 'big picture' to organize his thoughts, and he is also good at critical, analytical thinking.

Paul's strengths, by contrast, are in the bodily-kinaesthetic, visual/spatial and interpersonal intelligences. He is highly creative, good at sports and a talented dancer and actor. But he does not find it easy to express his thoughts in writing. Paul is also a strongly kinaesthetic learner. He needs to handle objects and to move around to learn new information effectively.

Paul has a strong right brain bias to his thinking. If given the opportunity (which is not often), he will produce highly original solutions to complex, open-ended problems and he enjoys sparking off ideas with others in group discussions. But he finds it extraordinarily difficult to think and learn effectively without the benefit of movement, discussion and a 'big picture' in which to contextualise his thoughts.

Now consider the classrooms in which Peter and Paul have to learn. In most of them there are rules of behaviour on the wall like those on page 31. The teachers mostly present new work in a logical, sequential manner, without a 'big picture'. Assessment is generally based on written work and is carried out by the teacher for grading purposes rather than to identify learning needs (see the quotations from **Inside the Black Box** on page 26).

Unsurprisingly, Peter is labelled an 'able' pupil. He is clearly highly intelligent and his standards of dress, behaviour and work presentation conform well to school policies on these issues. He is, of course, in the top set for all his examination subjects.

Unfortunately, the emphasis in most of these sets is on covering the maximum syllabus content in such a way as to gain high marks in the examinations, rather than developing deep understanding and effective thinking and learning skills. In other words, the emphasis is on using the 'neural' component of intelligence rather than developing the 'experiential' and 'reflective' components. Therefore, although he regularly picks up awards at school prize-giving and does very well in his school and university examinations, his understanding of much of the work is relatively insecure. Indeed, he epitomises Howard Gardner's claim that:

> '...even when school appears to be successful, even when it elicits the performances for which it has apparently been designed, it typically fails to achieve its most important missions.
>
> 'Evidence for this startling claim comes from a by-now overwhelming body of educational research that has been assembled over the last decades. These investigations document that even students who have been well trained and who exhibit all the overt signs of success - faithful attendance at good schools, high grades and high test scores, accolades from their teachers - typically do not display an adequate understanding of the materials and concepts with which they have been working.'

The Unschooled Mind, Gardner, H (HarperCollins Publishers Ltd., 1991)

Peter eventually embarks on a moderately successful career with an insurance company.

Paul, by contrast, is a problem! Talented perhaps, but not in academic activities. Paul is therefore labelled 'less able'.

Moreover, his behaviour causes problems for teachers and fellow pupils because he will not sit still and keep quiet in class for more than a few minutes at a time. He is regularly in trouble with the school's disciplinary system, leaves school at 16 and eventually joins a modern dance group. Paul goes on to become an outstandingly successful dancer and choreographer.

Of course, unlike Peter, many 'able' pupils do go on to highly successful careers in many walks of life. Unfortunately, unlike Paul, many 'less able' pupils fail to overcome the negative self-images created by (avoidable) lack of success in their school learning. At best they represent a waste of potential. At worst they become antisocial dropouts and a burden on society.

KEY PRINCIPLES OF LEARNING: A SUMMARY

The learning environment should -

- minimise threat and uncontrollable stress;
- promote positive self-image and high self-esteem;
- engage positive emotions;
- recognise that individual learners have legitimately different behavioural needs.

Learning activities should -

- encourage learners to perform their understandings;
- provide regular opportunities for review and reflection;
- include timely and accurate feedback;
- encourage the use of whole brain learning;
- cater for different thinking and learning styles;
- provide ample opportunities for learners to use and develop the full range of multiple intelligences.

Teachers should understand that -

- differences between pupils' abilities are complex and qualitative rather than simple and quantitative;
- there are no practical limits to the development of individual pupils' abilities;
- learning for understanding is achieved through the performance of challenging, open-ended tasks rather than by giving correct answers to closed questions.

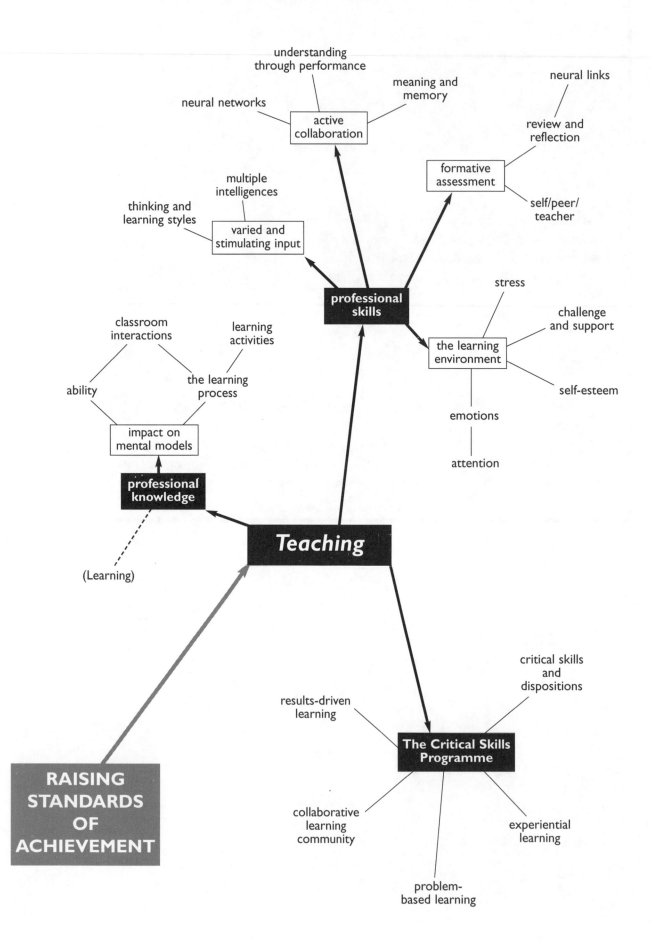

understanding
through performance

neural networks

meaning and
memory

neural links

active
collaboration

review and
reflection

formative
assessment

self/peer/
teacher

multiple
intelligences

thinking and
learning styles

varied and
stimulating input

professional
skills

stress

challenge
and support

the learning
environment

self-esteem

classroom
interactions

learning
activities

ability

the learning
process

emotions

attention

impact on
mental models

professional
knowledge

Teaching

(Learning)

critical skills
and
dispositions

results-driven
learning

**The Critical Skills
Programme**

**RAISING
STANDARDS
OF
ACHIEVEMENT**

collaborative
learning
community

experiential
learning

problem-
based learning

Section Two: Teaching

Section One outlines up-to-date knowledge of brain functioning and the learning process and identifies 13 key principles of learning which relate to three areas:

➡ *the learning environment;*

➡ *the design of learning activities;*

➡ *the beliefs and behaviours of teachers.*

These are summarised on page 47.

The purpose of Section Two is to describe how these key principles of learning can be applied to design and teach high quality learning activities for pupils.

Sections Three and Four then describe how these same principles can be applied to improve:

Staff Development (Section Three)

➡ *the design of learning activities for teachers*

➡ *the transformation of new knowledge into effective classroom practice*

Organizational Development (Section Four)

➡ *whole-school communications*

➡ *whole-school learning through collaboration and self-evaluation*

➡ *policy development and implementation*

➡ *development planning for learning schools*

Section Two consists of two chapters. The main issues addressed in these are (see also the visual layout opposite):

Chapter 2: Key Principles of Teaching

1. Teachers' Professional Knowledge

- the impact of new knowledge about the brain and learning on teachers' mental models of *ability* and the *learning process*; the consequences of these mental models for the ways in which teachers design learning activities and interact with their pupils.

2. Teachers' Professional Skills

- *managing the learning environment*: providing challenge with support; optimising levels of stress; raising self-esteem; engaging positive emotions and attention;
- *providing varied and stimulating input*: catering for different styles of thinking and learning, and multiple intelligences;
- *designing active, collaborative learning experiences*: to develop neural networks; encourage 'understanding through performance'; promote meaning and memory;
- *using formative assessment*: to consolidate and differentiate new neural links through timely and accurate feedback; review and reflection; self, peer and teacher-assessment.

Chapter 3: The Critical Skills Programme

A comprehensive and highly practical American teaching programme which combines the 13 key principles of learning into a coherent and powerful framework.

- *'critical skills and fundamental dispositions'*: for individual and organizational success in life and work;
- *experiential learning*: interaction in real-life contexts; constructing individual meaning; engaging in complex actions;
- *a collaborative learning community*: an intentionally structured classroom culture within which teachers and pupils support one another in pursuit of clearly articulated goals;
- *results-driven learning*: thoughtfully designed learning experiences which focus powerfully on curriculum targets for knowledge/understanding and skills/dispositions;
- *problem-based learning*: thoughtfully designed 'challenges' which create the 'need to know'; developing and applying knowledge/understanding; demonstrating skills/dispositions; attending to process; seeing the big picture.

Chapter 2: Key Principles of Teaching

> 'When we design learning around basic principles of how the brain learns, motivation, meaning and recall increase for all learners.'

Completing the Puzzle, *Jensen, E*

This chapter looks at the general implications of the principles of learning identified in *Section One* for the design of learning activities and the improvement of classroom practice. It consists of two main parts, which deal respectively with the issues of teachers' *professional knowledge* and *professional skills*. Chapter 3 then illustrates how these general principles are put into practice in a highly effective and comprehensive teaching programme.

1. Teachers' Professional Knowledge

This part of the Chapter deals with the following key principles of learning (see page 47).

Teachers should understand that -

- *differences between pupils' abilities are complex and qualitative rather than simple and quantitative;*

- *there are no practical limits to the development of individual pupils' abilities;*

- *learning for understanding is achieved through the performance of challenging, open-ended tasks rather than by giving correct answers to closed questions.*

> 'I recently met with Network Press' accountant and assumed, with some confidence, that he had an up-to-date knowledge of the relevant tax legislation. He'd be no use to us if he hadn't. My daughter recently contracted glandular fever and so we consulted our G.P. I assumed that he had an up-to-date knowledge of the relevant treatments, prescriptions and diagnoses. He'd be dangerous if he hadn't! Last week my daughter returned to school. How confident can I be that her teachers' professional knowledge matches that of my accountant and doctor?'

Chris Dickinson, West Lothian Headteachers Conference (1998)

> 'We have been made aware that many of our current actions and decisions are based on outdated mental models... We need to keep more up-to-date with current knowledge about learning... We need to design more appropriate learning tasks and to provide a rich curriculum which caters for different learning needs and preferences.'

West Lothian Headteachers Conference discussion groups (1998)

The new knowledge about learning described in Chapter 1 lies at the very core of teachers' professional practice - not least through its potential impact on their mental models of *ability* and the *learning process*. Unfortunately, many teachers are still unaware of much of this knowledge and so, as the West Lothian Headteachers pointed out, they continue to take inappropriate 'actions and decisions...based on outdated mental models'.

Prologue: A Tale of Two Teachers

* The use of female examples does not imply that outdated mental models are confined to one gender!

*See the quote from H.H.Goddard on page 37.

* See the postman cartoon and David Kolb's comments on page 42.

*The two 'Tunisia' worksheet examples (see also page 55) are taken from **Effective Learning Activities** by Chris Dickinson.

We can illustrate the problems caused by outdated mental models by considering the notional case of two geography teachers, *Ms. Fogg* and *Ms. Compass**, working in different schools and in departments with widely differing degrees of professional knowledge.

Ms. Fogg and her colleagues have a relatively low level of knowledge about the brain and learning. They believe that ability is essentially 'conditioned by a nervous mechanism that is inborn...and...but little affected by any later influence'*; and their concept of the learning process is the transmission model described on pages 41-44.

The transmission model assumes that new knowledge somehow slots into place in an 'accumulated storehouse of facts'* so that learning takes place when learners give correct answers to specific, closed questions. It ignores the need for learners to create their own meanings from new knowledge by constructing and strengthening new neural links.

Therefore Ms. Fogg makes regular use of worksheets such as the following* and assumes that correct answers to closed questions indicate that the pupils have learnt the information - as far as they are ever going to.

TUNISIA

Look at the two rainfall maps of Africa, figures 48 and 49, and answer these questions:

1   In which season does Tunisia have most rain - summer or winter?
    How much rain does the northern part of Tunisia receive each year?

2   Is there a big difference between the summer and the winter rain?
    In which part of the country is there the greatest difference?
    What is the difference?

3   Taking the year overall, which parts of the country are the driest and which are the wettest?

4   Does your home area receive as much, less or more rain than Tunisia for the year as a whole?

5   Where in Africa are there drier areas than Tunisia? Where are there wetter areas?
    Think of this question in terms of (a) latitude; (b) vegetation areas.

Unfortunately, written end-of-topic and end-of-session tests regularly show that many of Ms. Fogg's pupils have failed to remember even the basic information demanded by the worksheet questions. She rationalises this by assuming that these pupils have a low level of ability, i.e. their brains are so inherently ineffective that they are incapable of memorising even the most straightforward information for any length of time.

Even more unfortunately, very few of those pupils who can actually remember the basic information can use it to demonstrate real understanding by solving complex problems. Again, Ms. Fogg's mental model of ability comes into play and she assumes that the results are simply a reflection of the different levels of ability in her pupils. It does not occur to her that the problem might lie in the nature of the learning materials and her own teaching approach.

The following extract from an American History lesson transcript in James Dillon's highly insightful book **Using Discussion in the Classroom** (*1994*) is typical of Ms. Fogg's teaching approach, based on the 'transmission' model of learning. Sadly, it is still as widely prevalent in British as American schools.

> 'Teacher: OK, so we've covered leadership and some of the things that Washington brought with it. Why else did they win? ...
> Pupil: France gave 'em help.
> Teacher: OK, so France giving aid is an example of what? ...
> Pupil: Aid from allies.
> Teacher: Aid from allies, very good. Were there any other allies who gave aid to us?
> Pupil: Spain.
> Teacher: Spain. Now, when you say aid, can you define that?
> Pupil: Help.
> Teacher: Define help. Spell it out for me.
> Pupil: Assistance.
> Teacher: Spell it out for me (etc.).'

Using Discussion in Classrooms, *Dillon, J (Open University Press, 1994)*

Notice how the focus of the 'discussion' is on getting and giving the 'right' answers. When these are forthcoming the teacher responds positively ('very good'); but when the answer is not exactly what the teacher is looking for he/she responds with increasingly closed questions. As Paul Black and Dylan Wiliam observe in their recent authoritative review of research on formative assessment:

> '...the teacher is looking for a particular response and lacks the flexibility or the confidence to deal with the unexpected.* So the teacher tries to direct the pupil towards giving the expected answer. In manoeuvring the conversation in this way, the teacher seals off any unusual, often thoughtful but unorthodox attempts by the pupils to work out their own answers. Over time the pupils get the message - they are not required to think out their own answers. The object of the exercise is to work out, or guess, what answer the teacher expects to see or hear, and then express it so that the teaching can proceed.'

Black, P & Wiliam, D (op. cit.)

* The teacher is also clearly operating with an outdated, inappropriate mental model of the learning process, i.e. the 'transmission' model.

Unsurprisingly, relatively few of Ms. Fogg's pupils gain any real understanding of the climatic concepts involved in this topic but she consoles herself with the thought that this is largely because of their low levels of ability and/or inherent 'laziness'. Of course, her mental model of ability also influences her attitude and behaviour towards these pupils, whose self-image, self-esteem and motivation are consequently depressed. As Margaret Donaldson observed over 20 years ago:

> 'We are beings who ask questions; we are beings who make value judgements; ...and we are beings who build (mental) models of the world. In the course of time, these models come to include some representations of ourselves as part of the world. It is thus inevitable that we should arrive at the question: of what value am I? And it is also inevitable that the answer should matter to us a great deal.
>
> 'When a child first asks this question, how is he to get the answer? One obvious way will be to try to discover what value other people place upon him...they are bound to exert powerful influence on his self-esteem.'

Children's Minds, *Donaldson, M (HarperCollins Publishers Ltd., 1978)*

Ms. Fogg and her colleagues respond to this situation by employing the 'Motorway Model of Differentiation' (see the drawings on pages 38 and 56). They provide less demanding worksheets for the 'less able' like the one shown here. (Although this is from science rather than geography, it *is* a genuine example!)

Of course, this merely compounds the problem because it demands so little thinking that the pupils have no opportunity at all to develop understanding and memory - not to mention being totally bored and insulted! But this merely confirms Ms. Fogg's mental model. 'Low ability' clearly means *in*ability to operate at higher mental levels. Low ability brains are fundamentally deficient.

The end result of this approach was brilliantly described by Neil Postman and Charles Weingartner as long ago as 1969:

NAME..   CLASS.............

UNIT FOUR   ENERGY   SHEET 1

PART 1

It is very difficult to say what E.................. is, but when you have energy y...

Living things need energy to m......... and w........ and k...........
.... Machines need energy to be able to w............

Energy comes in quite a few different forms. Some of them are listed here with an example of something that has that sort of energy.

TYPE OF ENERGY	EXAMPLE
HEAT	A hot water bottle has heat energy.
LIGHT	A........................... has light energy
SOUND	A........................... has............ energy.
MOVEMENT	A........................... has............... energy.
STORED MOVEMENT	A.............. has........................... energy.
CHEMICAL	A........................... has ....energy.
ELECTRICAL	A ....has..................energy.
NUCLEAR	An atom bomb has.................... energy.

TEACHER   Ask your teacher to check your answers.

> 'The game is called 'Let's Pretend', and if its name were chiselled into the front of every school building in America, we would at least have an honest announcement of what takes place there. The game is based on a series of pretences which include: let's pretend that...this sort of work makes a difference to your lives; let's pretend that what bores you is important, and that the more you are bored, the more important it is; ...let's pretend that your intellectual competence can be judged on the basis of how well you can play Let's Pretend.'

Teaching as a Subversive Activity, *Postman, N & Weingartner, C*
(Pearson Education, 1969)

By contrast, *Ms. Compass* and her colleagues have a high level of professional knowledge about learning. They recognise that the mix of abilities and learning styles in their classrooms is complex and that learning for understanding occurs when pupils have to think and perform in a variety of modes. Therefore Ms. Compass' worksheet* for the same topic looks like this:

* This is a simplified version of a Critical Skills 'Challenge'. Further details are provided in Chapter 3, pages 87-92.

TUNISIA

A group of archaeologists are due to visit Tunisia and have asked you to advise them about its climate. Your task is to prepare some kind of document or presentation which gives them all the facts they need.

You may use any of the resources listed on page 2. Your document/presentation should include the following sections:

1   Rainfall - include details on how much rain; regional differences; seasonal wettest and driest regions.

2   Comparisons with UK and other parts of Africa - include details of rainfall compared with where you live; drier and wetter parts of Africa in terms of latitude and vegetation.

Provided you include the above information, your presentation could be:

● written (a report, handwritten or word processed; a letter; a script of an imaginary telephone conversation);

● spoken (a presentation; a cassette tape; a 'question time' event);

● visual (a poster; an annotated map; computer graphics);

● multi media.

Use this space to record data ... (etc.)

This approach encourages her pupils to think about - and with - their new knowledge, and to perform their developing understandings in a variety of ways. Consequently, they are able to develop strong neural links and to link newly developing neural networks to existing networks (i.e. 'schemata') which are extended and/or elaborated in the process.*

* See the comments by Neville Bennett (page 25) and Sally Brown (page 42).

Of course, not all of Ms. Compass' pupils score full marks on every test! But her first response in such circumstances is not to assume that this is due to a basic lack of ability. Instead, she encourages them to reflect on the reasons for their failures and to engage openly in discussion with herself and fellow pupils. She knows that this use of formative assessment will enable them to learn from their mistakes and that this will help them to develop stronger neural networks and *generative knowledge*.*

* 'Knowledge which does not just sit there but functions richly in people's lives to help them understand and deal with the world.' - See page 24.

Ms. Compass is convinced that *all* of her pupils have vastly underused thinking and learning potential, and that her responsibility is to help all of them to access as much of this as possible. Her classroom ethos is relaxed and supportive but also demanding. Both her own and her pupils' expectations of success are high - and more often than not achieved! In many ways her classroom resembles the typical Japanese situation described by Stigler and Hiebert (see page 38).

We can illustrate the essential difference between the two teachers' approaches to differentiation by revisiting the 'Motorway Model' shown on page 38.

* See the quote from **The Unschooled Mind** on page 45.

Because of her more up-to-date professional knowledge Ms. Compass has developed radically different mental models of ability and the learning process from Ms. Fogg. These have enabled her to provide more effectively differentiated learning experiences for her pupils by developing more effective professional skills. The details of these skills are the subject of part 2 and much of Chapter 3.

2. Teachers' Professional Skills

The following four sections examine the issues of:

(i)   Managing *the learning environment;*
(ii) Providing *varied and stimulating input;*
(iii) Designing *active, collaborative learning experiences;*
(iv) Promoting *regular formative assessment.*

(i) Managing the learning environment.

This section deals with the following key principles of learning (see page 47):

The learning environment should -

● *minimise threat and uncontrollable stress;*

● *promote positive self-image and high self-esteem;*

● *engage positive emotions;*

● *recognise that individual learners have legitimately different behavioural needs.*

Learning activities should -

● *encourage the use of whole brain learning.*

> 'Threat and induced learner helplessness have got to be reduced from the learning environment to achieve maximum potency... It's not stress that's bad, it's uncontrollable stress that's bad'

Completing the Puzzle, *Jensen, E*

Uncontrollable stress provokes primitive, survival behaviours.* Blood flows out of the cortex into the hind brain so that effective thinking and learning become impossible and learners start to exhibit typical 'reptilian' behaviours such as territoriality ('get away from me and my possessions') and ritualistic display (attention-seeking). These are usually labelled 'misbehaviour' but they are actually inevitable consequences of threat and stress!

*See the section on the hind brain, pages 19/20.

Of course, many pupils are subject to serious stress from factors (e.g. domestic problems) which are outside the control of schools and individual teachers. But there are a number of other factors which we can control, and which can greatly improve the quality of the learning environment by reducing threat and uncontrollable stress. These include:

- *promoting clarity and confidence about learning tasks;*
- *generating high expectations and an 'ethos of achievement';*
- *providing purposeful enjoyment in the classroom.*

Promoting clarity and confidence about learning tasks.

In **Completing the Puzzle** Jensen goes on to point out that:

> 'An example of a subtle threat to the learner is when an assignment or project is given, and the learner lacks the resources to carry it out. That might be not enough time, no pen or pencil or no one with whom to discuss it. The learner reacts and goes into a state of stress. In some cases, the threat may be perceived as indirectly aimed at one's self-esteem, confidence and peer acceptance.'

Jensen, E (op. cit.)

Clarity and confidence are promoted by teaching strategies which:

- *provide the big picture;*
- *enable pupils to clarify what they are expected to do and learn;*
- *identify long-term learning goals.*

Providing the big picture. It is important for learners to understand the context within which they are expected to achieve their learning targets. This does more than simply promote clarity and confidence. By encouraging pupils to use both halves of their brains it also promotes 'whole brain' learning in which critical and creative thinking are integrated more effectively.*

*See page 33.

One effective way of providing the big picture is through class 'debriefings' to find out what pupils remember from the previous lesson(s), before linking into new work. These can often provide a salutary lesson to the teacher on the difference between what she thought she had taught and what the learners had actually learnt!

Clarifying what pupils are expected to do and learn. Pupils are also often uncertain about the nature of their learning targets. As Black and Wiliam observe:

> 'Many...successful innovations have developed self and peer assessment by pupils... (but)...pupils can only assess themselves when they have a sufficiently clear picture of the targets that their learning is meant to attain. Surprisingly, and sadly, many pupils do not have such a picture, and appear to have become accustomed to receiving classroom teaching as an arbitrary sequence of exercises with no overarching rationale.'

Black, P & Wiliam, D (op. cit.)

Clarifying the learning task...

A particularly effective way of overcoming these uncertainties is through regular small group discussions in which pupils come to an agreement about what and how they are expected to learn before they start their learning tasks.*

* See also the description of 'chunking the challenge' in Chapter 3, pages 78-80.

Identifying long term learning goals. Regular discussion of the outcomes of learning activities through 'debriefings' helps to motivate pupils by focusing their attention on their successes. But just as importantly, it also provides the opportunity for them to identify any skills that they need to continue working on. This approach features particularly strongly in the Critical Skills Programme (see Chapter 3) in which pupils are also encouraged to collaborate with their teachers in designing activities to address these longer term goals.

...Debriefing: providing the big picture and identifying long term goals

Generating high expectations and an 'ethos of achievement'.

Classroom ethos is primarily determined by

- *classroom relationships*
- *the physical environment.*

Classroom relationships. The ways in which teachers behave in their classrooms hugely influence their pupils' beliefs and behaviours. Teachers with up-to-date mental models can minimise stress and maximise self-esteem by demonstrating through their actions that they genuinely believe that *all* their pupils can successfully tackle challenging learning tasks.

This is epitomised in the contrasting teaching approaches of Ms. Fogg and Ms. Compass, as described in part 1. Ms. Fogg responds to pupils' difficulties by simplifying the work and *reducing* the challenge. By contrast, Ms. Compass' genuinely high expectations lead her to encourage her pupils to *meet* the challenge by learning from their difficulties. Her interactions with her pupils are encouraging and supportive, and she also encourages them to interact with each other in supportive ways.*

* Further information about Ms. Compass' teaching techniques is provided in Chapter 3, page 76 onwards.

She knows that these interactions should not consist of closed questioning to elicit 'correct' answers but should be genuine and open explorations of the problem in the confident expectation that, given the right kind of opportunity to think through and talk about their difficulties, her pupils will be able to construct their own meanings from their learning experiences and so gain genuine understanding.

Finally, unlike Ms. Fogg, Ms. Compass realises that many of her pupils are prevented from learning effectively by simplistic behaviour rules that favour certain thinking and learning styles and intelligences more than others. This is not simply because these rules can directly hamper some pupils' learning. It is also because they can depress their self-images by sending implicit signals that their preferred styles and stronger intelligences are not valued in that particular classroom.*

* See the quote from Margaret Donaldson on page 54.

Hardly surprising, then, that Ms. Fogg regularly complains in the staff room about the 'misbehaviour' of many of her pupils and demands that senior management should 'do something about it'. She would do well to reflect on Robert Sylwester's observation that:

> 'Mobility is central to much that's human whether the movement of information is physical or mental. We can move and talk. Trees can't. Misguided teachers who constantly tell their students to sit down and be quiet imply a preference for working with a grove of trees, not a classroom of students!'

Art for the Brain's Sake, *Sylwester, R (Educational Leadership, November 1998)*

By contrast, Ms. Compass always negotiates an agreed 'learning contract' with her new classes. This is based on the demonstrably high expectations which she has of them and is derived from small group discussions and brainstorming. The Critical Skills Programme (Chapter 3), tackles this issue in a particularly effective way by encouraging pupils to develop a 'Full Value Contract' and criteria for 'Quality Discussion' and a 'Quality Audience'. The way in which this is done is described in some detail from page 78 onwards.

The physical environment. Classroom walls filled with positive messages and the products of pupils' learning activities can exert a powerful influence on the emotional and values centres within the brain's limbic system.* Ms. Compass knows this and has created a classroom environment which continually sends positive, reinforcing messages to her pupils - not least because her classes are heavily involved in creating wall displays which are substantially unique to each class. Because these are secondary pupils this does take extra time at the beginning and end of lessons as they put up and pack away their display materials, but since these are carefully and clearly stored this takes no more than a few minutes and the extra pay-off in attention and motivation of her pupils more than makes up for 'lost' time.

* See Section 2 of **Accelerated Learning in the Classroom** (Network Educational Press, 1996) for an excellent description of this issue.

Providing purposeful enjoyment in the classroom.

> 'When you have to do things and work together you have more fun than just sitting there and taking stuff off the board. It seems to get it into your head better, like you remember it better.'
>
> 'It's like fun, so we do things that are fun that helps to keep it in our brain.'

14 year-old pupils interviewed for **The Brain and Learning** *(video programme), ed. D'Arcagelo, M (ASCD, 1998)*

Positive emotions are crucial to effective learning. Our emotions drive our attention, and our attention determines what we learn. Enjoyable but purposeful classroom activities are therefore a very powerful means of generating an environment which supports learning.

One increasingly popular way of promoting purposeful enjoyment is through 'Brain Gym' ®.* Brain Gym ® activities are designed to improve brain functioning, mainly by improving communication between different parts of the brain. They can therefore be used to promote a real sense of purpose within the classroom.

* See Appendix 3 for further information about Brain Gym ®.

This sense of purpose can be conveyed to pupils by using the sporting analogy from Chapter 1*. Athletes take great care to warm up their muscles before any demanding sporting event. Active thinking and learning are also highly demanding activities and so we should prepare our brains equally carefully before intellectual activities.

* See the 'review and reflection' section on page 24/25.

The preface to the **Brain Gym ® Teacher's Edition** states that:

> 'Brain Gym ® activities...enable students to access those parts of the brain previously inaccessible to them. The changes to learning and behaviour are often immediate and profound, as children discover how to receive information and express themselves simultaneously.'

Brain Gym ® : Revised Teacher's Edition, *Dennison, P & Dennison, G (Edu-Kinesthetics Inc., 1994)*

So Brain Gym ® activities are an excellent way of improving self-image and self-esteem by bringing purpose to the learning environment. But they also have the great advantage of engaging pupils' positive emotions because they are *fun!* As the **Teacher's Edition** puts it:

> 'When students are introduced to Brain Gym ®, they seem to love it, request it, teach it to their friends, and integrate it into their lives, without any coaching or supervision.'

Dennison, P & Dennison, G (op. cit.)

There are many teachers who will testify to the ability of Brain Gym ® activities to help create a powerful learning environment within the classroom, especially when they are used in conjunction with appropriate music to re-energise or to create a state of 'relaxed alertness'.*

* Section 4 of **Accelerated Learning in the Classroom** also contains much valuable information about the use of Brain Gym ® and music to create different classroom moods.

(ii) Providing varied and stimulating input.

This section deals with the following key principles of learning (see page 47):

Learning activities should -

- *cater for different thinking and learning styles;*

- *provide ample opportunities for learners to use and develop the full range of multiple intelligences.*

> 'i'm actually a controlling person and I recognise that in myself. But to step back and to allow my students to be the centre of my classroom - as soon as you get a little bit of it and see the success of your students, it's like you want to try more and you want to give them more because it's amazing what they can do if you don't put limits on them.
>
> 'And it's amazing what they can produce if you say "OK, I want you to do X or Y or Z, however you get there is up to you." It's just phenomenal, ways that I never would have thought of because I'm a different thinker and learner than a lot of my students; and I would limit them because of my style of learning if the only way I accepted was "my way".'

Patty Ryan, Critical Skills Master Teacher, interviewed for **The Brain and Learning** *(op. cit.)*

> 'The danger is clear: Our preferred learning style becomes our preferred teaching style.'

Effective Learning Activities, *Dickinson, C (Network Educational Press, 1996)*

Pupils are more likely to learn for understanding if they can perceive and process new information in ways which best suit their individual learning needs. This means that learning activities should provide regular opportunities for all pupils to use their preferred styles of thinking and learning, and to perform their understandings with their strongest intelligences.

Unfortunately, as Chris Dickinson and Patty Ryan point out, it is all too easy for teachers who lack up-to-date professional knowledge to assume that 'their way' is the only valid way of learning. On the other hand, it is often claimed that catering for the immensely complex mix of styles and abilities that is the reality in any classroom is too demanding a task for the 'average teacher'. But such an assumption is based on a fundamental misunderstanding about the nature of learning, clearly identified by Eric Jensen when he observed that:

> 'Many now realise that we never had a coherent foundation for learning; it was merely a model for teaching and controlling the learners.'

Completing the Puzzle, *Jensen, E*

The problem is that many teachers continue to operate with the 'transmission' mental model of learning, in which the focus is on the content that the teacher 'delivers' rather than the meaning that the learner constructs by interacting with that content.* Consequently, it is assumed that the teacher will have to have almost superhuman powers to enable her to keep control of the learners' behaviour while at the same time

* See the first postman cartoon (page 42).

delivering packages of knowledge in a multitude of different ways to cater for the individual preferences of the learners.

Clearly this is an impossible task - even for 'super teachers'! But there is a solution to the problem - albeit still a demanding one. It was identified by Patty Ryan when she observed that:

> '...to step back and to allow my students to be the centre of my classroom - ...it's amazing what they can do if you don't put limits on them.'

What Patty is describing, of course, is true 'Student Centred Learning' - a concept which came into vogue with the TVEI programme of the 1980s and early 1990s but was rarely implemented effectively because 'stepping back and allowing my students to be the centre of my classroom' is a high risk strategy which can often be a recipe for chaos! To pursue such a strategy successfully, two key issues need to be addressed.

- **Pupils** - need well-designed learning tasks which encourage them to co-operate and collaborate in their learning. This is the subject of section (iii) and much of Chapter 3.

- **Teachers** - need high quality training and long-term in-school support to develop new and demanding professional skills. This is the subject of *Section Three*.

(iii) Designing active, collaborative learning experiences.

This section deals mainly with the following key principle of learning (see page 47):

Learning activities should -

- *encourage learners to perform their understandings.*

> 'Knowledge itself is useless unless it leads to fresh insights and understanding and that can only happen if the learner is able to share ideas with others.'

Targeting Excellence: Modernising Scotland's Schools, *Scottish Office Education Department, (HMSO, 1999)*

> 'Emphatically and in manifold ways schools address what might be called the "person-solo". It is the person-solo who should acquire knowledge and skills. It is the person-solo who should work out math problems and write essays...(but)...
>
> 'People normally function in their homes, workplaces, and play places in "person-plus" kinds of ways, with intensive use of physical and information resources, interaction and interdependency. Plainly this is no accident. People operate as persons-plus because it is empowering and engaging... The work of the world gets done in groups!'

Smart Schools, *Perkins, D (op. cit.)*

> 'If they can sit together in a group and discuss, just like businesses, just like our school and faculty meetings ... and have all those brains working together, brainstorming – that's when I get the real quality products.'

*Patty Lawson, Critical Skills Master Teacher, interviewed for **The Brain and Learning** (op. cit.)*

> 'Discussion, I feel, makes me see many arguments to a decision or statement. You can get actively involved and express your own view on particular topics.'

*13 year old pupil, quoted in **The Learning School**, Lincoln, P*
(Library and Information Report 62, British Library Publications, 1987)

Learning occurs when new links are formed between neurons in the cortex of the brain. These links form when we have to think, and the more we have to think the more secure do these links become.* In **Smart Schools**, David Perkins refers to this phenomenon as 'understanding through performance'. He goes on to claim that much current thinking about learning is 'back-to-front'.

* See the section on 'Thinking and Learning', page 23.

> 'The rationale can be boiled down to a single sentence: Learning is a consequence of thinking. Retention, understanding and the active use of knowledge can be brought about only by learning experiences in which learners think about and think with what they are learning.
>
> 'Notice how this single sentence turns topsy-turvy the conventional pattern of schooling. The conventional pattern says that, first, students acquire knowledge. Only then do they think with and about the knowledge that they have absorbed. But it's just the opposite: Far from thinking coming after knowledge, knowledge comes on the coattails of thinking. As we think about and with the content that we are learning, we truly learn it...
>
> 'Therefore, instead of knowledge-centred schools, we need thinking-centred schools. This is no luxury, no utopian vision of an erudite and elitist education. These are hard facts about the way learning works.'

Perkins, D (op. cit.)

This explains why Ms. Fogg's pupils are so poor at understanding and remembering new knowledge. Tasks such as those enshrined in the Tunisia and Energy worksheets shown on pages 52 and 54 do not ask pupils to 'think about and think with' new knowledge; they simply ask them to copy information from one place to another. As a result their brains form weak neural links which quickly dissipate through lack of use.*

* it's a 'use it or lose it' brain - see page 24.

By contrast, Ms. Compass provides challenging learning activities (such as the second Tunisia worksheet, shown on page 55) which engage her pupils' emotions and encourage them to think about the content and form of their learning product. They have to listen carefully to each other, justifying their own ideas and perspectives and trying to understand those of their colleagues.

All this thinking activity helps to strengthen and differentiate their developing neural links. Inappropriate links are rejected in favour of more appropriate ones which are then strengthened through repeated use in discussion and creative action. This is the process of 'extension, elaboration or modification of schemata' described by Neville Bennett.* It improves understanding and memory by enabling pupils to develop personal meaning from the content that they are learning. Other ways of encouraging this process are described in section iv below.

* See the quote from **Managing Learning in the Primary Classroom**, page 25.

In summary, the learning tasks that Ms. Compass and her colleagues have designed help their pupils to develop understanding and memory in three important ways:

1. They encourage *active thinking*, which develops and strengthens new neural links.
2. They promote *collaboration*, which encourages the extension, elaboration or modification of schemata.
3. They engage the *emotions*, which improves attention and promotes meaning.

Of course, 'collaboration' is much easier to extol in theory than to achieve in practice! This is why Ms. Compass and her colleagues use a number of powerful teaching strategies to build truly collaborative learning communities in their classrooms.*

* See, for example, the section on 'ethos of achievement', page 59.

Further details of these - as well as the design of challenging, collaborative learning tasks - are given in Chapter 3. Meantime, we need to consider one final professional skill: How to promote forms of *assessment* which actively support learning for understanding.

(iv) Promoting regular, formative assessment.

This section deals with the following key principles of learning (see page 47):

Learning activities should -

- *include timely and accurate feedback;*
- *provide regular opportunities for review and reflection.*

> '...innovations which include strengthening the practice of formative assessment produce significant, and often substantial, learning gains...(but)... There is a wealth of research evidence that the everyday practice of assessment in classrooms is beset with problems and short-comings... The collection of marks to fill up records is given greater priority than the analysis of pupils' work to discern learning needs.'

Black, P & William, D (op. cit.)

> 'The fundamental purpose of assessment is FEEDBACK to help students learn... Meaningful feedback is based on conceiving of assessment as a process not an event... We look to our environment constantly for clues about how well we are doing. If that feedback is readily available and unambiguous, we can internalise our needs and make corrections, or we can acknowledge our successes and press on to something new.'

The Critical Skills Programme Level 1 Training Manual *(Network Eductional Press, forthcoming)*

Learning for understanding involves the development and differentiation of new neural links; and timely, accurate feedback is essential to this process. When pupils work in a collaborative learning environment towards clear achievement criteria they gain much helpful feedback from each other. But not all of this feedback is sufficiently accurate. Therefore well-designed learning programmes also build in more formal opportunities for formative assessment which ensure that feedback is both timely *and* accurate.

Ms. Compass, for example, designs learning activities which present her pupils with clear goals and provide clear criteria by which they can judge how successful they have been in achieving those goals. Her interactions with her pupils are based on authentic engagement with their questions and ideas. Her own questions are mostly open-ended as she encourages them to achieve the criteria. Epitomising the spirit of collaboration, she often discusses and agrees some of the goals and criteria with her pupils before building them into a new learning activity.

When her pupils have completed a piece of work Ms. Compass uses various 'debriefing'* techniques (self- and peer-assessment) and 'anecdotal records'* (teacher-assessment) to enable her pupils to pinpoint what they have done well and what they still need to work on. Finally, she gives plenty of time for these reflective activities, knowing that they are vital if her pupils are to consolidate their learning by strengthening and differentiating their newly formed neural links.

* These techniques are fully described in Chapter 3, page 95 onwards.

By contrast, Ms. Fogg's pupils have little or no idea of the purpose of their learning activities. They see them as chores to be completed with the minimum of thought and effort. When they have difficulty in answering the worksheet questions, Ms. Fogg's response is to ask them more and more closed questions (see page 53) so that they eventually get the 'right' answer – the 'transmission' mental model of learning in full flow!

Ms Fogg's attempts to get her pupils to work in groups are always counterproductive and often chaotic for three reasons:

1. The work is so boring that most of them take the opportunity to talk about more interesting matters (boyfriends, football, etc.).

2. Because of her inappropriate mental models she does not see the need to encourage her pupils to work collaboratively. Therefore, although her pupils work *in groups*, they do not work *as groups*.

3. Because she sees assessment primarily as a means of grading her pupils' work, she does not *want* them to collaborate on tasks for fear that this will invalidate her marks system! As Black and Wiliam have observed:

> 'The giving of marks and the grading functions are over-emphasised, while the giving of useful advice and the learning function are under-emphasised.'

Black, P & Wiliam, D (op. cit.)

Throughout Chapter 2 frequent reference has been made to the American Critical Skills Programme. Chapter 3 takes a more detailed look at this immensely impressive teaching programme.

Chapter 3: The Critical Skills Programme

This chapter describes a comprehensive teaching programme that addresses all of the issues identified in Chapter 2 in a highly practical and outstandingly effective way. It has a firm base in up-to-date learning theory, a heavy emphasis on practical 'tools' for classroom use, and a strong commitment to involve practising teachers in training other teachers (see Chapter 4). It is important to note that, despite its relative length, this chapter represents only a relatively brief outline of this programme and that effective 'Critical Skills' teaching requires intensive training and regular support over a period of time.*

*Critical Skills Programme materials and training are supplied in the U.K. through Network Educational Press. For further details see Appendix 3.

After a general introduction the remainder of the chapter describes how the various teaching skills identified in Chapter 2 are consciously and powerfully addressed by the Critical Skills Programme.

Introduction

'In 1992, after 20 years of teaching English, I was so discouraged by the school climate that I seriously contemplated early retirement. Then I was offered the chance to take Critical Skills training. I went to this course and they were teaching teachers how to change their classrooms from traditional classrooms to ones that were experientially based. And I came back and I was just very, very enthusiastic again. The kids were having fun and I was having a ball!'

Peter Fox, Critical Skills Master Teacher at Gilboa-Conesville School, New York State, interviewed for **The Brain and Learning** *(op.cit.)*

'In 1992, out of 19 schools in our State District, we were bottom of the heap... Students were smoking pot in the school. Vandalism was rife... In the summer of that year Peter Fox took Level 1 Critical Skills training and we then gave him our full support to make the necessary changes to his classroom practice. When his colleagues saw the impact on his classroom, many of them asked to take the training too...

'And that was about the time when our test scores started to rise. Within four years they had jumped dramatically... The climate of the school has changed too. Now it's a really nice place to be. And it wasn't me; it was because those teachers did that training. All I did was to give them my full support in taking the inevitable risks involved in making the changes from traditional to experientially based teaching.'

Joe Beck, Superintendent of Gilboa-Conesville School, interviewed for **The Brain and Learning** *(op.cit.)*

The Critical Skills Programme (now known as Education By Design in the USA) was initiated in New Hampshire in 1981 by High School teacher Peter Eppig (now Professor of Education at the Antioch New England Graduate School, Keene, NH). It began as a partnership between the education and business communities, to answer two key questions. The first question, addressed by a group of educationists, was:

What skills and dispositions are vitally important for students to have by the time they leave school in order to be successful in their lives?

The second question, addressed by a group of business leaders, was:

What skills and dispositions are currently lacking in the workforce that impede individual and organizational success?

The two groups were deliberately kept apart to highlight differences in perspective between the two sectors but when they reported back it was found that their recommendations were remarkably similar. They culminated in the lists of 'Critical Skills' and 'Fundamental Dispositions' shown below.

Critical Skills	**Fundamental Dispositions**
● problem solving	● owners of life-long learning
● decision making	● self-direction
● critical thinking	● internal model of quality
● creative thinking	● integrity and ethical character
● communication	● collaboration
● organization	● curiosity and wonder
● management	● community membership
● leadership	

A group of practising classroom teachers was then asked to address a third question -

What would a classroom be like that gave conscious and purposeful attention to the development of these skills and dispositions?

- and to develop a course which would enable teachers to translate that vision into effective practice.

The development group first identified 'key indicators' of each skill/disposition. These indicators have a major influence on the design and use of the problem-solving 'challenges' that form the core of the Critical Skills teaching approach*. Some examples of these indicators are:

*For example, the 'Academic Challenge' (Teacher Version) shown on page 75 focuses on the development of the two skills indicators highlighted here in the **Skill** : Organization box. They have also been highlighted in the 'process criteria' section of that challenge.

Skill: Organization

Description: Individuals who can efficiently and productively organize time, space, materials, and tasks

Key Indicators (examples):
- understanding the interdependence of time, space, materials and tasks
- categorising and prioritising competing elements
- *optimising time and resources*
- *employing organizational tools, reviewing and revising plans*

Disposition: Collaboration

Description: Individuals who seek to optimise work through collaboration

Key Indicators (examples):
- valuing collaboration
- seeing conflict of issues and ideas as an essential aspect of collaboration
- valuing, building on and maximising ideas, abilities and perspectives of others
- distinguishing between 'buying in' and 'going along'

(*Adapted from* **The Critical Skills Programme Level 1 Training Manual**)

The group collected many examples of practical and effective classroom 'tools'* which teachers could use to help their pupils develop these skills and dispositions through the mainstream curriculum. They were particularly conscious of the fact that the modern, knowledge-based workplace environment differs from the traditional, hierarchical industrial environment in four fundamental ways:

* Several of these tools are described from page 78 onwards.

1. There is constant pressure on individuals to develop new skills throughout their working lives.
2. Workers are frequently presented with complex problems with a range of possible solutions.
3. There is a continuous focus on high quality products and high standards for processes.
4. There is a heavy emphasis on collaborative work skills.

They therefore based the developing programme on four 'broad ideas':

'Broad Idea' 1. Experiential learning - creates an environment in which pupils are allowed the opportunity to interact in real-life contexts, to construct individual meaning, and to engage in complex actions that reflect life outside school.

'Broad Idea' 2. A collaborative learning community - is an intentionally structured classroom culture within which teachers and pupils support one another in pursuit of clearly articulated goals.

'Broad Idea' 3. Results-driven learning - engages pupils in thoughtfully designed experiences that necessitate that they practise and develop the significant and demonstrable characteristics we desire to foster ... in terms of knowledge/understanding and skills/dispositions.

'Broad Idea' 4. Problem-based learning - is the use of thoughtfully designed and related challenges as the primary (yet not exclusive) instructional approach. These challenges pose a problem for pupils to solve as individuals, in small groups, or as a full learning community. They create the 'need to know' - allowing pupils to develop and apply their knowledge/understanding, demonstrate skills/dispositions, attend to their process, and see the big picture that makes the work worth doing.

'While each broad idea is powerful in itself, they work best ... (as) a cohesive whole where the *classroom culture* develops through *shared experiences* and *problem-solving* to help each student meet essential *curriculum targets*.'

(*Adapted from* **The Critical Skills Programme Level 1 Training Manual**)

The CSP 'Experiential Learning Cycle' shown below illustrates how these broad ideas are integrated into the overall teaching approach. It consists of six parts:

❶ *Specific curriculum targets* - the desired outcomes of the learning activity.

❷ A *problem-based 'challenge'* - a thoughtfully designed problem for pupils to solve.

❸ A *pupil cycle* - what the pupils do as they work to solve the problem (engage, exhibit, debrief). This is divided into two categories of curriculum targets: *knowledge / understanding* and *critical skills / fundamental dispositions*.

❹ A corresponding *teacher cycle* - what the teacher does to support the pupils (design, coach, feedback).

❺ The *meaningful context* - the big picture to which the challenge is connected.

❻ The *collaborative learning community environment* - what the classroom should look, sound and feel like.

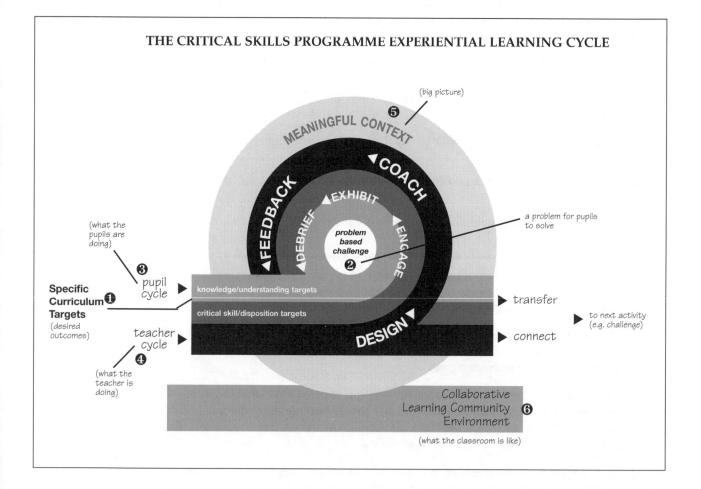

THE CRITICAL SKILLS PROGRAMME EXPERIENTIAL LEARNING CYCLE

The main links between the numbered parts of the cycle and the 'broad ideas' are:

Broad Idea	Part(s) of the Experiential Learning Cycle
'results-driven learning'	specific curriculum targets ❶ & pupil cycle ❸
'problem-based learning	problem-based challenge ❷ & teacher cycle ❹
'experiential learning'	meaningful context ❺
'collaborative learning community'	collaborative learning community environment ❻

A typical CSP classroom therefore displays the following characteristics:

Pupils -
- frequently *work in teams*
- *actively solve* meaningful problems
- *publicly exhibit* their learning
- *reflect* on what they are learning and doing
- *apply quality criteria* to their work
- *take responsibility and ownership* for their learning and the classroom community

Teachers -
- *mediate, coach and support* the learning process

Work -
- is *interconnected*

Curriculum, assessment and classroom culture -
- are guided by *specific curriculum targets*

(*Adapted from* **The Critical Skills Programme Level 1 Training Manual**)

The italicised words above relate closely to the teaching skills outlined in Chapter 2 – indeed 'Ms. Compass', who features in Chapter 2, is modelled on a CSP Master Teacher.* These relationships are explored in parts 1-3 of this chapter.

* See also Chapter 4, page 114 for a description of the role of CSP Master Teachers in promoting effective staff development.

As can be seen from the Experiential Learning Cycle, the core activities of the Critical Skills Programme are the problem-based '*Challenges*'.* These are designed at three levels of complexity and authenticity: '*Academic*'; '*Scenario*'; and '*Real Life*'. The descriptions which follow are adapted from **A Sampler of Critical Skills Challenges** (see *Appendix 3*).

* Design details of challenges vary depending upon the author(s) and the testing requirements of a particular US State. Some recent approaches to challenge design incorporate computerised templates which encourage participation by pupils in the design process.

Academic Challenges – 'Work which is structured as a "problem to solve" which arises directly from the area of study. Academic Challenges help students to

- acquire *essential knowledge and understanding*
- achieve *specifically targeted skill/disposition outcomes*
- work *co-operatively in a team setting*
- work toward *specified standards of quality*.'

Scenario Challenges - 'Work which is structured as a "problem to solve" which seeks to increase the authentic nature of the area of study by casting students in a real-life or fictive role. In addition to the behaviours listed for Academic Challenges, Scenario Challenges help students to:

- exercise *imagination and creativity* in simulating the conditions of the role or scenario
- understand a more *authentic context* for their work.'

Real-Life Problems – 'Work which is necessitated by a real problem in need of a real solution that has the potential for actual implementation at the class, school, community, regional, national or global level. In addition to the behaviours listed for Academic Challenges, these Challenges help students to:

- solve *real problems*
- receive *authentic feedback* from parties outside the classroom who have a vested interest in receiving a solution of quality
- use a broad range of skills, knowledge and strategies identical to those used by adults to solve challenges in the *real world*.'

* This challenge is adapted from one developed by Leading EDGE LLC, NY, for use in their Critical Skills training workshops. Sample Scenario and Real Life Challenges are shown in Appendix 1.

Two annotated extracts from a typical Academic Challenge* are shown on page 75: a simplified, pupil version and a teacher version which contains details of the 'product' and 'process' quality criteria that the pupils have to identify and work towards. The annotations indicate various features of the CSP teaching approach which address the key issues identified in Chapter 2 in a particularly powerful way, viz:

Challenges are designed to:

(i)   enable pupils to achieve *specific curriculum targets* (see teacher version)

(ii)   provide *clarity* about the learning task (pupil version)

(iii)   cater for different *styles of decision-making* (pupil version)

(iv)   promote *understanding through performance* (pupil version)

(v)   cater for different *styles of thinking and learning* (pupil version)

(vi)   provide regular opportunities to use and develop *multiple intelligences* (pupil version)

Teachers 'coach' their pupils through the experiential learning cycle by:

(iia)   helping them to gain further *clarity and confidence* about their learning tasks (teacher version)

(vii)   generating *high expectations* (pupil version)

(viii)   promoting supportive, productive classroom relationships through *collaborative learning* (pupil version)

(ix)   promoting regular, *formative assessment* (both versions)

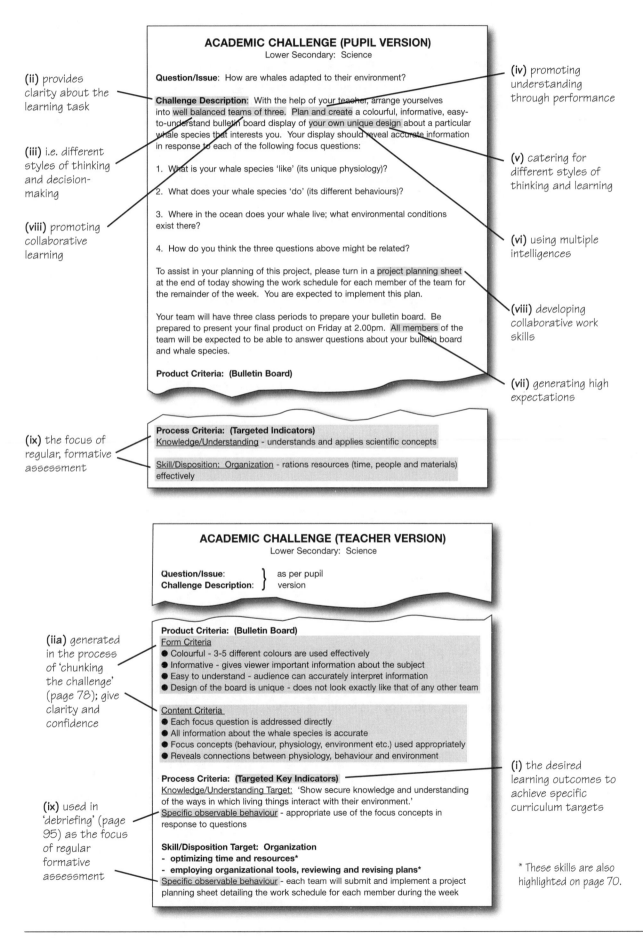

(ii) provides clarity about the learning task

(iii) i.e. different styles of thinking and decision-making

(viii) promoting collaborative learning

ACADEMIC CHALLENGE (PUPIL VERSION)
Lower Secondary: Science

Question/Issue: How are whales adapted to their environment?

Challenge Description: With the help of your teacher, arrange yourselves into well balanced teams of three. Plan and create a colourful, informative, easy-to-understand bulletin board display of your own unique design about a particular whale species that interests you. Your display should reveal accurate information in response to each of the following focus questions:

1. What is your whale species 'like' (its unique physiology)?

2. What does your whale species 'do' (its different behaviours)?

3. Where in the ocean does your whale live; what environmental conditions exist there?

4. How do you think the three questions above might be related?

To assist in your planning of this project, please turn in a project planning sheet at the end of today showing the work schedule for each member of the team for the remainder of the week. You are expected to implement this plan.

Your team will have three class periods to prepare your bulletin board. Be prepared to present your final product on Friday at 2.00pm. All members of the team will be expected to be able to answer questions about your bulletin board and whale species.

Product Criteria: (Bulletin Board)

(iv) promoting understanding through performance

(v) catering for different styles of thinking and learning

(vi) using multiple intelligences

(viii) developing collaborative work skills

(vii) generating high expectations

(ix) the focus of regular, formative assessment

Process Criteria: (Targeted Indicators)
Knowledge/Understanding - understands and applies scientific concepts

Skill/Disposition: Organization - rations resources (time, people and materials) effectively

ACADEMIC CHALLENGE (TEACHER VERSION)
Lower Secondary: Science

Question/Issue: } as per pupil
Challenge Description: } version

(iia) generated in the process of 'chunking the challenge' (page 78); give clarity and confidence

(ix) used in 'debriefing' (page 95) as the focus of regular formative assessment

Product Criteria: (Bulletin Board)
Form Criteria
● Colourful - 3-5 different colours are used effectively
● Informative - gives viewer important information about the subject
● Easy to understand - audience can accurately interpret information
● Design of the board is unique - does not look exactly like that of any other team

Content Criteria
● Each focus question is addressed directly
● All information about the whale species is accurate
● Focus concepts (behaviour, physiology, environment etc.) used appropriately
● Reveals connections between physiology, behaviour and environment

Process Criteria: (Targeted Key Indicators)
Knowledge/Understanding Target: 'Show secure knowledge and understanding of the ways in which living things interact with their environment.'
Specific observable behaviour - appropriate use of the focus concepts in response to questions

Skill/Disposition Target: Organization
- optimizing time and resources*
- employing organizational tools, reviewing and revising plans*
Specific observable behaviour - each team will submit and implement a project planning sheet detailing the work schedule for each member during the week

(i) the desired learning outcomes to achieve specific curriculum targets

* These skills are also highlighted on page 70.

* See also the
Experiential
Learning Cycle,
page 72.

The rest of the chapter examines these features in relation to *three major issues**:

1. *Creating and maintaining a collaborative classroom community*
2. *Designing the challenges*
3. *Coaching pupils through the learning cycle*

Parts 1 - 3 show how the CSP approach to these issues links powerfully to the key principles of learning and teaching identified in Chapters 1 and 2. For clarity, each issue is considered separately although there is considerable overlap between them in practice. Indeed, part 1 is considerably longer than parts 2 and 3 because it inevitably includes many aspects of all three issues.

1. Creating a Collaborative Classroom Community.

The main key principles of learning which relate to part 1 are:

The learning environment should -

- *minimise threat and uncontrollable stress;*
- *promote positive self-image and high self-esteem;*
- *engage positive emotions;*
- *recognise that individual learners have legitimately different behavioural needs.*

The intensely practical nature of CSP is most clearly seen in the way it uses a large number of highly effective teaching 'tools'. It is inappropriate to describe all of these in a relatively brief overview such as this; but some of them play such an important role in this phase of CSP development that they need to be described in sufficient detail to give a proper flavour of what a CSP classroom like that of Ms. Compass 'looks like, sounds like and feels like'.

The CSP approach to developing a collaborative community can itself be divided into three phases:

(i) *The initial phase*
(ii) *The first Challenge*
(iii) *Developing effective ground rules.*

(i) The initial phase. A teaching approach which relies heavily on collaborative team working is clearly headed for disaster unless early and thoughtful attention is paid to the development of positive, supportive relationships and collaborative working skills! Yet a number of aspects of this issue are in fact deliberately delayed in CSP, for very good reason.

CSP training emphasises that the process of building a collaborative community in the classroom can only be carried through effectively when it comes *after* pupils have been set group challenges so that they appreciate the *need* to develop ground rules and rituals that will enable them to work productively together. As Rick Gordon points out in the Training Manual:

> 'One of the most powerful and authentic ways to build community is through meaningful work. Note how communities come together in times of crisis as one example of this. In the classroom, this can occur through involving students in the process of collaboratively solving problems. The key here is using a problem that the students find important and for which they can take ownership.'

CSP Training Manual (*op. cit.*)

Of course, unless *some* initial attention is paid to relationships even the most basic and interesting of challenges will provoke discord and failure. So Ms. Compass will first spend time with a new class using 'ice-breaker' games* to help them get to know each other better. She may also use some of the Brain Gym ® activities described in Chapter 2 to promote enjoyment and a sense of purpose.

* CSP makes extensive use of ideas from **The Encyclopedia of Ice-breakers** - *see Appendix 3.*

MICHAEL!

(ii) The first Challenge. Once through this initial phase, Ms. Compass will give out a relationship-building 'Team Challenge', such as the one shown below. This asks the pupils to form 'balanced teams', introduce each member of their team to the rest of the class, identify their strengths and interests, and promote a team identity. Even a fun challenge such as this is likely to produce stresses and strains, especially as the deadline for presentation approaches!

The term 'balanced teams' (see illustration overleaf) refers to the notion of a mix of different learning, thinking and decision-making styles. These can be fairly accurately and quickly identified by asking pupils to move to different parts of the classroom according to the strength of their preferences for working with *text* versus *diagrams*; following *instructions* versus working by *intuition*; valuing new *ideas* versus meeting new *people*. They are then given three minutes to find three partners who are different from them and each other in as many of these ways as possible.

Early identification of these different styles of learning and decision-making helps to focus pupils' attention on the presence and

---

TEAM CHALLENGE (EXTRACT)

Question/Issue: Who are we? What are our strengths as individuals and as a group? How can we organize ourselves to work together productively?

Challenge Description: With the help of your teacher, create balanced teams of four.* These teams will work together to solve Challenges for some time, so try to ensure that you have a good mix of thinking styles in your team.

You will have one hour to prepare a presentation of no more than 5 minutes in which you introduce the members of your team to the rest of the class. Your presentation should include:
- your names
- some information about each of you (eg family, interests, things you have done, things you would like to do)
- one or two behaviours that your team thinks will be most important for you all to show if you are to meet the Challenges you will be presented with over the next few weeks.
- what strengths you have as individuals and as a team that will help you in your work

You should also produce a logo that includes the information in your presentation, and a name that you feel sums up who you are and what you intend to do.

As you organize your team, please be careful to stay within the comfort level of all team members.

* See also annotation (iii) in the Academic Challenge on page 75.

* See the description of the 'IP3' tool on page 83.

value of different approaches to problem-solving. At a later stage Ms. Compass will explore this issue in more detail with them.* Feedback in the debriefing phase can then focus on how each team worked at a challenge in the light of these differences, giving pupils important insights into the nature of group work and reinforcing the need for effective ground rules.

A vital coaching skill for CSP teachers involves helping pupils to become time-conscious (an important element of the critical skill of 'Organization'). So Ms. Compass will ensure that they are put under sufficient pressure to test their relationships by limiting their 'time on task' - in this case to one hour. This also helps them to appreciate the need for effective ground rules!

(iii) Developing effective ground rules. Undoubtedly the most important component of the CSP collaborative community is the Full Value Contract. This is a comprehensive collaborative working tool originally developed by Project Adventure in Massachusetts. It incorporates a set of ground rules that all members of the class (including the teacher!) agree to follow. In this way it epitomises the whole concept of a 'collaborative community'. It also epitomises in the clearest possible way the principles of learning listed at the beginning of part 1 on page 76 and is a powerful means of promoting *appropriate behaviour* and *purposeful, effective learning* in the classroom.

However, it is clearly unrealistic to expect pupils to subscribe willingly to rules of behaviour which are developed out of context. Therefore Ms. Compass ensures that the Full Value Contract *emerges from*, rather than precedes, challenging work. To do this, she first introduces a number of more specific collaborative working tools, including:*

* More comprehensive descriptions and demonstrations of these tools are given in the Network Educational Press **Introduction to CSP** and **Level 1 CSP Training** workshops as well as the **CSP Level 1 Training Manual** booklet - see Appendix 3.

- *chunking the challenge;*
- *quality discussion standards;*
- *the sweep;*
- *the thumb tool;*
- *quality audience standards;*
- *the full value contract;*
- *the IP3 tool;*
- *the carousel brainstorm.*

'Chunking the challenge', 'quality discussion standards' and 'the sweep'.
Once the class has formed into suitable teams Ms. Compass will ask them to look again at the Team Challenge and think how they are going to tackle it. At this stage she will introduce the concept of *'chunking the challenge'* in which the groups identify what the challenge description is asking them to do, and then 'chunk' this down into manageable bits – the 'quality criteria' for their group product.*

* Further information about this procedure is given in part 2: 'Designing the challenges' (see page 87).

In the case of Ms. Compass' Team Challenge these criteria include: announcing individual names; agreeing on a team name; identifying helpful behaviours; designing and drawing a logo; etc. Clearly, if they are to meet these criteria within the time-scale they will need to talk and listen to each other efficiently and effectively - in other words, to engage in a *'quality discussion'*.

The next stage is to give them two minutes (time-pressure again!) to identify what they think such a discussion will 'look like and sound like'. At this point Ms. Compass may ask the groups to organize themselves internally to carry out different roles - facilitator, recorder, reporter etc. Alternatively, depending on the age and attitude of the class, she may judge it better to leave them to find out the need for these roles themselves!

When the time is up she will ask them to spend a further minute prioritising their lists of criteria and then she will record their ideas by using 'the sweep'. This is a valuable tool for ensuring that everyone is able to contribute to a whole-class activity*. Each group reporter is invited in turn to report *one only* of their group's suggested criteria.

* The sweep is also a valuable tool for collaborative work within groups, as a means of ensuring that everyone has an opportunity to contribute to group discussions.

After every group has reported, Ms. Compass will 'sweep' again and/or invite further contributions in any order from the reporters. The insistence on only one criterion at a time is an effective way of ensuring that every group feels that they have made an important contribution to the exercise, thus promoting 'ownership' and commitment to the quality discussion standards.

There is a common tendency to avoid the notion of conflict and disagreement when thinking about ideal discussion. And yet constructive disagreement is an essential element in effective collaboration and often an important means of creative problem-solving. Therefore, if necessary, Ms. Compass will raise this topic herself and perhaps suggest a criterion such as 'giving reasons for disagreement'.

QUALITY DISCUSSION STANDARDS
· Purposeful
· Respectful
· Listening
· Trust
· One person speak at a time
· Friendly

The important concept here is that *Ms. Compass is a fellow learner and fully paid-up member of the classroom community, subject to the same rules as her pupils.*
Therefore she is equally entitled to make a contribution to the development of the community's ground rules - indeed, making genuine contributions like this can add authenticity to the teacher/class relationship.

The 'thumb tool'. Once the contributions have finished, Ms. Compass will invite the class to discuss the draft criteria in their groups, with two questions in mind:

a) Do they all understand what each criterion means? (e.g. 'respectful' will probably have to be clarified further with specific, observable behaviours* such as 'asking everyone for ideas', 'making sure everyone understands', 'listening carefully to everyone', 'using positive body language' etc.)

b) Are they prepared to live by them?

* Role-play can be a useful way of identifying specific, observable behaviours - indeed, collaboration with a drama department can be a highly productive way of taking this whole process forward.

She will then ask them all to signal their commitment by using the *'thumb tool'*:
-    thumb up = 'I'm happy with all of these.'
-    thumb horizontal = 'I can go along with them but I'm not totally happy with (named one)...'

- thumb down = 'I can't agree with (named one) because (must give a reason!)... I would prefer (alternative suggestion) because ...'

Note that in the case of a thumb down the group or individual concerned has to say why and suggest an alternative - again, to ensure that everyone in the class feels a genuine sense of ownership.

The final, agreed version of the Quality Discussion Standards is then written up neatly and displayed whenever the class is in Ms. Compass' room,* as a constant reminder of the high standards of behaviour expected and agreed to by every member of the class (including Ms. Compass!).

* For further details see the section on 'the physical environment' in Chapter 2, page 60.

OUR QUALITY DISCUSSION STANDARDS

- Keeping to the task
- Respecting each other
- Using positive body language
- Getting everyone's ideas
- Checking that everyone understands
- Listening carefully to each other
- Trusting each other
- Taking turns to speak
- Being friendly to each other
- Stopping to think before disagreeing
- Giving reasons for disagreeing

With these quality discussion standards in mind Ms. Compass will then ask the groups to spend five minutes 'chunking the challenge' and this time she will use 'the sweep' to record the definitive view of the whole class on the details of their challenge. Once these have been generally agreed and recorded they are posted on the wall as a reminder, and the class is then ready to tackle the challenge.

CHUNKING THE CHALLENGE

Names
Information –
       family
       hobbies
       ambitions
Important behaviours

Like many CSP challenges, Ms. Compass' Team Challenge culminates in a performance by each team in front of their peers - not always the easiest thing for pupils to carry off well, either as performers or audience! Therefore, before starting the presentations, she will invite the class to develop one further building block of effective collaborative group work – the 'quality audience' standards.

Quality audience standards. Ms. Compass will introduce this tool by pointing out to the class that they are all going to have to perform in front of their classmates and that if this is to go well they will need to provide a 'quality audience' for each other. So, what do they think a quality audience will 'look like and sound like'?

The procedure is similar to that for the 'quality discussion' standards, including the use of the 'sweep' and 'thumb' tools; and again the outcome is a wall poster, unique to that class, which reinforces the message that all have agreed to high standards of behaviour in all aspects of their work together.

OUR QUALITY AUDIENCE STANDARDS

●   Make eye contact

●   Nod and smile

●   Be forgiving

●   Be supportive

●   Applaud

●   Look for the positive things

The details of challenge design and operation are discussed in part 2 of this chapter. At this point we will simply assume that the class has completed their Team Challenge - and probably gone on to complete one or two more challenges - and observe how Ms. Compass facilitates the development of the *Full Value Contract*.

The Full Value Contract. As already indicated, the Full Value Contract epitomises the notion of a collaborative community and also represents a powerful and practical application of the principles of learning listed at the beginning on page 76. This can be appreciated from the following definition in the CSP Level 1 Training Manual, in which the highlighted phrases clearly relate to the need to *reduce stress; raise self-esteem; engage positive emotions*; and *respect differences*:

> 'The Full Value Contract is a social contract that helps to create a "*safe place to be*" for each individual in a community and for the interactions among community members. It provides a structure within which *expectations are established* and to which members can hold one another accountable. The notion of "full value" refers to assigning *full value to others* rather than "discounting" them.'

(op. cit. - emphases added)

The manual continues:

> 'The following three commitments are the foundation for the Full Value Contract:
>
> 1. Agreement to work together as a group and to work toward individual and group goals.
> 2. Agreement to adhere to certain safety and group behaviour guidelines.
> 3. Agreement to give and receive feedback, both positive and negative, and to work toward changing behaviour when it is appropriate.
>
> 'The contract can be oral or written, and should give consideration to guidelines for what it means for a group to -
>
> ● play/work hard
> ● play/work safe
> ● play/work fair
>
> 'The Full Value Contract is most effectively established after a group has had some initial experience together. Group experiences create a context or a need for such a contract.'

(op. cit.)

The timing and method of developing the Full Value Contract will vary according to circumstances - notably the age, experience and maturity of the class. As previously indicated, it may be necessary to take a class through several academic challenges before the teacher judges that they are ready to develop the contract; and many CSP teachers will renegotiate it to suit changing circumstances, especially at the start of a new school session. Ms. Compass' general approach is as follows:

* Debriefing is more fully described in part 3: 'Coaching pupils through the experiential learning cycle', page 92.

a) Debriefing* the Team Challenge. She will start by drawing the class' attention to the 'quality discussion' and 'quality audience' wall charts they have developed together and then ask them to discuss the following question in their groups:

'How does setting these kinds of expectations of our behaviour affect our willingness to work well with each other?'

Again, she will give them a precise time-scale (30 seconds thinking; 2 minutes discussion) and ask them to observe the 'quality discussion' standards as they discuss the question.

Then she will use the sweep to collect answers from the group reporters. These answers and the subsequent class discussion will usually highlight the fact that people tend to feel anxious when they have to work and perform with others they don't know well. Ms. Compass will then focus their attention on the way in which this anxiety can be reduced by following specific guidelines for behaviour which have been discussed and agreed (e.g. the 'quality discussion' and 'quality audience' standards) and that these also help groups to work and play together safely and productively.

b) Tackling Academic Challenges. Ms. Compass will then take the class through one or more Academic Challenges* and apply a judicious amount of pressure by continually emphasising the need to keep to time. Following the completion of this/these challenge(s), she will focus attention more closely on their group dynamics by introducing the *IP3 tool*.

* See part 2: 'Designing the Challenges', page 87.

c) Using the 'IP3' tool. IP3 was developed by Bruce Bonney of Leading EDGE LLC, New York, with the assistance of Peter Fox of Gilboa-Conesville School (see page 69). It is derived from the work of Ichak Aziz on 'Mastering Change' and is an immensely powerful way of gaining insight into the dynamics of group behaviour. In 'CSP schools' such as Gilboa it is also used to facilitate staff and organizational development activities (see Chapter 5: 'Creating a Collaborative School Culture'). Suffice to say here that it is a way of identifying different *styles of thinking and decision-making* and of prompting discussion about the effects these differences have on the ways people work together.

'IP3' stands for the initials 'I,P,P,P' and indicates that there are four basic styles of thinking and decision-making. As with styles of learning, most people use all of these styles to some extent and at different times*. But most people also have distinct preferences which come to the fore in stressful circumstances - e.g. working with people with different preferred styles under time pressure! The four styles are:

* Pupils can be tempted to use IP3 as an excuse for avoiding certain activities that they find difficult! However CSP teachers encourage them to work on their weaker styles at every opportunity.

- 'I' = 'Ideas people' who need *flexibility and choice* in what they do. They hate rigidity and don't readily follow rules. They like activities like *brainstorming* and *debriefing*.

- 'P1' = 'People people' - who are sensitive to the *feelings* of others. They hate to see people excluded from group activities and are always looking for harmony and common ground. They like activities such as *small group discussions* - and *debriefing*.

- 'P2' = 'Product people' - who live on *results* and need *clear goals and answers*. They hate drift in discussion and demand accuracy and high quality ('ideas people' drive them up the wall!). They like activities like *chunking the challenge*, setting *criteria* for success – and *debriefing*!

- 'P3' = 'Process people' - who bring *discipline and efficiency* to group work. They need rules to follow and hate chaos ('ideas people' also drive them up the wall!). They like to organize tasks in *logical steps* and to follow *rituals*. They also like – *debriefing*!!

Ms. Compass initially used a 'rough-and-ready' method of identifying these styles (see 'The first Challenge' on page 77). Now, however, she uses an appropriate version of the more sophisticated *Decision Making Styles Questionnaire* (see *Appendix 1*) which helps pupils to identify their styles more accurately and comprehensively by plotting them on flipchart paper as shown.

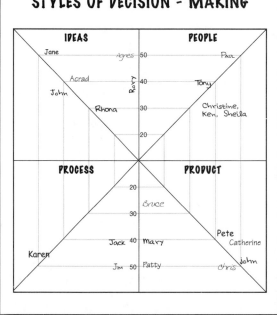

STYLES OF DECISION - MAKING

Unsurprisingly, when Ms. Compass takes her classes through this exercise they are amused and fascinated by what it tells them about themselves and each other. This provides an ideal opportunity for her to ask what it tells them about the problems they encountered in working together. She also asks them to discuss how the 'quality discussion' standards and any informal agreements they came to helped them to cope with these problems, and again uses the sweep to record their responses.

HOW DID OUR STANDARDS AND AGREEMENTS HELP?

- Felt safer
- Made more progress
- Felt more like a team
- Felt more confident
- Gave everyone a chance
- Worked better together

This leads into a class discussion about the importance of having more open and comprehensive agreements about behaviour towards each other, especially in the light of the significant differences exposed by the IP3 tool. Ms. Compass is now ready to tackle the final stage of developing the Full Value Contract, in which she uses another collaborative work tool – 'the carousel' - to help the class brainstorm and distil their ideas for creating and maintaining a classroom where everyone 'plays hard, safe and fair'.

Using the carousel tool. The carousel is a particularly effective form of brainstorming because it generates maximum involvement and the maximum number of ideas in minimum time. It also involves quite a bit of movement and so highlights the need for the 'play safe' element of the Full Value Contract - as well as catering quite well for the more kinaesthetic learners (mostly boys!) in the class.

THE FULL VALUE CONTRACT

- Play/work hard
- Play/work safe
- Play/work fair

Ms. Compass introduces the activity by referring to the different styles identified by 'IP3'. She points out that each of these styles is essential to productive group work and asks how they can create a classroom environment in which they can work well together and use these styles productively.

She will probably employ a sporting analogy by introducing the notion that successful sports teams are those which best use the different strengths of their members. Then she will show them the outline Full Value Contract and discuss its links to the quality discussion standards and other, informal, agreements they came to. Finally, she will divide them into four new groups* to brainstorm ideas about what the classroom would be like if everyone followed each of the Full Value Contract guidelines.

* CSP training includes advice and techniques for forming groups to suit different circumstances.

It is important to emphasise again that the development of an effective Full Value Contract is crucial to the creation of a collaborative learning environment. Therefore, it should only be introduced when the teacher feels that the class has had sufficient experience of challenging group work to appreciate the need for such comprehensive ground rules.

To start the brainstorming activity Ms. Compass refers to the following questions on her flip chart:

> - What will our classroom look like and sound like if we all play hard?
> - What will our classroom look like and sound like if we all play safe physically?
> - What will our classroom look like and sound like if we all play safe emotionally?
> - What will our classroom look like and sound like if we all play fair?

She discusses these questions with the class, stressing the importance of identifying *specific, observable behaviours* - though she may well use different terms! Then she will take them through the carousel brainstorming procedure, as follows.*

* The diagram at the foot of page 60 shows the carousel brainstorm in action.

1. Each group is given a different colour marker pen.

2. She reviews the basic rules of brainstorming, which are also displayed on a flip chart:

> RULES FOR BRAINSTORMING
>
> - Record ideas quickly and accurately
> - Work for quantity not quality
> - Don't judge or criticise other people's ideas
> - Encourage 'piggy-backing' (building on other people's ideas - but NOT discussing them!)
> - Be forgiving
> - Have fun! ☺

On the wall behind the stand is another piece of flip chart paper which displays the 'filter funnel' diagram.

3. She refers to this diagram to illustrate the purpose of the exercise.

4. She puts four pieces of flip chart paper, each with one of the 'looks like, sounds like' questions on four separate tables ('stations').

5. The groups spend three minutes at each station brainstorming responses to the question.

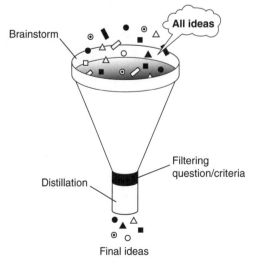

Brainstorm — All ideas

Filtering question/criteria

Distillation

Final ideas

6. When they move to a new station, they take their marker pen with them but change to a new recorder. They can then either add to (but not alter) previous responses, tick ones that they agree with, and/or add new ideas of their own.

7. When they return to their original station, they 'distil' the total list of ideas down to a small number of agreed priorities by asking two questions: a) Is this behaviour *relevant and significant?* b) Is the description *specific and observable?*

8. Ms. Compass then uses the sweep to record the groups' responses as a list on her flip chart.

9. Following general discussion she asks the groups to discuss the list for 2 minutes in their groups and then checks for agreement with the thumb tool.

10. The final, agreed list of behaviours, unique to that class, is written up neatly and subsequently displayed on the wall whenever the class is in Ms. Compass' room.

* Note that Ms. Compass is a secondary teacher. The approach described above would clearly be modified for early primary classes.

Extracts from early primary* and middle/upper secondary Full Value Contracts are shown below. These are adapted from The Critical Skills Training Manual.

Extracts from a Full Value Contract produced by an early primary class

'We agree that we will honour the following list of Peaceful Classroom behaviours:

1. Sharing

2. Teamwork and cooperation...

5. When it is your turn to speak, you speak and when it is your turn to listen, you listen

6. Use inside voices that are loud enough to be heard*

7. Decisions are made

8. Problems are worked out...

11. People have fun.'

* Note the very positive way of saying 'don't shout'!

Extracts from a Full Value Contract produced by a middle/upper secondary class

'As a full and responsible member of this learning community, I agree to:

1. Respect the privacy of other group members...

3. Ask for what I want and need, but not expect to get everything that I want

4. Speak only for myself and not others...

6. Express my feelings in a way that shows respect for myself and for others...

9. Decide on if or how I want to be different as a result of my experience in this community and develop a plan for changing...

11. Be willing to receive and to give open and honest feedback...

16. Seek quality in both individual and collaborative work and in my interactions with others

17. Maintain a sense of humour.'

The effective development of a Full Value Contract is undoubtedly a time-consuming process and requires teaching skills of a high order. But there is also no doubt that it represents time very well spent because of its crucial importance in creating an effective, collaborative learning environment in the classroom. As Gilboa-Conesville teacher Lisa Collins observes in **The Brain and Learning** video programme:

'...it takes a lot of hours but the pay-off is enormous. I strongly believe that you cannot get the kind of pay-off that we're getting by doing traditional "chalk-and-talk" kind of lessons.'

2. Designing the Challenges

The main key principles of learning (page 47) which relate to this part are:

Learning activities should -

- ● *encourage the use of whole brain learning;*

- ● *encourage learners to perform their understandings;*

- ● *cater for different thinking and learning styles;*

- ● *provide ample opportunities for learners to use and develop the full range of multiple intelligences.*

* The process of challenge design is not described here because it is relatively complex and requires at least Level 1 CSP training.

The main *features** of challenge design were identified in the introduction to this chapter (page 74), as follows. CSP challenges -

(i)   enable pupils to achieve *specific curriculum targets*

(ii)/(iia)   provide *clarity and confidence* about the learning task

(iii)   cater for different *styles of decision-making*

(iv)   promote *understanding through performance*

(v)   cater for different *styles of thinking and learning*

(vi)   provide regular opportunities to use and develop *multiple intelligences*

These features will each be discussed with reference to the relevant extracts from the annotated Academic Challenge, previously shown on page 75. The numbering of the features corresponds to the numbering of the annotations.

(i) Achieving specific curriculum targets. One of the most frequent reservations expressed by hard-pressed teachers about experientially-based learning is that it is so time-consuming that it is bound to prevent them from 'covering the syllabus'.*

* It is worth asking the question: 'Who's actually covering the syllabus - the pupils or the teacher?'!

CSP tackles this problem head-on by consciously focusing the design of challenges on important curriculum targets. Indeed, the phrase 'a thoughtfully designed problem for pupils to solve' (see the description of the 'Experiential Learning Cycle' on page 72) indicates that each challenge focuses on a number of specific curriculum targets in a systematic way.

Well designed challenges therefore address several *desired outcomes* (knowledge/ understanding; skills/dispositions) in one problem-based activity. And at the more advanced levels of CSP teaching, where challenges are consciously linked to each other via the 'debriefing' process (see pages 96 and 102-104), considerable amounts of time are gained by reducing the need to reteach concepts and skills that pupils readily forget in less experiential courses. As Eric Jensen points out:

* i.e. in 'experiential/problem -based learning' – see 'Broad Idea' 1 and 4 on pages 71/72.

> 'Teachers ought to spend 55 to 80 percent of their time allowing students to process information.* Most teachers don't set aside this time and therefore do an enormous amount of reteaching.'

How Julie's Brain Learns, *Jensen, E (Educational Leadership, November, 1998)*

This clear focus on specific targets is illustrated in the 'process criteria' section of the sample Academic Challenge (see top of next page) where it can be seen that the challenge is designed to help pupils develop:

knowledge and understanding of the interrelationship between the concepts of *behaviour, physiology* and *environmental conditions;* and

the critical skill of *organization.*

A key point to note here is that CSP training insists that process criteria include *specific, observable behaviours,* i.e. things to 'look for/listen for'. These then form a powerful means of formative assessment in the 'debrief' phase (see page 95 onwards).

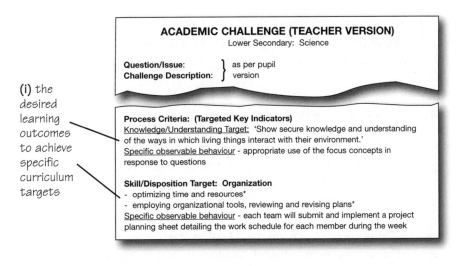

(i) the desired learning outcomes to achieve specific curriculum targets

Of course, a number of other skills and dispositions are developed as pupils go through the challenge process - notably in relation to the Full Value Contract - and regular attention is also given to the long term development of these in the debrief. But as shown in the sample, each challenge also focuses specifically on one or two key indicators of a critical skill such as 'organization' so that pupils and teacher can concentrate their attention on monitoring its development as effectively as possible.

(ii) (iia) Providing clarity and confidence about the learning task. Clarity about the learning task is important for two reasons. Firstly, by raising confidence and reducing stress it promotes higher order thinking in the cortex. Secondly, by providing the big picture as well as the procedural details it promotes whole brain learning (see page 58).

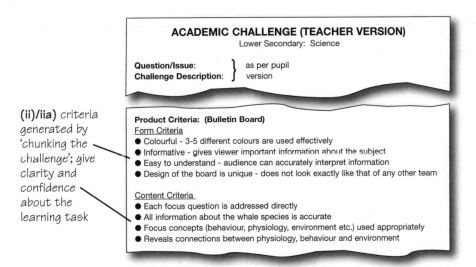

(ii)/iia) criteria generated by 'chunking the challenge'; give clarity and confidence about the learning task

In CSP, clarity is generated largely through the process of *chunking the challenge* (see pages 78-80) in which pupils identify the 'product criteria' by reading and discussing the 'challenge description'. The Teacher Version provides a full list of these criteria so that the teacher can ensure that they are all identified before the groups start work on the challenge.

'Chunking' is therefore a classic whole brain approach to learning in that it requires pupils to read and discuss the overall learning task (the big picture = 'right brain'); and then go systematically through it to identify its components (the sequential steps = 'left brain').*

* See the section on 'Brain Laterality' in Chapter 1, pages 27-34

(iii) Catering for different styles of thinking and decision-making -

i.e. *processing* information - is also very effectively done through the 'chunking' process because it involves two questions which appeal to quite different styles (see page 83). These are:

a) 'What have we got to do?' - which caters for

- *'Ideas people'* ('I've got lots of ideas for what we can do!') and
- *'Product people'* ('Let's focus on one idea that meets the criteria and get the job done.')

b) 'How are we going to do it?' - which caters for

- *'Process people'* ('These are the steps we must take to reach our goal.') and
- *'People people'* ('This is how we must work together to achieve our goal.')

A skilled teacher who understands the complex, qualitative nature of differentiation can therefore use the 'chunking' tool to raise expectations and self-esteem by emphasising the value of all four styles and the importance of working to improve weaker styles.

(iv) Promoting understanding through performance. In Teaching for Understanding (*1998*) David Perkins makes the following observation about promoting understanding:

'...to gauge a person's understanding at a given time, ask the person to do something that puts the understanding to work - explaining, solving a problem, building an argument, constructing a product... What learners do in response not only shows their level of current understanding but very likely advances it. By working through their understanding in response to a particular challenge, they come to understand it better.'

Teaching for Understanding ed. Wiske, M (© Jossey Bass Inc., 1998. Reprinted by permission of Jossey Bass Inc., a subsidiary of John Wiley & Sons, Inc.)

ACADEMIC CHALLENGE (PUPIL VERSION)
Lower Secondary: Science

Question/Issue: How are whales adapted to their environment?

Challenge Description: With the help of your teacher, arrange yourselves into well balanced teams of three. Plan and create a colourful, informative, easy-to-understand bulletin board display of your own unique design about a particular whale species that interests you. Your display should reveal accurate information in response to each of the following focus questions:

Your team will have three class periods to prepare your bulletin board. Be prepared to present your final product on Friday at 2.00pm. All members of the team will be expected to be able to answer questions about your bulletin board and whale species.

(iv) promoting understanding through performance

CSP challenges always require pupils to develop their understandings by performing in one way or another. In the case of the sample Academic Challenge the performance involves *planning, creating* and *answering questions* about a bulletin board on their chosen whale species but there are many other ways in which pupils can be challenged to develop and demonstrate understanding through performance.

CSP Level 1 training actually provides a list of over 100 different 'products' which can produce 'evidence of desired content understanding and competence.' These include:

---

writing and performing a rap/song/short play; planning a field trip; designing a game show; organizing a fund raiser; creating a museum; creating a video presentation, etc..

(v) Catering for different styles of thinking and learning - i.e. *perceiving* information.

(vi) Using and developing multiple intelligences.

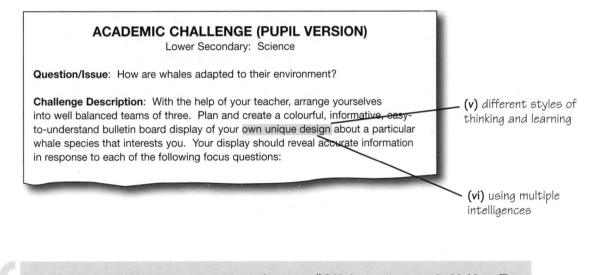

ACADEMIC CHALLENGE (PUPIL VERSION)
Lower Secondary: Science

Question/Issue: How are whales adapted to their environment?

Challenge Description: With the help of your teacher, arrange yourselves into well balanced teams of three. Plan and create a colourful, informative, easy-to-understand bulletin board display of your own unique design about a particular whale species that interests you. Your display should reveal accurate information in response to each of the following focus questions:

(v) *different styles of thinking and learning*

(vi) *using multiple intelligences*

'...it's amazing what they can produce if you say "OK, I want you to do X, Y or Z, however you get there is up to you". It's just phenomenal, ways that I never would have thought of because I'm a different thinker and learner than a lot of my students; and I would limit them because of my style of learning if the only way I accepted was my way.'

Patty Ryan, Critical Skills Master Teacher interviewed for **The Brain and Learning** *(op. cit.)*

As well as emphasising the *performance* aspect of understanding, CSP challenges also allow pupils to choose *how* they will develop and demonstrate that understanding. A particularly successful example of the benefits of this choice is shown in a challenge devised by Jane Fox of Gilboa-Conesville School for her early primary class.   This involved creating a class video on nocturnal animals, to be watched by their parents while waiting to meet Jane at a Parents' Evening.

There were certain product criteria that all the groups had to meet - creating visual representations of their chosen animal's habitat; providing certain specified kinds of information about the animal; writing, timing and recording a commentary for their section of the video, etc.. But as Jane herself comments in **The Brain and Learning** video:

'They make a lot of decisions about their learning themselves, in terms of what facts they think are important to report. They decide for themselves what they want to put in their presentation, and the way in which they express the facts about their animals is totally up to them.'

(op.cit.)

The great advantage of an approach such as this is that it allows pupils to perform and develop their understandings by using their preferred styles of learning and strongest intelligences in the first instance - though experienced CSP teachers are also keenly aware of the need to encourage pupils to use and develop their weaker styles and intelligences.

The benefits of the overall CSP approach to challenge design are perhaps best summed up by Jane Fox's final comment in **The Brain and Learning** video:

> 'What I am doing now is much more natural. The students are allowed a lot more freedom so I'm not trying to tell them to do something that they really can't do - like sit still and keep quiet! They don't do that naturally but they can use their enthusiasm and their excitement in producing things - in making a book, or a story or a presentation.'

(op. cit.)

3. Coaching Pupils Through the Experiential Learning Cycle.

The main key principles of learning (page 47) which relate to this part of the chapter are:

Teachers should understand that -

- *differences between pupils' abilities are complex and qualitative rather than simple and quantitative;*

- *there are no practical limits to the development of individual pupils' abilities;*

- *learning for understanding is achieved through the performance of challenging, open-ended tasks rather than by giving correct answers to closed questions;*

Learning activities should -

- *include timely and accurate feedback;*

- *provide regular opportunities for review and reflection.*

The CSP Level 1 Training Manual describes coaching in a CSP classroom as follows:

* See the postman cartoon on page 63.

> 'The notion of teacher as coach may be the hardest part of the CSP model to grasp. However, it is so important, this entire manual is framed as a tool to support the role of teacher as coach. In the traditional school paradigm, teachers are more often seen as the transmitter of knowledge, authority figure, expert, boss, encourager, evaluator... In short, teachers do everything for or to the pupils. Not only is this a recipe for overwhelming teachers*, but it lessens the opportunity for pupils to develop the most important outcome of school - *the ability to be able to do things for themselves...*

> 'Coaching involves **moving pupils through an experience** and helping them to **debrief that experience and to connect it to other experiences**. Coaching combines the skilful and timely use of the related roles of facilitator, mentor, inspirational leader and mediator - employing tools that strengthen work towards desired learning results... You are less the "sage on the stage" than the "guide along the side"...
>
> 'But be careful. "Along the side" is not the same as "on the side". We are not suggesting that teachers simply step back and let pupils "play the game" while the coach watches or calls in a few instructions. There are any number of interconnected and interdependent roles that teachers need to assume to be effective and responsive to their pupils...it is important to remember that the role of coach weaves in and out of all phases of the student learning cycle.'

CSP Level 1 Training Manual (*op. cit. - emphases added*)

It was pointed out in the Introduction (pages 74-76) that CSP teachers coach their pupils by

(iia) helping them to gain *clarity and confidence* about their learning tasks;
(vii) generating *high expectations*;
(viii) promoting supportive, productive classroom relationships through *collaborative learning*;
(ix) promoting *regular formative assessment*.

Essentially, issues (iia), (vii) and (viii) are about '*moving pupils through an experience*'; while issue (ix) relates primarily to '*debriefing that experience and connecting it to other experiences*'. Since *collaborative learning* (viii) and *clarity and confidence* (iia) have already been dealt with in parts 1 and 2 respectively, the remainder of part 3 will be mostly concerned with the issues of *high expectations* and *formative assessment*. The section and chapter will then conclude with a short description of the way in which CSP coaching improves learning by helping pupils to make better *connections* between their learning experiences. As before, the relevant extracts from the 'Whales' Academic Challenge are provided for reference.

ACADEMIC CHALLENGE (PUPIL VERSION)
Lower Secondary: Science

Question/Issue: How are whales adapted to their environment?

Challenge Description: With the help of your teacher, arrange yourselves

Your team will have three class periods to prepare your bulletin board. Be prepared to present your final product on Friday at 2.00pm. All members of the team will be expected to be able to answer questions about your bulletin board and whale species.

(vii) generating high expectations

(vii) Generating high expectations. This aspect of coaching is primarily influenced by teachers' mental models of two key concepts - *ability* and *the learning process* - in the following ways:

Ability. It was pointed out in Chapter 1 that the 'simplistic, quantitative model of ability has a particularly pernicious impact on teachers' and pupils' levels of expectation'. In Chapter 2 this was illustrated by the classroom practice of Ms. Fogg who 'rationalises the poor achievements of many of her pupils by assuming that they

---

have a low *level* of ability, i.e. their brains are... inherently ineffective... Her mental model of ability also influences her attitude and behaviour towards these pupils, whose self-image, self-esteem and motivation are consequently depressed.'

By contrast, experienced CSP teachers like Ms. Compass are well aware of the complex, qualitative nature of differentiation and of the vastly underused potential of the human brain. Consequently, she continually signals through her classroom behaviour that she has genuinely high expectations of all her pupils. This is reinforced in the challenges she writes (see the Challenge extract overleaf) where she typically signals her high expectations by requiring *all* her pupils to be able to understand the key concepts sufficiently well to be able to explain them to their classmates.

The learning process. Ms. Compass has a thorough grasp of constructivist principles of learning. She understands that her pupils need to *think with - and about -* new knowledge before they can truly understand it. Therefore she often engages in discussion with her pupils as a fellow learner, genuinely interested in their ideas. Unlike Ms. Fogg*, she encourages *them* to ask questions and any questions she herself asks are open, and genuinely seeking after information.

*See, for example, the passage from an American History lesson quoted on page 53.

As Paul Black and Dylan Wiliam observed in their recent review of research on formative assessment:

> 'The dialogue between pupils and a teacher should be thoughtful, reflective, focused to evoke and explore understanding, and conducted so that all pupils have an opportunity to think and to express their ideas.'

Black, P & Wiliam, D (op. cit.)

And over ten years ago James Dillon commented memorably on his extensive research into classroom discourse, as follows:

> 'Every time a student question arises, a child's mind opens to learning...(but)...no one has ever walked into a sample of classrooms in any school at any level and heard a lot of student questions. To the very contrary. You can go and see for yourself. Children may well ask a lot of questions, but not in school.'

Questioning and Teaching: A Manual of Practice, *Dillon, J (Routledge, 1988)*

Sadly, this observation still remains substantially true today. Happily, it is manifestly *not* true of the ways in which Ms. Compass and her fellow CSP teachers engage with their pupils. They are aware that the role of coach in a CSP classroom involves -

- *motivating* - raising *self-image and expectations*; communicating the *interest and relevance* of the learning challenges;
- *facilitating* - ensuring that all pupils are *clear and confident* about the task; helping them to *think and express their ideas*; helping them to *organize themselves* to complete the challenges successfully; and

- *being a role model* - demonstrating what *high quality product and process criteria* look like; providing models of products which help to clarify expectations and the development of an *internal model of quality* (see the 'Fundamental Dispositions' table on page 70). Or as CSP Master Teacher Jack Drury puts it:

> '1. It means living the golden rule in my classroom - treating students as I would like to be treated and living with the messy consequences of that - allowing democracy within my classroom and living without arbitrary authority.
> 2. It means modelling. I cannot do one thing while expecting my students to do the opposite. One of my favourite quotes is by Robert Fulghum: "Don't worry that your children don't listen to you. Worry that they are watching everything you do."
> 3. It means having your pupils set standards and you helping them hold themselves accountable to them.'

CSP Level 1 Training Manual

(ix) Promoting regular, formative assessment.

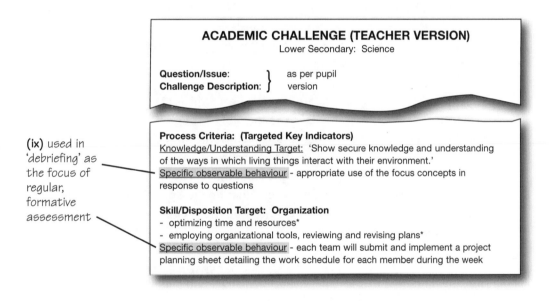

ACADEMIC CHALLENGE (TEACHER VERSION)
Lower Secondary: Science

Question/Issue: ⎫ as per pupil
Challenge Description: ⎭ version

(ix) used in 'debriefing' as the focus of regular, formative assessment

Process Criteria: (Targeted Key Indicators)
Knowledge/Understanding Target: 'Show secure knowledge and understanding of the ways in which living things interact with their environment.'
Specific observable behaviour - appropriate use of the focus concepts in response to questions

Skill/Disposition Target: Organization
- optimizing time and resources*
- employing organizational tools, reviewing and revising plans*
Specific observable behaviour - each team will submit and implement a project planning sheet detailing the work schedule for each member during the week

> 'Our own review has selected at least 20...studies...(which) show that innovations which include strengthening the practice of formative assessment produce significant, and often substantial, learning gains... Opportunities for pupils to express their understanding should be designed into any piece of teaching, for this will initiate the interaction whereby formative assessment aids learning.'

Black, P & Wiliam, D (op. cit.)

Undoubtedly one of the most striking features of CSP is the considerable amount of time and effort given to formative assessment - i.e. *feedback*, *review* and *reflection* - particularly in the *'debrief'* phase of the experiential learning cycle (see overleaf). On the face of it, this should make it even more difficult to cover the syllabus but again it is well to note Eric Jensen's observation about the 'enormous amount of reteaching' that is typically required because inadequate time is given to this process. Or as the CSP Training Manual puts it in the section on debriefing:

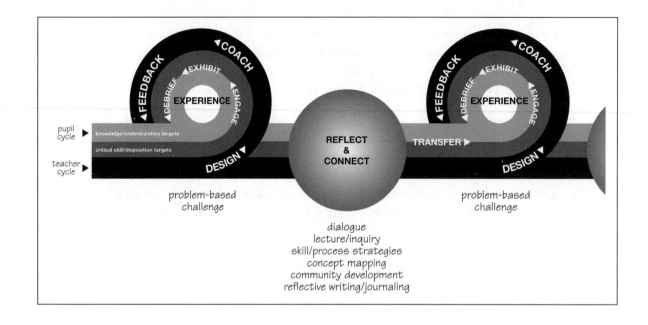

problem-based
challenge

dialogue
lecture/inquiry
skill/process strategies
concept mapping
community development
reflective writing/journaling

problem-based
challenge

'Pupils do a great deal in school. What is too often missing is the opportunity to think about what they are doing - its meaning, how it connects to other things they have done, how it connects to their lives. *The process of learning is diminished when it is based on unexamined experience alone*. Thinking time is learning time; furthermore, learning is most effectively transferred to new experiences through the process of reflecting on the work.

'...Through *debriefing*, pupils are given time to think about the meaning of their experiences. Debriefing may take the form of a group discussion, or it may involve journal writing or other reflective techniques. In the debriefing phase, pupils are encouraged to look at the completed challenge 'event' from the perspective of 'What happened?' (non-evaluative reflection); 'What is the significance of what happened?' (evaluative reflection); and 'What do we do with what we have learned from this experience?' These three might be more directly stated as: 'What?'; 'So what?'; and 'Now what?'

CSP Training Manual (*op. cit.- emphasis added*)

Debriefing, then, is a powerful way of focusing pupils' attention on their learning progress by using feedback from themselves, each other, and the teacher. Some of the specific CSP techniques for promoting feedback are described on pages 98-102. However, before looking at the specifics, it will be helpful to examine first the programme's general approach to formative assessment.

The 'Feedback and Assessment' section of the CSP manual contains the following powerful advice:

'Feedback is critical to the learning process, especially when behaviours are being learned. We look to our environment constantly for clues about how well we are doing. If that feedback is readily available and unambiguous, we can internalise our needs and make corrections, or we can acknowledge our successes and press on to something new...

> 'Feedback can be *unintentional**, *informal*, or *formal* in nature. We need to give consideration to all three kinds in the classroom - addressing the unintentional through a *supportive classroom culture*, the informal through the development of *coaching schemes*, and the formal through a *quality approach to assessment*. In the classroom feedback comes from multiple sources - self-reflection, peers, teachers, and perhaps from the larger community.'

* For example, the negative feedback caused by Ms. Fogg's outdated mental model of ability is presumably unintentional but no less harmful for that!

(*op. cit.*- emphases added)

The development of a supportive classroom culture and classroom coaching schemes have already been dealt with. Therefore, the remainder of this section will focus on the formal, 'quality approach to assessment.'

Some of the most outstanding features of formative assessment in a CSP classroom are -

---

1. ***It is a shared process*** - i.e. both pupils and teachers set product and process quality criteria and work together to assess both individual and group development towards curriculum targets.

2. ***Input comes from the teacher, peers and self-observation*** - in answering questions such as 'Am I doing this well?' or 'Could I do this a better way?'

3. ***It focuses on both individual and group development*** - which strengthens both interdependence and individual accountability.

4. ***It consists of a 'dialogue' in which the pupils are actively engaged***. Pupils regularly reflect on their performances and on how well they are progressing towards long-term learning goals; and they share these thoughts with each other and the teacher.

5. ***A wide variety of assessment 'tools' are used by both teacher and pupils*** - as they monitor pupils' progress towards their learning goals.

6. ***Assessment informs practice*** - i.e. evidence of pupils' development is used to design and connect one problem-based challenge to another.

(*Adapted from* **CSP Level 1 Training Manual**)

CSP has a range of over 60 different assessment tools to promote feedback and reflection. The most straightforward way of illustrating the above features is by examining how a small number of these tools are used for self, peer and teacher assessment. For the sake of clarity these will be dealt with as separate issues, though in practice there is a good deal of synergistic overlap.

Self-assessment.

> 'For formative assessment to be productive, pupils should be trained in self-assessment so that they can understand the main purposes of their learning and thereby grasp what they need to do to achieve... Self-assessment by pupils, far from being a luxury, is in fact an essential component of formative assessment... (But) pupils can only assess themselves when they have a sufficiently clear picture of the targets that their learning is meant to attain. Surprisingly, and sadly, many pupils do not have such a picture...'

Black, P & Wiliam, D (op. cit.)

It should be abundantly clear by now that CSP places great emphasis on helping pupils to be clear about their learning targets by playing an active role in identifying them and monitoring their development. Unsurprisingly, therefore, many of the CSP assessment tools are designed to promote self-assessment of both individual and group progress.

Two outstanding examples of self-assessment tools are *pupil journals* and *learning logs*. These are designed to encourage pupils to 'review and reflect' - i.e. to take the time to gather their thoughts and reinforce their learning by forming new neural connections (see the section on 'Review and Reflection' in Chapter 1, page 24).

Pupil journals. The **CSP Level 1 Manual** describes journals as follows:

> 'A journal is a periodic piece of writing completed and kept by pupils. A journal has an open-ended format. It might include unstructured reflections on what happened during an experience, how pupils felt about their experiences, their thought about the essential question under consideration, what they learned, and so on. Through a periodic review by the teacher/coach, pupils can receive individual feedback.'

CSP Training Manual *(op. cit.)*

In **The Brain and Learning** video Patty Ryan comments graphically on the powerful way in which these journals can promote productive dialogue between teacher and pupils as they work towards their long-term learning goals:

> 'A journal entry is a good way for them to sit back, think about what they've done and why they've done it... I want them to walk away knowing that there was a purpose to their activity... When I respond to journal writing it's directed to them. They know I've read their journal, I've taken it into account and I've responded, so I can touch them individually as a person - their strengths, their weaknesses - and not just slap a percentage on a paper.'

It is clear from Patty's description that the journal is a very effective way of promoting productive dialogue between pupil and teacher. It is also worth noting that Patty, like many of her CSP colleagues, writes her journal responses on 'Post-it' stickers which pupils can remove once read. This is an excellent way of signalling that ownership of the journal and its contents resides firmly with the learner.

Learning logs. According to the **CSP Level 1 Manual**:

> 'A log is similar to a journal but has more structure. Students may respond in writing to questions regarding a *specific challenge*... Or they may use a log format to respond to a *basic set of questions* throughout the year, reflecting back on earlier answers for comparison.'

An extract from a 'specific challenge' log sheet* is shown below.

* The assessment tools shown here are all from CSP Level 1 training workshops run by Leading EDGE LLC.

Challenge - Self Assessment

Pupil Name   **Date:**

Challenge Title:
Group/Team Members:

Directions: Think about how much you contributed to the challenge just completed. Please respond to the statements below by circling the word which best describes your level of contribution. Please write some specific examples of your contributions that support your response.

1. On this project I shared my ideas, opinions and suggestions appropriately with the rest of the group.

rarely - sometimes - often - consistently

Describe at least one idea or suggestion which you shared -

4. On this project I helped the group to meet the standards of quality that went with this project.

rarely - sometimes - often - consistently

Describe at least one way that you helped the group meet the standards of quality that went with this project -

Leading EDGE LLC - Workshop Handout

Two points worth noting are:

1. The way in which the directions and questions promote *review and reflection* on individual and group performance during the challenge;

2. How pupils are required to justify their judgement by describing *specific, observable behaviours*. These can then form a powerful focus for the 'Now what?' question which encourages pupils to make connections between challenges (see pages 96 and 102).

It is also worth noting how powerfully CSP addresses David Perkins' concept of 'learnable intelligence' (see Chapter 1, page 37). Perkins maintains that intelligences

---

have three components - *neural, experiential* and *reflective* - and that the latter two are undoubtedly 'learnable', viz:

Experiential intelligence – 'is learned (as) the result of extensive experience thinking and acting... over long periods of time.' Clearly, the typical CSP challenge epitomises the kind of experience designed to promote this component of intelligence.

Reflective intelligence – 'is in effect a control system...bent on deploying (neural and experiential) intelligence wisely.' Equally clearly, the heavy emphasis given to personal review and reflection in the debrief phase of CSP is a powerful way of developing this crucial component of intelligence.

Peer assessment. Two CSP tools which provide particularly valuable opportunities for effective peer feedback are the *huddle* and the *check-in*.

The huddle. This is commonly used during the 'exhibition' phase of the CSP cycle (see page 96), e.g. when each group is asked to make a display or presentation. Generally, after each group has presented their work to the class the other groups are given a minute to agree on *one* specific thing they liked about the presentation. As confidence and sensitivity grow with the development of the collaborative classroom community, they can also be asked to identify one thing that could be improved. As the **CSP Manual** explains:

> 'The huddle is a positive way to structure peer feedback. When it is used after pupil presentations, it can:
>
> ● provide a model for pupils on how to give constructive feedback to their peers
>
> ● engage pupils in the process of attending to and supporting one another to strengthen the learning community.'

(op. cit.)

The huddle can also be used for group self-assessment, in conjunction with other feedback tools such as the *pro/con debrief* (see the extract on page 101). This is a simple device for focusing attention on what went well and what did not. Normally, the teacher will then use 'the sweep' (see page 79) to collect observations and stimulate class discussion.

The check-in. This is similar in format to the well-known 'Circle Time' in that teacher and pupils sit in a circle at the beginning of the lesson so that everyone can see everyone else. They are each given 30 seconds, in turn, either to share an experience they have had since the class was last together or share a thought or question arising from the previous lesson (the latter may well be stimulated by completing a learning log sheet and/or journal entry for homework). Everyone also has the option to 'pass'.

Despite the fact that this can take several minutes out of a lesson, many CSP teachers employ the check-in regularly because they find it so helpful in building a collaborative classroom community and supportive learning environment. It also provides an opportunity to clarify issues about previous work and make connections to future work, especially in conjunction with self-assessment tools such as journals and learning logs. This process is briefly described in the 'reflection and connection' section (page 102).

```
┌─────────────────────────────────────────────┐
│                  DEBRIEF                      │
│                  PRO/CON                      │
│                                               │
│        PRO          │      NEEDS WORK         │
│  ───────────────────┼──────────────────────  │
│                     │                         │
│                     │                         │
│                     │                         │
└─────────────────────┴─────────────────────────┘
```

Teacher assessment. Two particularly significant teacher assessment tools are the *anecdotal record* and the *product quality checklist*.

The anecdotal record. This is perhaps the most innovative and powerful of all the assessment tools. It was first devised by Peter Fox who describes its development and use in the following way:

> 'I can run their activities but that's not really my job. My job is to teach them to do it themselves... (So) I had to find something else to do with myself... So I got myself a clipboard and I sat over in a corner of the room and I just started taking notes on whatever it was that the kids did. So assessment became fairly easy because I had extensive anecdotal records that I could play back to the students.
>
> 'And I think that actually helps with the assessment because when the kids begin to hear their exact words being reflected back to them it changes the way in which they view their own behaviours.'

Peter Fox, interviewed for **The Brain and Learning** *(op. cit.)*

Peter devised a record sheet to record his observations. The one shown overleaf is for the 'Whales' challenge, first shown on page 75. It can be seen that the record sheet allows the teacher to focus attention on the 'process criteria' specific to that challenge, as well as long-term quality criteria associated with the Full Value Contract, for example.

When the pupils have completed their challenge by producing and presenting their product (e.g. display and/or performance), the anecdotal record sheet enables the teacher to feed back to them how they went about their task in relation to the agreed quality criteria. This provides a very powerful way of helping pupils to reflect on their individual and group performances and to prepare individual and group 'action plans' for further development, using peer- and self-assessment tools such as those as described in the previous two sections.

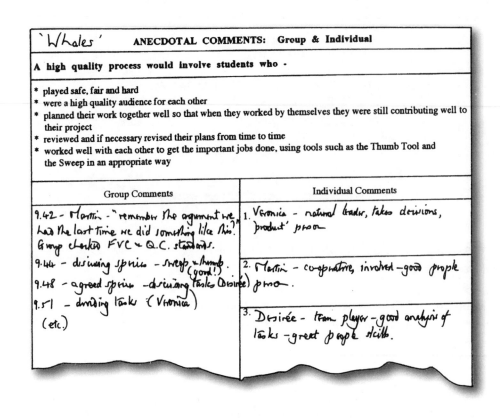

Peter's colleague and fellow CSP Master Teacher Patty Ryan comments about the anecdotal record technique:

> 'The assessment that means the most to them, which really surprised me when I first started using it, is the anecdotal record. I just take notes and then I throw those out at the end of the class and say 'here are my notes' and they just *attack* it!'

Patty Ryan, interviewed for **The Brain and Learning** *(op. cit.)*

The anecdotal record, then, is a means of assessing individual and group development towards agreed quality *process* criteria. By contrast, the final tool to be described in this section - the product quality checklist - monitors progress towards agreed quality *product* criteria.

Product quality checklist. This can actually be used for both teacher and peer assessment - indeed, parts of it can also be used for group self-assessment. The extract shown here relates to the 'Whales' challenge first shown on page 75.

The checklist is completed during the 'exhibit' phase of the learning cycle by the teacher and/or one or more of the other class teams. Along with the anecdotal record feedback it then becomes the focus of discussion during the 'debrief' phase and provides further information to inform individual and group reflection on their learning progress.

Note that points can be allocated for each criterion. If the teacher uses this facility she will ensure that the pupils know this beforehand, so that they focus most of their effort on the important criteria.

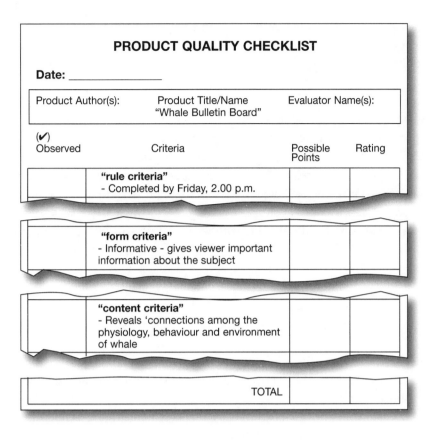

PRODUCT QUALITY CHECKLIST

Date: _____

Product Author(s):	Product Title/Name "Whale Bulletin Board"	Evaluator Name(s):

(✔) Observed	Criteria	Possible Points	Rating
	"rule criteria" - Completed by Friday, 2.00 p.m.		
	"form criteria" - Informative - gives viewer important information about the subject		
	"content criteria" - Reveals 'connections among the physiology, behaviour and environment of whale		
	TOTAL		

Reflection and connection. Following the reflective activities of the debrief phase (journals, logs, huddle and check-in discussions, etc.), experienced CSP teachers will help their pupils to make connections with previous and future learning experiences.

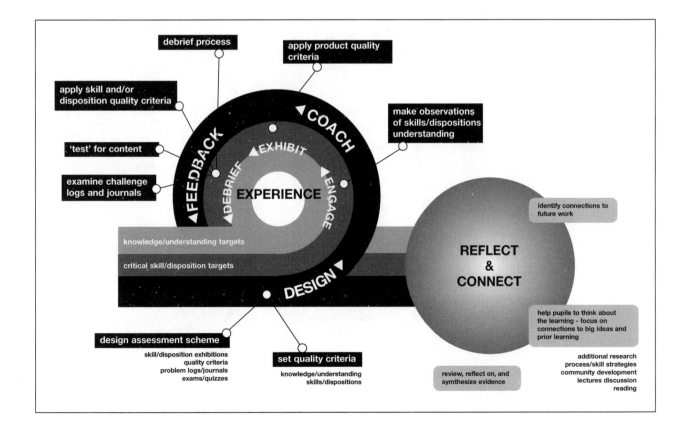

This final aspect of the learning cycle is in some ways the most sophisticated aspect of CSP coaching and as such features in Level 2 rather than Level 1 training. The following outline of its main features is adapted from the last part of the Level 1 Manual.

*See the comments, and the quote from Eric Jensen, on page 88.

'Moving into a period of reflection and connection between challenges is taking the opportunity to bring closure to the previous experience, to make sense of it in a larger context, and to prepare for the next challenge. This is the opportunity for further inquiry or research and for discussions or 'lectures'...it is the time to work on concept mapping techniques and to work on 'standard operating procedures' for specific core skills. In short, it is the time to think about what it is pupils now know, understand and can do that they can carry over to future experiences.'*

(op. cit.)

Essentially, the reflection and connection phase improves learning in four ways:

- *It enhances understanding* - by encouraging pupils to identify the *key concepts* of a challenge and to think about how well they understand them and their interconnections.

- *It focuses attention on the big picture* - by asking pupils to consider how the knowledge/understanding they have gained from a challenge connect to *other work* they have done; to other, *bigger ideas*; and why the work is *relevant and important*.

- *It identifies particular skills that need further attention* - especially those that will enable pupils to tackle the *next challenge* more effectively.

- *It focuses attention on the class as a learning community* - is there immediate need for further *community building or maintenance*, or for *conflict resolution* skill development?

(Adapted from **The Critical Skills Programme Level 1 Training Manual***)*

A final comment on the significance of this phase comes from CSP Master teacher Patty Lawson. It is also a fitting way to end this chapter since it well describes the outstandingly effective nature of the Critical Skills Programme as a whole.

'These kids really want to come to class; they're having a good time. They come back the next day: 'Do you remember this?' when we go through a debrief. They're talking about 'Oh this' and they're comparing what this challenge was to a previous challenge. So they're linking their year's work and that's what I have been looking for, the link from different *themes*, different *topics*, different *words*.'

Patty Lawson, interviewed for **The Brain and Learning** *(op. cit.)*

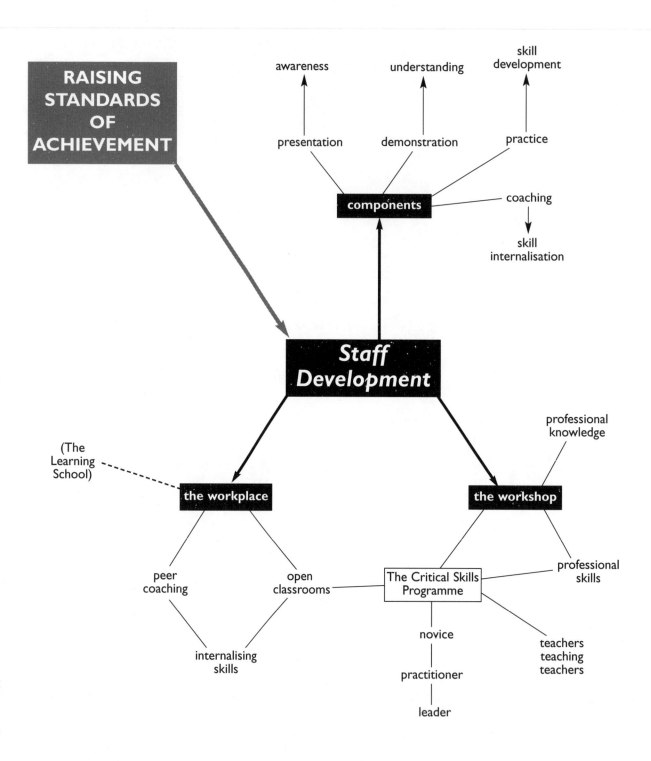

Section Three: Staff Development

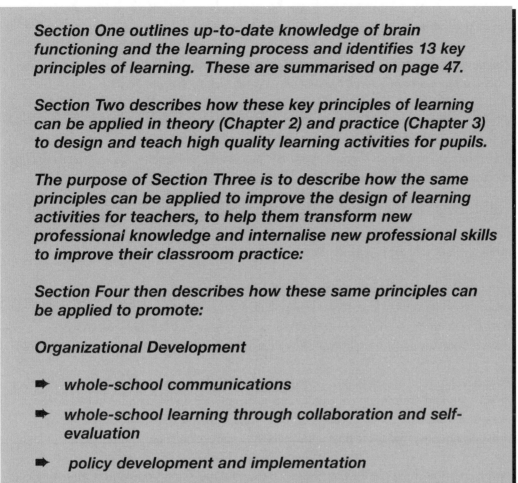

Section One outlines up-to-date knowledge of brain functioning and the learning process and identifies 13 key principles of learning. These are summarised on page 47.

Section Two describes how these key principles of learning can be applied in theory (Chapter 2) and practice (Chapter 3) to design and teach high quality learning activities for pupils.

The purpose of Section Three is to describe how the same principles can be applied to improve the design of learning activities for teachers, to help them transform new professional knowledge and internalise new professional skills to improve their classroom practice:

Section Four then describes how these same principles can be applied to promote:

Organizational Development

➡ **whole-school communications**

➡ **whole-school learning through collaboration and self-evaluation**

➡ **policy development and implementation**

➡ **development planning for learning schools**

Section Three consists of one chapter -

Chapter 4: Promoting Effective Teaching.

The main issues addressed in Chapter 4 are (see also the visual layout opposite):

1. The Components of Effective Staff Development Programmes

- *presentation*: raising awareness and understanding of the principles;
- *demonstration*: developing understanding of the underlying theory;
- *practice*: developing the skills in the 'workshop'
- *coaching*: internalising the skills in the 'workplace'.

2. The Critical Skills Programme and Effective Staff Development

- *the 'Critical Skills' model*: 'teachers teaching teachers'; novice, practitioner, leader; collaboration and peer coaching; the 'open classroom'; the 'learning school'.

Chapter 4: Promoting Effective Teaching

This short chapter addresses issues which, though relatively briefly stated, are of crucial importance to the improvement of learning and teaching and have profound implications for the ways in which schools are organized and managed.

The key question to be addressed is: *'How can we best enable teachers to develop the levels of professional knowledge and skills described in Section Two?'*

The contention is that the most effective way to do this is by applying the key principles of learning identified in *Section One* to the design of staff development activities and programmes. In other words, *teachers' own professional learning experiences should be based on the same principles of learning that should underpin their teaching.*

The format and content of the chapter is heavily based on the extensive research of Bruce Joyce and Beverly Showers, internationally acknowledged leaders in the field of staff development. It is divided into two parts:

Part 1 looks at the relationship between the *components* of staff development programmes and their long-term *impact* on classroom teaching and learning. It shows how this relationship reinforces the important message that teachers' learning experiences should be based on the key principles of learning identified in Chapter 1.

Staff development should also incorporate two key elements - the *workshop*, where staff receive 'off-site' training in controlled and relatively stress-free conditions; and the *workplace*, where the skills developed in the workshop are translated into effective practice 'on-site', under the day-to-day stresses of the classroom.

Part 2 describes how the Critical Skills Programme provides a powerful framework for effective staff development. Unfortunately, relatively few schools have made good use of this framework. Part 2 therefore concludes by examining the practical problems of translating professional skills from the 'workshop' to the 'workplace' through examples of successful and unsuccessful approaches to the implementation of CSP.

1. The Components of Effective Staff Development Programmes

The main key principles of learning (see page 47) which relate to this part of the chapter are:

Learning activities should -

- *cater for different thinking and learning styles;*
- *provide ample opportunities for learners to use and develop the full range of multiple intelligences;*
- *encourage the use of whole brain learning;*
- *encourage learners to perform their understandings;*
- *include timely and accurate feedback;*
- *provide regular opportunities for review and reflection.*

> 'Nothing has promised so much and has been so frustratingly wasteful as the thousands of workshops and conferences that led to no significant change in practice when the teachers returned to their classrooms.'

The New Meaning of Educational Change, *Fullan, M (Continuum International Publishing Group Ltd., 1991)*

Michael Fullan's devastating comment on the ineffectiveness of most staff development programmes derives largely from the work of Joyce and Showers, whose landmark book **Student Achievement through Staff Development** (*Longman USA, 1995*) describes more than 20 years of research on this issue. They have shown quite conclusively that *most staff development activities and programmes fail to produce significant long-term improvements in classroom teaching and student achievement.*

From a detailed analysis of the characteristics of successful and unsuccessful development programmes Joyce and Showers conclude that teachers need to go through four stages* in order to translate newly learnt teaching skills into long-term effective practice in the classroom.

* But see the comments about a fifth stage in The Critical Skills Programme in part 2, page 114.

These stages are shown as 'components' down the left-hand side of the diagram below, which also shows the potential impact of each component on long-term teacher behaviour.

Components of Effective Staff Development Programmes

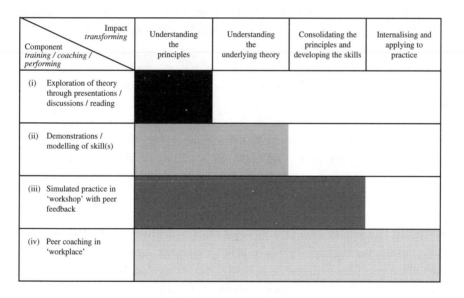

Component *training / coaching / performing* — Impact *transforming*	Understanding the principles	Understanding the underlying theory	Consolidating the principles and developing the skills	Internalising and applying to practice
(i) Exploration of theory through presentations / discussions / reading	██			
(ii) Demonstrations / modelling of skill(s)	██	██		
(iii) Simulated practice in 'workshop' with peer feedback	██	██	██	
(iv) Peer coaching in 'workplace'	██	██	██	██

(Based on Joyce & Showers (op. cit.). Original concept by Professor Ray Bolam of Cardiff University)

As the diagram shows, Joyce and Showers have identified four key components of staff development programmes.

(i) Exploration of the basic theory behind a teaching skill or strategy - e.g.
through presentations, discussions and reading. Presentations which take good account of *thinking and learning styles*, encourage use of *multiple intelligences* and promote *whole brain learning* as described in *Sections One* and *Two* are likely to make a significant impact on teachers' awareness and understanding of the principles and rationale that underpin a skill or strategy. Therefore, high quality in-service presentations on relevant teaching issues can prepare teachers well to gain maximum benefit from the second component.

(ii) Demonstration and modelling of skills and strategies - at in-service workshops. Many good in-service workshop programmes actually combine components (i) and (ii) - i.e. basic theory with practical demonstrations - to powerful effect. As Joyce and Showers observe:

> '...the theory and modelling components...have reciprocal effects. Mastery of the rationale of the skill facilitates discrimination, and modelling facilitates the understanding of underlying theories by illustrating them in action.'

Student Achievement through Staff Development, *Joyce, B & Showers, B (Longman USA, 1995)*

Therefore high quality workshops based on components (i) and (ii) are likely to have a beneficial effect on staff morale, motivation and performance - in the short term! But as Joyce and Showers have also observed, no matter how high the quality of the workshops, *programmes which fail to go beyond this point almost invariably fail to make any long-term impact on classroom practice.* Indeed, they can often be counter-productive if teachers are enthused and then frustrated by the inability of their school system to provide appropriate long-term support. As Sparks and Hirsh pungently comment:

> 'Soon to be gone forever, we hope, are the days when (teachers) sit relatively passively while an 'expert' exposes them to new ideas or 'trains' them in new practices, and the success of the effort is judged by a 'happiness quotient' that measures participants' satisfaction with the experience and their off-the-cuff assessment regarding its usefulness.'*

A New Vision for Staff Development, *Sparks, D and Hirsh, S (ASCD, 1997)*

* cf. the typical end-of-course 'Evaluation Sheet'!

To gain significant long-term benefits we need to move beyond such 'relatively passive' in-service experiences by providing activities in which teachers, like their pupils, are given opportunities to *perform their understandings* and internalise new skills through regular practice with appropriate *feedback*, and time to *review and reflect* on their progress. This involves two further components.

(iii) Practising the skills and strategies under simulated conditions - i.e. 'off-site' training in the 'workshop', in which teachers practise and discuss new skills with colleagues. This provides experience of being at both the 'teacher' and 'pupil' ends of new techniques, and allows teachers to provide helpful feedback to each other.

It also enables them to identify and correct errors of understanding or performance through review and reflection in a safe and relatively stress-free environment. In doing so, it presents a powerful model to teachers of the kinds of experiences that they in turn should provide for their pupils.

Many staff development programmes fail to include component (iii) on the grounds of cost. But costly though it might be, it is still insufficient to ensure long-term classroom impact. This requires a fourth, even more demanding component.

(iv) Peer coaching - i.e. 'on-site' coaching in the 'workplace', in which teachers work actively and collaboratively together to solve problems and questions arising from attempts to implement the new skills in the stressful circumstances of the typical classroom. Joyce and Showers claim that peer coaching of this nature is essential if teachers are to transform new knowledge and internalise new skills to the point where they become so intuitive that they can resist 'the bungee rope syndrome' (see page 10).

It must be stressed that peer coaching is about more than teachers getting together to be nice to each other! To have any beneficial impact on classroom practice it must be sharply focused on specific teacher behaviours and therefore involve well structured observations based on clear and agreed criteria.* This can place quite a strain on relationships and so it is crucially important to develop a truly collaborative whole-school culture, as described in Chapter 5.

* See page 48 of **Effective Heads of Department** Jones, P and Sparks, N (Network Educational Press, 1996) for a concise description of structured lesson observation based on the Joyce and Showers model.

As Chris Dickinson pointed out to the West Lothian Headteachers (see Introduction, page 8):

> 'Off-site experiences are the easy, low risk / low cost bits. They're necessary, certainly, but by no means sufficient. Unfortunately, they typify the common hit-and-run approach to INSET - "Learning and teaching is one of our development priorities this year; so we'll get in a good speaker, run one or two workshops, tick the box in the development plan and move on!"
>
> 'The hard but essential part, if we're going to make in-service experience worthwhile, is what we do "on-site", back in the classroom, in high-risk situations where we need to generate our own solutions to real, everyday classroom problems.'

Chris illustrated these concepts with the diagram overleaf, pointing out that

> 'the difficult issue we have to face is that INSET that has the most impact on the classroom is also the most difficult to provide.'

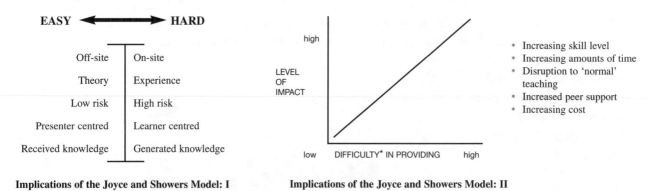

Implications of the Joyce and Showers Model: I　　**Implications of the Joyce and Showers Model: II**

(After David Oldroyd, School of Education, Bristol University)

We should hardly be surprised that programmes which are confined to presentations and demonstrations fail to bring about significant long-term improvements, since they clearly epitomise the 'transmission' model of learning described on pages 41-44 and 52-55. By contrast, 'off-site' simulated practice followed by 'on-site' peer coaching epitomise the 'transformation' model of learning (pages 23-27 and 55-57) by providing opportunities for teachers to *perform*, receive *feedback*, *review* and *reflect*.

There are therefore at least two good reasons to stress the importance of incorporating simulated practice and peer coaching into all staff development programmes.

● Teachers are unlikely to be able to internalise new teaching skills without them.

● A programme based on an outdated model of learning encourages teachers to retain this same mental model, to the detriment of their teaching.*

* See the description of Ms. Fogg's teaching, page 52.

Peer coaching epitomises the teaching approach of the Critical Skills Programme, as shown in the table below.

Peer Coaching	**'Critical Skills'**
● teachers working actively and collaboratively together	● creating and maintaining a collaborative learning community
● solving problems arising from implementation	● problem-based learning
● transforming and internalising new knowledge and skills from training to classroom	● experiential learning - constructing meaning from experience

These basic similarities are considered further in the next section of this chapter and in Chapter 5.

In a political climate of tight budgetary controls, local education authorities are now firmly (and rightly) wedded to the concept of 'best value'. Therefore, in view of the cost implications of the Joyce and Showers model it is important to emphasise that 'value' itself has two components: *cost* and *quality*.

In the case of effective staff development, 'quality' must include more than the usual 'happiness quotients' which measure participants' satisfaction with the experience and their off-the-cuff assessment regarding its usefulness (see page 110). Crucially, it must relate to the *long-term impact on the kinds of learning experiences teachers are able to provide for their pupils* as a result of their own in-service learning experiences.

Therefore, staff development programmes which fail to provide adequately for workshop practice and peer coaching on the grounds that they are too costly and time-consuming are likely to prove, in Michael Fullan's ringing phrase, 'frustratingly wasteful'. And by focusing attention on cost to the exclusion of quality they are also likely to end up providing 'worst' rather than 'best value'.*

* cf. the phrase 'Knowing the cost of everything and the value of nothing'!

Schools and education authorities must therefore recognise the awkward fact that public commitments to 'raise standards' by providing 'learning and teaching of the highest quality' will be little more than empty rhetoric unless 'hard choices' are made about resource prioritisation for effective staff development.

In the Introduction to this book a group of West Lothian Headteachers was quoted as saying to Chris Dickinson:

> 'We were struck by the potential effectiveness of the staff development model* you described... Teachers need to see each other teach more often and to engage in peer coaching so that staff development becomes part of the normal school day. There are significant organizational implications here, for schools and the authority as a whole.'

* i.e. the Joyce and Showers model.

These 'significant organizational implications' will be addressed in *Section Four*. Meanwhile, it will be valuable to see how the Joyce and Showers model can help to explain why even high quality training programmes like 'Critical Skills' are not always successfully translated from 'workshop' to 'workplace'.

2. The Critical Skills Programme and Effective Staff Development

In addition to the principles addressed in part 1, the main key principles of learning which relate to this part of the chapter are:

The learning environment should -

- *minimise threat and uncontrollable stress;*
- *promote positive self-image and high self-esteem;*
- *engage positive emotions;*
- *recognise that individual learners have legitimately different behavioural needs.*

Part 2 starts with a description of the overall CSP staff development framework. It then analyses this framework in terms of the Joyce and Showers model and draws conclusions that have significant implications for the ways in which schools are currently organized and managed.

'Critical Skills' training is offered at three levels:

Level One - takes teachers to the 'Novice' stage, where they are ready to design individual challenges (see pages 87-92) and attempt to create a 'collaborative classroom learning community' by using a range of teaching 'tools' as described on pages 76-87. In the words of the CSP Level Two Training Manual:

> 'Level One presents the conceptual framework, and includes individual strategies, tools, and examples to help teachers take the first steps toward implementation. To keep it simple and of value to the novice, Level One is consciously designed as a collection of ideas and practices that help teachers to get started.'

Critical Skills Training Manual (*op. cit.*)

Level One training consists of six days of intensely active workshops in which teachers experience CSP activities as 'pupils', and plan for classroom implementation. The six days are split into two sessions (either 5+1 or 3+3), with several weeks of 'on-site' classroom practice in between.

Level Two - takes teachers to the 'Practitioner' stage where they gain further understanding of the basic theory and learn how to make effective connections between challenges so as to focus pupils' attention on long term learning goals and promote the 'far transfer' of knowledge and skills to new situations. Level Two training consists of three further days of workshops followed by an extended period of 'on-site' practice.

'Practitioners' are therefore experienced and competent teachers of the CSP classroom model and are encouraged to act as mentors to colleagues. They are also expected to provide 'open classrooms' where teachers from within and without the school can observe CSP in action. This notable feature of CSP provides significant extra help to 'Novice' teachers in making the difficult transition from 'workshop' to 'workplace' and is a powerful additional component to the Joyce and Showers model described on page 109. It is shown as component (iv) in the diagram below.

The Critical Skills Programme Staff Development Model

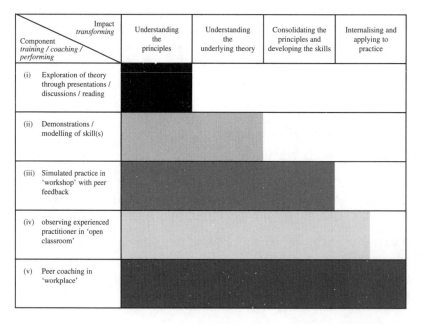

(Based on the Joyce & Showers / Bolam model)

Level Three training is essentially 'training for leadership'. It takes a comprehensive approach to designing and teaching the entire curriculum and leads to the qualification of 'Master Teacher'. Master Teachers have a deeper understanding of theory and mastery of practical skills; and crucially to the CSP staff development model, they also have the capacity and desire to teach other teachers in both 'off-site' training workshops and 'on-site' coaching/mentoring situations. This adds considerable authenticity to the CSP staff development model and is enshrined in the CSP motto: 'Teachers Teaching Teachers'.

The overwhelming majority of post-training evaluation comments testify to the fact that Critical Skills training workshops are demanding, enjoyable and of very high quality. In terms of the modified Joyce and Showers model they provide:

Components (i) and (ii) - *presentations and demonstrations* which cater well for different *thinking and learning styles, multiple intelligences* and *whole brain learning* and therefore promote good understanding of the basic theory and principles behind CSP practice;

Component (iii) - *simulated workshop practice* which:

- enables teachers to *perform*, receive *feedback*, *review* and *reflect*;

- provides a *supportive, threat-free environment*;

- promotes *self-esteem* and *positive emotions* through success and enjoyment;

- provides powerful insights into the *different behavioural needs* of different learners.

As more than one CSP trained teacher has observed: 'Everyone else tells you where to go' (i.e. Components (i) and (ii)), 'CSP also tells you how to get there' (Component (iii)).

But CSP trainers are acutely aware that teachers also need 'help to get there' if they are to apply CSP skills and strategies successfully in the classroom. In the CSP version of the Joyce and Showers model this help is available in the form of:

Component (iv) - *open classrooms* where novice CSP teachers can observe experienced practitioners;

Component (v) - *peer coaching*, by asking schools to send groups of teachers who can provide follow-up support for each other.

Despite these efforts, effective long-term implementation of the complete CSP model in the classroom is still the exception rather than the rule. For example, in a comment that finds many an echo in the research of Joyce and Showers, CSP Co-Director Rick Gordon observes that:

> 'We have improved our implementation by only working with schools or districts that send multiple participants to a workshop and by offering follow-up support. Still, back in their classrooms, many teachers are relatively isolated and don't have the support to bring about the changes they hope to make.'

Personal communication (August 1999)

CSP follow-up support is offered in a number of ways, including periodic 'on-site' visits to individual classrooms by CSP trainers; local after-school follow-up meetings; regional day-long follow-up workshops; and the development of authority-wide mentoring and leadership programmes designed to help teachers provide more effective in-school peer support for each other. But as Training Co-ordinator Bruce Bonney reports:

> 'None of these approaches is totally successful unless the individual school has the capacity and the will to provide an appropriate context in which collaborative peer coaching and support can flourish.'

Personal communication (May 2000)

Or as Chris Dickinson graphically expressed it:

> 'We frequently ask teachers to do new things in old contexts - that is, we attend to curriculum and staff development aspects without addressing key aspects of organizational development. It's a bit like asking someone to bake a cake on a spit!'

(See Introduction, page 12)

The relatively rare instances of effective school-wide implementation of CSP such as Gilboa-Conesville (see page 69) have produced strikingly successful results, from which important lessons can be learned about whole school organization and management. Indeed, by applying the CSP classroom model with great success to whole-school management, Gilboa epitomises the concept of the 'learning school' which forms a major subject of *Section Four: Organizational Development*.

Before turning to the issue of organizational development, however, it is worth concluding this chapter with an observation from Peter Fox which illustrates how the CSP model has been used to such good effect at Gilboa-Conesville. Peter has recently pointed out that the emphasis throughout CSP on developing a collaborative classroom community means that pupils, too, are encouraged to give critical but supportive feedback to the teacher. Such 'pupils' eye' views of the learning and teaching process are a particularly effective way of reducing stress and promoting the internalisation of skills. As Peter comments:

* See the passage on 'Quality Discussion Standards' from page 78.

> 'If I could go back and redo the training for Gilboa teachers after all these years, there is one change I would make. I would assert over and over again that the teacher is a member of the community of learners in the classroom... * This means that, yes, teachers must be willing to obey the rules themselves (and this is not something that older teachers always want to do)... (But) just as teachers cannot excuse themselves from the rules, teachers are also community members who have needs.
>
> 'It is legitimate for a teacher to say: "I have this need that must be met." State it openly and clearly. Students also need to recognise that about their teachers. To me the community that is built is stronger because we all share our vulnerabilities as well as our strengths. I was immensely relieved by this when I started using the model. I cannot begin to tell you how much it has helped me, and my teaching, to have my kids genuinely care about me as a person. Teachers who are willing to risk an open admission of their needs actually model the community that needs to be formed.'

Personal communication (May 2000)

Peter's comment identifies in a particularly powerful way the importance of real collaboration at all levels of the school. This is an issue which dominates much of *Section Four*.

Section Four: Organizational Development

Section One outlines up-to-date knowledge of brain functioning and the learning process and identifies 13 key principles of learning. These are summarised on page 47.

Section Two describes how these key principles of learning can be applied in theory (Chapter 2) and practice (Chapter 3) to design and teach high quality learning activities for pupils.

Section Three describes how these principles of learning can also be applied to help teachers transform new professional knowledge and internalise new professional skills to improve their classroom practice.

The purpose of Section Four is to describe how these same principles of learning can be applied to raise standards of achievement by creating and leading 'learning schools'.

Section Four contains two chapters. The main issues addressed in these are (see also the visual layout opposite):

Chapter 5: Creating a Collaborative School Culture

1. Collaborative Processes

- effective communications; self-evaluation and collaborative policy development; leadership style.

2. Collaborative Structures

- the 'cadre' group - communications; policy development; staff development; case study.

Chapter 6: Development Planning for Learning Schools

1. Some Basic Principles of Planning for Learning Schools

- minimising teacher stress; shared vision; shared understandings; focusing on classroom learning and teaching.

2. A 'Whole Brain' Approach to Development Planning

3. Introducing a Holistic Element to the Planning Process

4. Integrating the Holistic and Sequential Elements

Chapter 5: Creating a Collaborative School Culture

> 'Research and experience have taught us that widespread, sustained implementation of new practices in classrooms, principals' offices, and central offices requires a new form of professional development (which) not only must affect knowledge, attitudes and practices of individual teachers, administrators and other school employees, but it also must alter the cultures and structures of the organizations in which those individuals work.'

Sparks, D & Hirsh, S (op. cit.)

> 'In the Learning School:
>
> - the focus is on children and their learning;
> - individual teachers are encouraged to be continuing learners themselves;
> - the group of teachers (and sometimes others) who constitute the 'staff' is encouraged to collaborate by learning with and from each other;
> - the school (i.e. all those people who constitute 'the school') learns its way forward. The school as an organization is a 'learning system';
> - the headteacher is the leading learner.'

Holly, P & Southworth, G (op. cit.)

In Chapter 4 it was argued that significant, long-term improvements to teachers' classroom practice and pupils' learning achievements depend upon effective collaboration at all levels of the school. Indeed, as Holly and Southworth's definition makes clear, collaboration is in many ways the defining activity of a true 'learning school'. For example, there is no doubt that the peer coaching component of Joyce and Showers' staff development model (see page 111) will be unable to flourish without real collaboration based on mutual respect and desire to 'learn with and from each other.' Therefore, this chapter looks in some depth at the issue of promoting effective whole-school collaboration. It comprises two parts, which examine the two main aspects of collaboration.

Part 1 - identifies the key *processes* involved in effective collaboration. It starts by highlighting the crucial role of *effective communications* in the whole collaborative enterprise. It then considers the process of *self-evaluation* - as important to institutional learning as self-assessment is to individual learners - and illustrates this with a case study from Gilboa-Conesville School (see pages 69 and 116) which shows how collaborative self-evaluation can lead to effective *policy development*. Part 1 concludes by examining some implications of these issues for *leadership* in a learning school.

Part 2 - looks at the kinds of *structures* needed to promote collaboration. In particular, it examines the suggestion by the Cambridge University *Improving the Quality of Education for All* project (IQEA), derived from the work of Joyce and Showers, that schools should establish a small staff *cadre group* to promote and co-ordinate peer coaching and other collaborative activities. A group such as this can provide a powerful means of promoting self-evaluation, policy development and staff development by improving communications within and without the school. It is also an important element in the development planning model described in Chapter 6 and *Appendix 2*. Part 2 concludes with a case study illustrating how such a group operates effectively in a primary school.

1. Collaborative Processes

This part of the chapter deals with the issues of *effective communications; self-evaluation and policy development;* and *leadership style.*

(i) Effective communications.

The key principles of learning highlighted in this section are:

The learning environment should -

- *minimise threat and uncontrollable stress;*
- *promote positive self-image and high self-esteem;*
- *engage positive emotions.*

Learning activities should -

- *encourage learners to perform their understandings.*

It cannot be stressed often or strongly enough that in a learning school, communication is about much more than giving and receiving information.

Communication systems are the means by which an organization's real values (as opposed to its publicly professed ones!) are translated into practice. In effect, they represent the 'specific observable behaviours' (see page 85) which show an organization's values in action. Therefore, in a learning school, communication systems have three functions:

● **The instrumental function** - i.e. *giving and receiving information* as clearly and unambiguously as possible.

The section on 'Clarity and Confidence about Learning Tasks' (page 58) describes how important clarity is in reducing pupil stress in the classroom. *Communicating information clearly and regularly throughout the school is equally important in reducing teacher stress.*

● **The intrinsic function** - i.e. motivating people by demonstrating that they and their ideas are *valued.*

Collaborative policy development, as described in the next section and in part 2 of this chapter, generates high expectations by signalling clearly to staff (and pupils) that their ideas are valuable to the life and work of the school. *High expectations and an ethos of achievement are as important in promoting self-esteem and commitment amongst staff as amongst pupils.*

● **The learning function** - i.e. enabling people to *collaborate* effectively in tackling problems and developing policies.

As Holly and Southworth point out, in a learning school teachers need to be 'continuing learners themselves'. Above all, they need to develop greater understandings of the key learning and teaching issues described in Chapters 1 and 2. *As with their pupils, therefore, teachers need to be able to develop their understandings through performance,* i.e. by 'learning with and from each other' in collaborative staff and school development sessions. As Neville Bennett puts it:

> 'Learning is believed to be optimised in settings where social interaction is encouraged and where co-operatively achieved success is a major aim.'

Bennett, N (op. cit.)

The communication systems of a learning school can be usefully compared to the neural networks in the cortex of the brain ('principles are indivisible' again!) The section on 'thinking and learning' in Chapter 1 (pages 23-27) describes how active, collaborative learning experiences help to develop and consolidate neural networks by encouraging the development and myelination of new axon links between individual neurons. And it is by using these neural communication networks regularly that we develop 'generative knowledge' that helps us 'understand and deal with the world' (Perkins)

Similarly, regular, active collaboration between individual teachers and pupils in a learning school develops and strengthens communication networks which promote the intrinsic and learning functions described above. And the regular use of these networks will enable a school to become a 'learning system...(which)...learns its way forward' (Holly & Southworth).

The intrinsic and learning functions are vividly demonstrated in the management of Gilboa-Conesville School, as described in the next section; while part 2, *Collaborative Structures,* describes how the Joyce and Showers concept of a cross-hierarchical 'cadre' group of staff can be used to promote all three functions in a highly effective way.

(ii) Self-evaluation and policy development in a learning school.

The key principles of learning highlighted in this section are:

Learning activities should -

- *include timely and accurate feedback;*
- *provide regular opportunities for review and reflection.*

> 'Organizational learning is the process by which an organization obtains and uses new knowledge, tools, behaviours and values. (It) is not the same thing as individual learning, even when the individuals who learn are members of the same organization. There are too many cases where organizations know less than their members. There are even cases in which the organization cannot seem to learn what everybody knows.'

Organizational Learning: a Theory of Action Perspective *Argyris, C & Schon, D (Addison Wesley, 1978)*

The role of self-evaluation is one of the most striking examples of the *indivisibility of principles' principle* (see page 10), i.e. that in a true 'learning school' the same principles of learning apply to pupils learning in classrooms; to the professional development of their teachers; and to the leadership of the school as a whole. Self-evaluation is, in effect, formative assessment at the school level and therefore performs the same valuable functions as those prescribed by Black and Wiliam for individual learners (see pages 26 and 95):

> '...innovations which include strengthening the practice of formative assessment produce significant, and often substantial, learning gains... Self-assessment*...far from being a luxury, is in fact an essential component of formative assessment.'

* and self-evaluation

Black, P & Wiliam, D (op. cit.)

Programmes such as 'Critical Skills' (CSP - see Chapter 3), which place great emphasis on the development of a collaborative classroom culture, provide an ideal model from which to develop whole-school self-evaluation involving pupils as well as staff. This is indicated, for example, by the comments of Peter Fox quoted at the end of Chapter 4. And Peter's comments are reinforced by the following observation in the report of a seminar on school improvement held by the Cambridge University *Improving the Quality of Education for All* (IQEA) group in 1996:

> 'The inclusion of pupils' observations and views can be a powerful factor in effective school development. Through observations and evaluations of classroom innovation, and even participation in staff development workshop sessions, pupils can play a vital role in the creation of a "learning community".'

Improving the Quality of Education for All, *seminar on School Improvement, West Lothian Council, 1996*

The power of the CSP model to promote self-evaluation and collaborative policy development is powerfully illustrated at Peter's school, Gilboa-Conesville, where the collaborative, problem-solving 'challenge' approach to the mainstream curriculum for pupils has been adapted to promote highly effective self-evaluation and policy development planning sessions with the whole staff. A typical 'Administrator's Challenge', as used at Gilboa, is shown over the page.

Collaborative self-evaluation of this nature has the potential to increase the effectiveness of school development planning significantly, for two particular reasons.

● Teachers who have themselves learnt to create collaborative classroom cultures are much more able and willing to work productively together.

● By asking staff to focus primarily on classroom learning and teaching issues that are of priority concern to them, collaborative self-evaluation greatly facilitates the audit phase of development planning. This issue is discussed further in Chapter 6.

Before leaving the issue of policy development, however, it is important to make a clear distinction between 'collaboration' as exemplified by the Gilboa example, and the more common but less effective process of 'consultation'.

The *consultation* process typically starts with a policy document drafted by an individual (e.g. headteacher) or small group (e.g. senior management). This is then circulated to staff who are invited to respond to its contents. Unfortunately, because this draft has

Administrator's Challenge

Addressing our major concerns

Question Issue: How can we address some of the major concerns that face us at the beginning of each school year?

The Challenge

We have listed a number of problems that we face as we begin the new school year. We have discussed some of them with each other and brainstormed possible solutions to those problems. We must now narrow down those possibilities and devise a specific strategy to use for the start of school in two weeks. Working in your 'home' teams, devise a strategy (i.e. a clearly described sequence of steps to be taken) to solve your problem or concern.

- Clearly describe the problem/concern you want to address
- List the steps you recommend we take to solve this problem. These steps should be reasonable
- Lay out a time line for the completion of your strategy and identify who is responsible for completing the various steps
- Describe your plan for involving the rest of the faculty in the solution to the problem so that they 'buy in'
- Include some graphic image of your strategy which succinctly communicates the essence of your plan

Please be prepared to present your team's ideas to the whole staff in 45 minutes. We ask that each of your presentations take no more than five minutes.

Product criteria: Problem Strategy

- Problem is described clearly
- Steps for a solution are reasonable and described clearly
- Staff accountability for each step of the strategy is described and will contribute to likely success
- Solution invites faculty involvement
- Graphic image is clear and supports an understanding of the strategy

Evidence of:

- Knowledge
- Skill
- Disposition

Targeted Standard/Indicator(s):

- Knowledge - staff develops sound strategies to solve problems facing the school
  Look for/Listen for > vigorous discussion regarding the advantages and disadvantages of various solutions

- Problem Solving - construct a problem solving strategy
  Look for/Listen for > debate regarding the appropriate sequence of steps to be implemented as part of a given strategy

been prepared by one person, or at best a few like-minded people, it rarely represents the full range of relevant thinking on the issue. Yet its very existence can inhibit the wider expression of critical and creative ideas - especially if the school has a strongly hierarchical management structure and the draft has been produced by senior management!

There is often also a certain defensiveness on the part of the original drafters so that 'consultation' degenerates into a process of justification against criticism and staff relationships become severely strained! As a result, the policy statements which emerge from such a 'consultative' process often fail to take account of all relevant perspectives, overlook some useful ideas and, above all, are imperfectly understood and weakly committed to by those who have to put them into practice. As the IQEA team observe:

> 'In some ways, involvement in planning activity is more important than producing the plans - it is through collective planning that goals emerge, differences can be resolved and a basis for action created. The 'plan' is really a by-product from this activity, and will almost always need to be revised, often several times.* *The benefits of the planning activity, however, will often outlast the currency of the plan.'*

Improving the Quality of Education for All: Progress and Challenge,
Hopkins, D, West, M & Ainscow, M (David Fulton, 1996 - emphases added)

* see Appendix 2, page 180 for a description of this process in action in 'whole brain' development planning.

This is graphically illustrated by the following comment from Gilboa-Conesville Business Studies teacher Lisa Collins:

> 'The thing that surprised me most is the bonding that has occurred between the teachers that have worked together on the project... There's a respect level that has grown enormously - and it's wonderful!'

Another of Lisa's comments equally graphically illustrates the power of true collaboration to promote effective peer coaching:

> 'We're very fortunate at our school to have supportive management and fellow teachers, to allow you the opportunity to try different methods of teaching and realise that it's a risk and it may work and it may not; and if it doesn't you can learn from that, pick up and go on, and do something different next time.'

Interviewed in **The Brain and Learning** *(op. cit.)*

In echoing Eric Jensen's comment that 'Superior learners learn by systematic trial and error' this again highlights the fact that *key principles of learning apply as much to teachers' professional development as to their pupils' learning.*

It is clear, then, that effective policy development - i.e. development which leads to the *effective implementation* of agreed policy changes - depends crucially on an initial collaborative, self-evaluation phase in which ideas and perspectives are openly shared. This can then be followed by a more focused, consultative phase in which specific proposals are examined and agreed, as in the Gilboa Conesville 'Administrator's Challenge' shown opposite.

(iii) Leading a learning school.

Clearly, effective leadership of a learning school involves the application of all the key principles of learning identified in *Section One.*   But those of particular relevance to this section (suitably modified) are:

(Head!)teachers should understand that -

- *differences between (teachers') abilities are complex and qualitative rather than simple and quantitative;*

- *learning for understanding is achieved through the performance of challenging, open-ended tasks rather than by giving (prescribed responses to 'consultative' documents).*

> 'In the Learning School: ...
>
> - the headteacher is the leading learner.'

Holly, P & Southworth, G (op.cit.)

The description in the previous section of collaborative staff planning activities at Gilboa-Conesville School highlights the crucial importance of leadership style in creating and maintaining a learning school. As the 'Administrator's Challenge' shows, the headteacher's leadership style is heavily based on the learning principles listed above.

For example, it is clear that staff have taken part in one or more brainstorming sessions before reaching the 'Challenge' stage of identifying development priorities, and strategies for addressing them. The CSP approach to brainstorming (see page 84) caters well for the *complex, qualitative nature of learning and behavioural differences*, particularly in relation to thinking and decision-making styles. And the Challenge itself obviously provides a *challenging, open-ended task* which invites staff to use various 'multiple intelligences' in preparing and delivering their presentation.

In his presentation on 'Leadership for the Learning School' at the West Lothian Headteachers Conference (see page 8) Professor John MacBeath of Strathclyde University* described some typical outcomes of an activity from his Quality in Education group's 'Leadership' seminars for headteachers. This involves asking them to sketch an image to illustrate how they see their job.

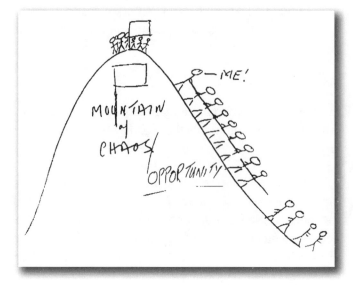

* Dr. MacBeath is now Professor of Educational Leadership at Cambridge University. His QIE group has also developed a range of valuable 'tools' for school self-evaluation.

The sketch shown here is quite typical and is well worth considering in relation to the concept of a learning school. As Professor MacBeath himself commented:

'The concept of leadership illustrated here is very much a line-management, hierarchical model. The head clearly sees herself at the top of a hierarchy, coping as best she can with the problems created by the 'mountain of chaos' and trying to pull her staff along to a particular destination - the top of the mountain. Notice that not all the staff seem to be able or willing to pull together. Two have become detached, though they are still struggling along in roughly the same direction; but another two have set off in a different direction altogether!

'Contrast this perspective with Joe Murphy's description of the kind of leadership style that is essential in a learning organization:

"(Leaders) must learn to lead not from the apex of the organizational pyramid but from the centre of the web of personal relationships."'

John Macbeath, West Lothian Headteachers Conference Report (1998)

The contrast between these two perspectives on leadership is nicely encapsulated by Peter Senge in his best-selling book on business leadership, **The Fifth Discipline**:

'Our traditional views of leaders - as special people who set the direction, make the key decisions and energise the troops - are deeply rooted in an individualistic and non systemic worldview...(which) reinforces a focus on short-term events and charismatic heroes rather than on systemic forces and collective learning. At its heart, the traditional view of leadership is based on assumptions of people's powerlessness, their lack of personal vision and inability to master the forces of change.'

The Fifth Discipline: The Art and Practice of the Learning Organization, *Senge, P (Hutchinson, 1990)*

Senge's comments resonate strongly with Douglas McGregor's observations on patterns of management behaviour which are referred to in Chapter 6 (page 150). They also strike a notable chord at the whole school level with the observations of Douglas Barnes at the classroom level (see page 43).

'It is the teacher who is using language to shape meanings, not the pupils, who are given only slots to fill in with single words. If they are to understand it must be through his eyes.* ...the traditional teacher-dominated lesson...is based upon an implicit distrust of children's ability to learn.'

Barnes, D (op. cit.)

* See the description of the 'consultation' process on page 123.

It is hardly surprising that teachers behave in this way towards their pupils if the headteacher's leadership style is 'based on assumptions of people's powerlessness, their lack of personal vision and inability to master the forces of change.' Yet again we see how crucially important it is to apply key principles of learning at all levels if we are to create 'learning schools'.

Senge's observations on the importance of collective, systemic (i.e. collaborative) approaches to the management of learning organizations are revisited in some depth in Chapter 6. Meantime, it is worth concluding this section by quoting the comments of Gilboa Principal, Matthew Murray, on his own leadership style:

> 'I think there needs to be a relationship of trust with my staff. As a leader, I also have to model what I believe. I am a role model to the kids and to the teachers as well; and if I'm living and doing the kinds of things that I'm asking them to do, they're going to do them much more easily.'

Matthew Murray, interviewed for **The Brain and Learning** *(op. cit.)*

The importance of leaders modelling desired behaviour cannot be over-exaggerated. In any group of people, behaviour is 'infectious' (consider, for example, how difficult it is to resist responding to a noisy pupil by raising your voice!). But the group leader's behaviour is usually much the most infectious. *This is why regular opportunities for pupil and staff feedback in an open, collaborative climate can provide a powerful means of modifying leadership style, to the considerable overall benefit of the would-be 'learning school'.*

2. Collaborative Structures

In a relatively small school like Gilboa-Conesville (420 pupils) where a high proportion of the teaching staff is knowledgeable about learning, and skilled in teaching a collaborative, experiential teaching programme like CSP, there is perhaps less need for formal structures to promote whole-school collaboration. But for most, especially larger secondary schools, it will be important to ensure that appropriate formal structures are put in place to facilitate the kinds of processes described in the previous section.

One structure with strong potential for promoting effective collaboration is what the IQEA project calls a *cadre group* - i.e. a small group of staff with primary responsibility for co-ordinating *communications and policy development*; and for organizing and supporting *staff development* activities within the school. The potential of such a group to promote the collaborative processes identified in Part 1 is illustrated at the end of this section by a case study from a Scottish primary school.

The key principles of learning highlighted in Part 2 are:

Learning activities should -

- *include timely and accurate feedback;*

- *provide regular opportunities for review and reflection;*

- *cater for different thinking and learning styles.*

The cadre group.

The concept of the cadre group has been developed by the IQEA team (see page 123) from the work of Joyce and Showers (see Chapter 4). IQEA describe the cadre as follows:

'One of the things that we had learned from research and our previous work is that change will not be successful unless it impacts all levels of the school organization. Specifically, our focus is on...three levels...and the ways in which these levels interrelate. The *school level* is to do with overall management and the establishment of policies, particularly with respect to how resources and strategies for *staff development* can be mobilised... At the level of *working groups* the concern is with...*supporting improvement activities*. Finally, at the *individual teacher level* the focus is on *developing classroom practice*.

'...a specific aim of the IQEA project (is) to devise and establish positive conditions at each level and to co-ordinate support across these levels. It is in this connection that we require the establishment of a team of co-ordinators in each school whose task includes the integration of activities across the various levels. We refer to these co-ordinators as the *cadre group*... In many schools members of the cadre establish an *extended cadre group* which serves to extend involvement...within the school.'

Hopkins, D, West, M & Ainscow, M (op. cit. - emphases added)

IQEA suggest that a cadre group should number between four and six teachers - though, as they also point out, larger schools may establish an extended cadre. The group should epitomise the collaborative philosophy of a learning school in two ways:

Structurally, it should be cross-hierarchical - i.e. it should contain a member of senior management (preferably the headteacher, to signal commitment to the collaborative philosophy at the 'highest' level); at least one middle manager (senior teacher/head of department); and at least one unpromoted teacher.

Functionally, it should be representative - i.e. the staff as a whole should be confident in its ability to represent and/or take on board all significant perspectives when policy is being developed. In this context there is clear merit in the non-senior management members of the group being elected by their colleagues in some way so that they have a mandate to represent their views when development activities are being planned.

The representative nature of such a group is clearly of great significance in terms of *effective communications and policy development*. It can also provide a highly effective way of promoting the kind of collaborative peer coaching and support that is so crucial to ensure that *staff development* activities lead to long-term improvements in classroom practice (see page 111). Both of these aspects are illustrated in the diagram overleaf which shows how the group has responsibility for these two areas:

Communications and policy development. These aspects of the group's work are shown in the left-hand side of the diagram. Here, the *upper half-arrows* indicate that the group has responsibility for the *instrumental function* of communication - i.e. it ensures

---

through both paper and personal communications that parents, staff and pupils are kept as fully informed as possible about key aspects of the school's development.

In this context the group clearly needs to cater for different *thinking and learning style preferences* by ensuring that *written* communications are clear and include *visual* representations wherever relevant; and that these are backed up by regular formal and informal *oral* communications.

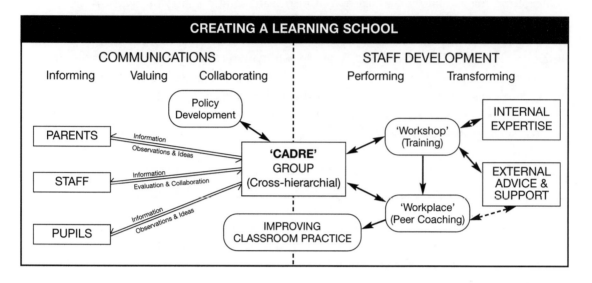

The *lower half-arrows* indicate the *intrinsic and learning functions* of communication. By promoting self-evaluation and the free flow of ideas between all 'levels' of the school the group is responsible for promoting the 'specific observable behaviours' which demonstrate the school's professed collaborative values in action and lead to effective policy development as described on pages 122-125.

Staff development. This aspect of the group's work is shown in the right-hand side of the above diagram. It relates closely to the issues identified in Chapter 4, particularly in relation to the Joyce and Showers model (see page 109). As will be seen in the following case study, the group has responsibility for taking forward initiatives agreed in collaborative policy development planning sessions. To do this it will normally organize workshops, initially with external advice and support.

For example, in the case of 'learning and teaching' policy development, the group will typically start by arranging for a number of staff (including themselves) to take *external training* - e.g. in CSP - to a level where they can begin to provide internal *'workshop' training* and *'workplace' mentoring* (i.e. peer coaching) to their colleagues (see Chapter 4). They will then be responsible for monitoring the effectiveness of the implementation programmes as described in the following case study - albeit in relation to the development and implementation of a discipline rather than a learning and teaching policy.

The 'cadre group' in action - a case study. This case study in a Scottish primary school provides a striking example of the value of a cross-hierarchical cadre group in improving communications between senior management and the rest of the teaching staff. It started when the headteacher arranged for an external consultant (myself) to lead a workshop on 'The Brain and Learning', following which she hoped to set up a cadre group to work with me to identify and address agreed learning and teaching development priorities.

The headteacher's expectation was that the staff would wish to follow up this workshop by working immediately on ways of applying new knowledge about the brain and learning to their classroom teaching. In the event there was significant disagreement amongst the staff about the merits of this suggestion! There was, however, a warm welcome for the proposal to set up a cadre group - though the word 'cadre' was disliked and was replaced by the term 'development group'. Staff nominated three members to join the headteacher and myself. Further details of the composition and work of the group are given in the extract from its first evaluation report below.

At the first meeting of the group the nominated staff members confirmed that most of their colleagues wished to focus on discipline, albeit in relation to a discussion on the uses of behaviourist learning principles which had taken place at the original workshop. Unsurprisingly perhaps, the headteacher was initially disappointed that her staff did not seem willing to take a more positive stance towards learning and teaching.

However, after some discussion, it became clear that progress on learning and teaching, as such, would need to be postponed until the teachers in general felt more confident about developing an appropriate classroom ethos. *This initial meeting thus provided a striking example of the value of such a cross-hierarchical cadre group in promoting effective self-evaluation and collaboration.* It also provided a major stimulus towards the development of the learning school development planning model outlined in Chapter 6, and illustrated in some detail in *Appendix 2.*

The remainder of the policy development is described in the following extracts from an evaluation report prepared by a member of the group.

'Introduction

'As part of the school's development plan...learning and teaching was a key area for focus and development during INSET. An external facilitator whose expertise lay in this field, led these sessions, discussing with staff the differences in learning styles, multiple intelligences theory and our role, as teachers, in catering for these differences...

'Concern was raised amongst staff regarding discipline within the school... The external facilitator continued to work alongside staff encouraging openness in airing views from all staff members to develop an ethos of shared understanding... It was decided that a development group would be established to work with staff in producing a discipline policy for the school.

'The members of the 'cadre' or development group representing the staff consisted of a probationer teacher working in Primary 5, a senior teacher working in Primary 1 and a special needs teacher working with Primary 4-7, as well as the headteacher and external facilitator... Time was initially allocated to allow formulation of the group and for its members to peruse suggested reading by the facilitator. All members of the group represented and undertook the concerns of staff and held discussions with them during planned activity times, INSET and staff meetings...

* See Appendix 3, page 193 for further information about Circle Time.

*This networking model proved to be a valuable way of developing mutually respectful staff relationships which were sufficiently robust to withstand the focused and critical observations that are essential for effective peer coaching – see page 111.

'Much time was spent in planned activity time workshops discussing with the staff what was perceived to be problematic behaviour. All suggestions were recorded and the development group then condensed these into specific categories... Classroom charters were discussed fully and since *Circle Time** was conducted by all staff, this was seen as a possible forum for involving children in the formulation of their own set of classroom 'rules'...

'An active Pupil Council...brought forward suggestions from their classes and produced a playground charter which was issued to all classes. Non-teaching members of staff, nursery nurses, auxiliaries and playground supervisors were involved in discussion of this charter... Members of the development group also discussed the developing policy with the Parent Teachers' Association...

'With charters being the suggestion for improving playground and classroom behaviour, a solution was needed for the more constant disruptive types of behaviours. It was suggested that 'networking', whereby two members of staff team up to support each other by referring pupils who caused disruption for 'time out' of their own classroom*...

'The policy was agreed, with a vision statement, specific aims, methodology and procedures... A whole school assembly informed all children of the agreed policy...'

'**Conclusions**

'The high percentage of returns to the staff evaluation questionnaire indicate the level of commitment staff have in promoting this policy... The numbers of discipline referrals had reduced since the implementation of the policy... Networking has reduced the variety that previously were referred to senior management... The management team felt there was better communication...

'There was a perception of better ethos amongst the staff. They were more positive and there seemed to be more discussion, with teachers exploring their own behaviour as well as the children's. The Pupil Council was also monitoring and evaluating discipline. They appeared more reflective and wanted to look for solutions to other problems... When the children made the decisions rather than being told, it held more meaning for them...

'There was also a sense of better and smoother running in the school, but further issues needed to be addressed. Not everything could be "brushed with success" but this was seen as positive - being active, not complacent... All members of the management team were impressed with the way the policy had been formulated... Everyone had a purpose, an opportunity to speak up and then see the changes.

'The openness and honesty of staff during this process has been marked. The level of sharing has increased and staff are more open to suggestion from one another.'

It is clear from this extract that the work of a 'cadre' group epitomises the concept of collaboration in a number of ways, viz:

Leading the Learning School

Communications and policy development. The members of the group provided written information and met regularly with non-teaching staff and other school 'stakeholders' in formal communication structures such as the Pupil Council, the P.T.A, the School Board, etc. They also took on a particular responsibility to keep their colleagues informed on a daily basis through informal conversations.

With the help of myself they also organized and ran highly effective staff workshops at which the school's new discipline policy was so successfully (and collaboratively) developed. The high degree of involvement of staff, pupils and parents throughout the collaborative and consultative phases of the development resulted in the successful implementation of the policy described in the above extract. But perhaps of greater importance, it also significantly improved relationships and brought a greater level of commitment by all parties to work productively together. To quote the IQEA team again (see page 125):

> 'In some ways, involvement in planning activity is more important than producing the plans - it is through collective planning that goals emerge, differences can be resolved and a basis for action created. The 'plan' is really a by-product from this activity, and will almost always need to be revised, often several times. *The benefits of the planning activity, however, will often outlast the currency of the plan.*'

Hopkins, D, West, M & Ainscow, M (op. cit. - emphases added)

Staff Development. The staff workshops in the collaborative phase of the discipline policy development* provided a valuable basis for future in-school staff development workshops, while the networking structure which developed from this phase provided a powerful basis for the peer coaching 'workplace' element of the Joyce and Showers staff development model.

* See the diagram on page 130.

The network system had a further benefit. As a result of discussions about behaviourist learning principles at the original 'Brain and Learning' workshop and the subsequent policy development workshops, staff were aware of the important role of positive feedback in improving pupils' behaviour. Many of them then began to use the network system for positive - rather than negative - referrals, with notably beneficial results.

Following the successful implementation of the discipline policy a majority of the teaching staff indicated that they wished to address some of the learning and teaching issues that the headteacher had attempted to interest them in originally. Certainly, there had been a year's delay; but the outcome of the collaborative process mediated through the cadre group and the other collaborative structures (Pupil Council, staff workshops, etc.) had produced a much more collaborative school culture which provided a sound basis for future development.

But perhaps the most significant outcome - as in so many instances when things initially 'go wrong' - was the realisation that the different perspectives which the group members brought to the initial discussions generated important insights into the relationship between 'learning and teaching' in classrooms and the other key areas of a development plan. A classic example, in fact, of the phrase 'Every problem is an opportunity'! These development planning issues are considered in some depth in Chapter 6.

Chapter 6: Development Planning for Learning Schools

'In the Learning School:

● the focus is on children and their learning; ...

● the school...learns its way forward. The
  school as an organization is a 'learning system"

Holly, P & Southworth, D (op. cit.)

'How do we work with our school development plan in a 'learning for understanding' way? Are we stuck with a model which basically involves ticking boxes every so often or can we apply the *Teaching for Understanding* model* to whole-school as well as classroom management?'

Maggie Farrar, Principal of the University of the First Age, speaking at the West Lothian Headteachers Conference, May 1998 (see page 8)

* The Harvard University **Teaching for Understanding** programme is very similar to the **Critical Skills Programme** described in Chapter 3.

This chapter looks first at the basic requirements for effective development planning in a learning school. It then examines some limitations of current approaches to development planning in this context and concludes with some suggestions for an alternative approach which is more clearly based on the principles of learning.

Appendix 2 contains two examples which show how the proposed learning school development planning model would work in practice. The first example is based on the work with a primary school which was described in Chapter 5, and which actually stimulated the development of this model. The second is a notional example showing how the approach could significantly improve the implementation of a programme to raise standards of achievement in a secondary school.

Since its introduction to the United Kingdom by David Hargreaves and David Hopkins in the late 1980s, school development planning has gained widespread acceptance and has undoubtedly led to greater clarity and openness in school management. Nevertheless, there are still doubts about whether the current model does actually help to raise standards of achievement. As Professor Sally Brown has recently observed:

'It is assumed that a top-down development planning model will be effective in improving classroom teaching and learning but there is very little research on this aspect and as yet no evidence to support such an assumption.... Indeed, the only conclusion for which there seems incontrovertible evidence thus far is that development planning improves schools' abilities to construct development plans!'

School Effectiveness, *West Lothian Education Seminar No 1, April 1997*

David Hargreaves himself now lays great stress on the importance of planning within the context of a 'learning school'. At a 1995 seminar on development planning, for example, he emphasised the importance of schools developing as learning organizations with the following characteristics:

> **'Schools as Learning Organizations**
>
> - self-managing, self-monitoring, self-evaluating & self-improving
> - distinctive and shared ethos
> - teams replace hierarchical structures
> - enabling and empowering chiefs
> - dispersed leadership & management
> - collaborative culture of teaching
> - coaching and mentoring for learning
> - knowledge producing as well as knowledge transmitting'

Managing School Development, *seminar in Edinburgh, February 1995*

And in his presentation on leadership to the 1998 West Lothian Headteachers' Conference, Professor John Macbeath quoted Per Dalin's claim that:

> 'The only way schools will survive in the future is to become creative learning organizations. The best way students can learn to live in the future is to the experience the life of the "learning school".'

Changing the School Culture, *Dalin, P & Rolff, H (Continuum International Publishing Group Ltd., 1993)*

This concept of 'learning schools' has since gained widespread recognition. For example, South Gloucestershire's current **Guide to School Strategic Planning** (*1999*) opens with the following statement:

> **'A school is effective if it:**
>
> - promotes progress for all its pupils beyond what would be expected
> - ensures that whatever the pupils achieve is at their highest level
> - enhances all aspects of pupils' achievement and development
> - maintains these positive effects consistently from year to year
>
> **'Research suggests that an effective school accomplishes this by:**
>
> - benefiting from strong leadership
> - ensuring everyone involved has a shared vision for the school
> - keeping an emphasis on teaching and learning, with the highest expectations all round
> - maintaining a climate conducive to learning, actively involving pupils and their parents
> - learning from evaluation
>
> *'In other words it is an effective school because it is a learning school'*

(Emphases as in original)

Clearly, there is now widespread backing for the notion that the most effective way to raise standards of achievement is by creating learning schools. And in this context there are two outstanding requirements of development planning:

(i) The planning process should be firmly based on key principles of learning – i.e. 'principles are indivisible' (see page 10). Or as Holly and Southworth so graphically put it: 'The school as an organization is a "learning system".'

(ii) The prime focus of the plan should be on the improvement of classroom learning and teaching - i.e. 'the focus is on children and their learning' (Holly and Southworth).

These requirements are considered in the four main parts of this chapter under the following headings:

1. Some *basic principles* of planning for learning schools;

2. The need for a *'whole brain'* approach to planning;

3. Introducing a *holistic element* to the planning process;

4. *Integrating* the holistic and sequential elements.

1. Some Basic Principles of Planning for Learning Schools

The issues dealt with in part 1 are:

(i)   *Minimising teacher stress;*

(ii)   *Promoting a shared vision;*

(iii)   *Promoting shared understandings; and*

(iv)   *Focusing on classroom learning and teaching.*

(i) Minimising teacher stress.

The key principle of learning which relates to this section is:

The learning environment should -

- *minimise threat and uncontrollable stress.*

The important role of a collaborative culture in reducing teacher stress is discussed in some depth in Chapter 5. As one of the West Lothian Headteacher discussion group reporters put it (see page 8):

> 'As leaders we need to work at helping people to feel good about themselves if they are to perform at their best. We need to provide more positive feedback and so reduce stress on staff through the development of a collaborative culture.'

But it's not simply a question of relationships. There are also significant implications for the way in which the actual development planning process is managed. As Eric Jensen points out*, a major cause of stress is 'learner helplessness' caused by an inappropriate learning environment:

* See Chapter 1, page 20.

> 'Threat and induced learner helplessness have got to be reduced from the learning environment to achieve maximum potency.'

And a major cause of learner helplessness is lack of clarity about the nature of tasks to be carried out (see Chapter 2, page 58).

Clearly, a major feature of the teaching staff's learning environment is the school's development plan and so an important way of reducing stress on teachers is through an approach to planning that provides clarity about the nature of the tasks they are required to do. One significant way of doing this is by constructing a plan which gives the 'big picture' as well as the step-by-step procedures involved in achieving the aims of the plan (see the section on 'Promoting Clarity and Confidence about Learning Tasks', page 58). This issue is discussed further in 'A Whole Brain Approach to Planning' (page 143).

(ii) Promoting a shared vision.

The key principles of learning which relate to this section are:

The learning environment should -

- *promote positive self-image and high self-esteem;*

- *engage positive emotions.*

> 'For the brain to validate learning there must be an emotional connection. The learning must be associated with a purpose which the learner has set.'

Accelerated Learning in the Classroom, *Smith, A (Network Educational Press, 1996)*

The role of the *reticular formation* (see Chapter 1, page 21), is particularly relevant to development planning. This structure links the hind and mid brains and is essentially responsible for deciding which information will be filtered through into the cerebral cortex for higher order thinking and storage. Information which has a positive emotional connection, i.e. which is linked to values which are important to the individual, is much more likely to be filtered through and processed effectively. And of course individuals tend to value information which supports their self-image and self-esteem.

This clearly has profound implications for the kinds of learning experiences we provide for children in classrooms. *But it has equally profound implications for the development planning process, since it is clear that teachers will be more likely to embrace and deal effectively with planning priorities if these reflect their own values.*

In his widely acclaimed book **Change Forces** (*Falmer Press, 1993*), Michael Fullan points out that most teachers have a clear sense of their own values in relation to teaching, which he calls 'moral purpose'. And importantly, this almost always relates to classroom practice. Thus:

> 'Scratch a good teacher and you will find a moral purpose. ...We recently examined why student teachers wanted to enter the profession... The most frequently mentioned theme was "I want to make a difference" reflected in the following sample of quotes:
>
> "...I care about children and the way that children are learning."
>
> "I want to effect positive change in students' lives."
>
> "I've always thought that if I could go into a classroom and make a difference in one kid's life...then that's what I am here for".'

Change Forces, *Fullan, M*

Therefore, if we seriously wish to help teachers to deal effectively with the competing pressures on their time and energy, we need to involve them in the planning process in a way which helps them to pursue their personal visions - to achieve their individual 'moral purposes' - by improving what they do, day by day, for their pupils in their classrooms.

Two important consequences flow from this conclusion:

● The development plan itself must be based on a *shared vision* which clearly reflects and supports individual *personal visions*.

* See 'Vision and Strategic Planning Come Later', page 140.

Here again we see the vital role that a truly collaborative school culture can play in helping individuals to share their personal visions and so create a larger vision which can support them in pursuing these visions. This issue is developed further in the next section.*

● The clear and permanent focus of the plan should be on supporting individual teachers to *improve their classroom practice*. This issue is dealt with on page 141.

(iii) Promoting shared understandings.

The key principles of learning which relate to this section are:

Learning activities should -

- *encourage learners to perform their understandings;*
- *provide regular opportunities for review and reflection.*

* See Chapter 2, page 51, especially the quotation from Chris Dickinson.

Learning is manifestly the core process in education. Yet as we have seen,* relatively few teachers have an adequate knowledge of fundamental learning issues. This has serious implications for whole school as well as classroom management, for without such knowledge it is clearly impossible to identify appropriate planning criteria with any confidence or accuracy. So the kinds of judgements needed for effective *auditing* and *prioritisation* within the development planning cycle become problematic, to say the least.

This is presumably what Sally Brown had in mind when she observed that:

> '...management seems often to fill the role of a displacement activity when educational thinking about the problem looks as if it might be difficult.'

Raising Standards: factors influencing the effectiveness of innovations,
Scottish Council for Research in Education Fellowship Lecture, 1992

While in **Change Forces** Michael Fullan goes even further by claiming that:

> '...wrong solutions to complex problems nearly always make things worse (worse than if nothing had been done at all)!'

Fullan, M (op. cit.)

So the process of development planning in a learning school should provide regular opportunities for all teachers to develop 'understanding through performance' of fundamental learning issues, so that they can engage in 'educational thinking' about these issues in relation to key planning decisions at all levels of the school. As Kurt Lewin once famously remarked:

> 'There's nothing so practical as good theory.'

Experiential Learning: Experience as the Source of Learning and Development, Kolb, D © 1984
(Reprinted by permission of Practice-Hall, Inc., Upper Saddle River, NJ)

And as David Perkins might respond:

> 'Good theory comes from practical performance.'

Therefore, teachers need to be actively and collaboratively involved in 'learning about learning', so as to develop shared understandings of key learning and teaching issues.

There should also be a strong emphasis on *review and reflection* through the processes of self-assessment and self-evaluation. The vital role of school self-evaluation in promoting whole school learning is discussed in Chapter 5 . But self-evaluation on its own is not enough. If the process is to be effective it is equally vital that those involved in it have adequate *professional knowledge*, and adequate opportunities to use this knowledge for 'educational thinking about the problem' through *collaborative planning*. This issue is also discussed in some depth in Chapter 5.

In a typically challenging section of **Change Forces** headed 'Vision and Strategic Planning Come Later', Michael Fullan comments on these issues in the following way:

* See the quotation on page 146 for an explanation of this term.

> 'Visions are necessary for success but few concepts are as misunderstood and misapplied in the change process. Visions come later for two reasons. First, under conditions of dynamic complexity* one needs a good deal of reflective experience before one can form a plausible vision. Vision emerges from, more than it precedes, action... Second, shared vision, which is essential for success, must evolve through the dynamic interaction of organizational members and leaders... Visions coming later does not mean that they are not worked on. Just the opposite. They are pursued more authentically while avoiding premature formalization.'

Fullan, M (op. cit.)

There is clear resonance here with Perkins' concept of 'understanding through performance', reinforcing once again the message that 'principles are indivisible'.

Fullan goes on to quote Peter Senge:

> 'Today, 'vision' is a familiar concept in corporate leadership. But when you look carefully you find that most 'visions' are one person's (or one group's) vision imposed on an organization. Such visions, at best, command compliance - not commitment... A shared vision is a vision that many people are truly committed to, because it reflects their own personal vision.'

Senge, P (op. cit.)

The key point here is that the effectiveness of a development plan is hugely affected by the way in which it is constructed and put into operation. *In learning schools, development plans emerge from, and are implemented through, a collaborative culture in which knowledgeable professionals continually improve their understandings of fundamental issues of learning and teaching; engage in real educational thinking about these issues; and so are able to make insightful, relevant decisions and take effective actions.* This is powerfully exemplified by the way in which the Critical Skills Programme has been used so effectively in Gilboa-Conesville School (see Chapter 5).

As Michael Fullan, again, characteristically observes:

* See the 'Secondary School Example' in Appendix 2 (page 180) for a description of how this sequence would work in practice.

> '*Ready, fire, aim* is the more fruitful sequence... *Ready* is important, there has to be some notion of direction, but it is killing to bog down the process with vision, mission, and strategic planning, before you know enough about dynamic reality. *Fire* is action and inquiry where skills, clarity, and learning are fostered. *Aim* is crystallizing new beliefs, formulating mission and vision statements and focusing on strategic planning. Vision and strategic planning come later; if anything they come at step 3, not step 1'.*

Fullan, M (op. cit.)

Just how these issues might be reflected in the format and operation of a learning school's development plan will be considered shortly. Meantime, it is necessary to consider the other major requirement of such a plan, i.e. a permanent focus on the improvement of classroom learning and teaching.

(iv) Focusing on classroom learning and teaching.

The key principle of learning highlighted in this section is:

Teachers should -

● *continually update their professional knowledge about learning and teaching.*

Here are some typical extracts from local authority documents on educational planning:

'At the *heart* of our work lies the aim to raise levels of achievement...(by)... improving the quality of teaching and promoting and providing learning opportunities of the highest quality.'

'High quality learning and teaching is at the *heart* of an effective school.'

'The improvement of learning and teaching should be at the *heart* of the plan.'

(emphases added)

Yet official advice on development planning at both local and national levels does not obviously reflect this kind of rhetoric.

Take, for example, the Scottish HM Inspectors of Schools Audit Division's booklet: **The Role of School Development Plans in Managing School Effectiveness** (*HMSO 1994*), which lists the following core set of 'key areas' as a 'Basic Framework for Audit':

● quality of the curriculum

● quality of learning and teaching

● pupil progress and attainment

● staff

● curriculum planning

● finance and resources

● accommodation

● ethos

It seems clear from this list that 'quality of learning and teaching' is given the same status as the other key areas of planning. Yet the rhetoric – e.g. 'the improvement of learning and teaching should be at the *heart* of the plan' - suggests a different status altogether. This is discussed further in part 3 of this chapter.

The 'Primary Plan Action Section' of the same document gives examples of current and future action projects, as shown below.* This is followed by an outline description of Project 4 - 'To improve the balance in teaching approaches'.

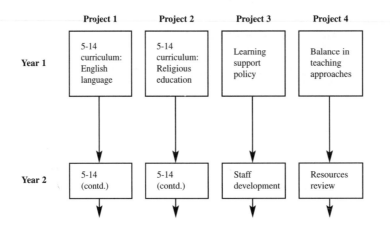

Project 4: To improve the balance in teaching approaches throughout the school (outline description)

Target:
'To change the balance in teaching approaches throughout the school in order to increase opportunities for pupils to be engaged in active learning, including group/individual activities; problem-solving situations; and other activities which encourage independent thinking, group discussion and decision-making.'

The criteria for success are:

i.   every teacher has introduced 2 major projects to their class work which have a significant emphasis on active learning and problem solving.

ii. every pupil has undertaken an individual project, appropriate to the class/stage, which requires independent thinking.

iii. group discussion and decision making are features of learning and teaching throughout the school.

Implementation strategies:

i.   discussion of active learning approaches during PAT and INSET days, including input from advisers/staff tutors.

ii. attendance at college INSET courses for appropriate staff (and report back).

iii. introduction of agreed techniques and applications into teachers' project plans and classroom practice.

Timescale:
1 school year

Resources and staff development requirements:

People
i.   AHT in lead   ii. Whole staff.   iii. EA advisers and staff tutors.
Time
i.   4 x 1 hour PAT sessions.   ii. 1 x ½ day INSET sessions..   iii. 2 staff on 2 days' INSET course.
Materials
i.   paper/reprographics materials for production of project materials
Cost
i.   cost of 2 x 2 days' college in-service course (course fees, travel expenses, supply teachers).
ii. cost of materials.   iii. EA costs.
(NB: these costs should be quantified).

Evaluation procedures:
HT and AHT to evaluate progress using a set of performance indicators relating to quality of learning and teaching, including the performance indicator 'Involvement of Pupils in Learning' by:
i   discussion with individual teachers.
ii. classroom observation
iii. discussion with pupils
iv. examination of teachers' plans and records of work
v.   discussion among whole staff at PAT session

Extracts from **The Role of School Development Plans in Managing School Effectiveness,** *HM Inspectors of Schools (Scotland) Quality, Standards and Audit Division (HMSO 1994)*

Clearly, Project 4 is from the key area 'quality of learning and teaching' (see page 141); and yet the outline description gives little indication that it will address such important learning and teaching issues as *lack of professional knowledge about learning*, and *misleading mental models* (see Chapter 1). Furthermore, the evaluation procedures suggested for the project - e.g.: 'HT and AHT to evaluate progress...' - are clearly derived from a line-management, hierarchical model of development planning, so heavily criticised by Professors John MacBeath, Sally Brown and David Hargreaves.

There is no suggestion, for example, of the kind of peer coaching and evaluative feedback that will be essential if teachers are to make significant, long-term improvements to their teaching practice (see Chapter 4). Neither is there any indication of a long-term focus on learning and teaching. Indeed, there is little evidence of it at all in Year 2 of the plan. Yet if the improvement of learning and teaching really is 'at the *heart* of the plan' then '*quality of learning and teaching' must become the permanent focus of the planning process, year in, year out* (see the diagram on page 152).

2. A 'Whole Brain' Approach to Development Planning

The key principles of learning which relate to part 2 are:

Learning activities should -

- *encourage the use of whole brain learning;*

- *cater for different thinking and learning styles.*

This part of the chapter makes a direct analogy between a *learning organization* (i.e. a school) and a *learning organism*, pointing out that both have to survive and carry out their functions in a complex world of threats and opportunities. This analogy reinforces yet again the argument that *the same principles of learning that should be applied to help individual learners should also be applied to the management of learning schools.*

In his recent book **The Right Mind** (*1997*), noted neurologist Robert Ornstein describes research which shows that left-brain/right-brain differences are not exclusive to humans. They seem to occur, to varying degrees, in all mammals. Commenting on this from a biological viewpoint he says:

> 'Having an overall picture...(from the right hemisphere)...would serve very well for an animal getting around in the world. We quickly have to recognise situations that are safe or that have difficulties... At the same time the animal needs to make a series of precise...decisions, and this decision-making seems best done by the left hemisphere... An animal can't spend its life forever searching the horizon.'

Ornstein, R (op. cit.)*

* See also the section on 'Brain Laterality', page 27.

Nor, of course, can it spend its life forever making 'a series of precise decisions' since ignoring the overall picture would leave it vulnerable to threats from predators and competitors; or cause it to miss out on opportunities for feeding and mating.

In other words, as learning organisms our brains have evolved to carry out two essentially different kinds of functions - holistic (right brain) and sequential (left brain) - because this combination is best suited to enable us to survive in a highly complex and demanding world, and to carry out our biological purpose - the reproduction of our species.

Schools, too, exist in a world of opportunities and threats; and they too have a purpose, which might be characterised as the reproduction of our culture. In **Smart Schools** (*1992*) David Perkins makes the following observations about the purpose of schools, and in so doing makes a powerful case for a permanent focus on the key area 'quality of learning and teaching':

> 'What do we want of education?... Of course, in a broad sense, we know all too well what we want. It can be put in a single word: *everything*... But we should also wonder whether the educational enterprise has a core... One reason to worry about a core is that the 'everything' agenda for schools is an energy vampire. It drains teachers, students and managers... So even though we want everything, what do we want most?... Here at a minimum is what we want... These are goals almost no one would argue with:
>
> ● Retention of knowledge
> ● Understanding of knowledge
> ● Active use of knowledge
>
> 'A summary phrase for the goals taken together might be 'generative knowledge' - knowledge that does not just sit there but functions richly in people's lives to help them understand and deal with the world...* These goals...follow directly from the core function of education, passing knowledge from one generation to the next. Whatever else a school is doing, if a school is not serving these goals well, it hardly deserves the name of school.'

Perkins, D (op. cit)

* See also the section on 'Thinking and Learning' in Chapter 1, page 23.

* A classic example of the value of a whole brain approach to problem solving at group level is the discovery of the structure of DNA. Wilkins and Franklin provided the essential information through logical analytical thinking and investigation (left brain). Crick and Watson provided the creative thinking which synthesised this information to provide the helical model (right brain). Neither team would have succeeded in unravelling the mystery of life without the work of the other.

Schools undoubtedly operate in highly complex political and social environments. Therefore, if they are to achieve their core purpose of raising standards by passing 'generative knowledge' from one generation to another, they too will need to operate in a whole-brained way. In other words, *just as a learning organism needs to process information with both sides of its brain if it is to achieve its biological goals, so does a learning school need to use a whole-brained approach to development planning if it is to fulfil its educational goals.* This is illustrated in the illustration opposite, which is itself based on the original rabbit and fox illustration on page 28.

But the model of development planning shown on page 142, for example, seems to be essentially a 'left-brained' approach to management. No doubt it will enable a school to make a series of precise, sequentially related planning decisions; but it is unlikely to be so helpful in terms of seeing the interrelationships between planning areas, or the wider context (big picture) to which these decisions must relate.

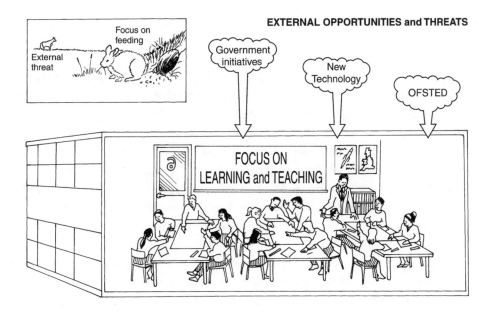

The effects of left-brain/right-brain differences are readily observable in any group discussion of development planning, where views commonly polarise. For example, Professor Sally Brown's criticisms of the hierarchical, line-management approach to planning (see page 134) provoked strong differences of opinion amongst the participants at the seminar in question - differences which almost certainly reflected the different thinking and learning style preferences of the individuals concerned.

One typical consequence of a focus on detailed decision-making at the expense of the wider picture is seen in a common response to unexpected events, whether these be opportunities or threats. This can be characterised as:

'We've agreed our priorities for this year, so please go away world.'

Unfortunately, the real world does not go away. It is full of unexpected surprises! As Michael Fullan points out:

> 'There are fundamental reasons why the change process is uncontrollably complex, and in many circumstances 'unknowable'. The solution lies in better ways of thinking about, and dealing with, inherently unpredictable processes.'

Change Forces, *Fullan, M*

And, of course, it is precisely *because* of the need to think and deal in better ways with inherently unpredictable processes that our brain has evolved its two distinct ways of dealing with information about the world; and why learning schools should use 'right-brained' as well as 'left-brained' approaches to planning and management.

Notice, however, the 'as well as' in the last sentence. It is important to stress that a holistic (right brain) approach to development planning must be *in addition to*, not *instead of* the current sequential (left brain) approach. To go from the one to the other would be to leave the school in the same position as Ornstein's animal – 'forever scanning the horizon' rather than 'forever making a series of precise decisions'. Both kinds of activities, on their own, are equally (and literally) 'half-witted'!

In a typically penetrating analysis of an all-too-common situation, Fullan goes on to say:

'How is change complex? Take any educational policy or problem and start listing all the forces that could figure in the solution and that would need to be influenced to make for productive change. Then, take the idea that unplanned factors are inevitable - government policy changes or gets constantly redefined, key leaders leave, important contact people are shifted to another role, new technology is invented, ...a bitter conflict erupts, and so on. Finally, realize that every new variable that enters the equation - those unpredictable but inevitable noise factors - produce ten other ramifications, which in turn produces tens of other reactions and so on...

'Senge makes the distinction between 'detailed complexity' and 'dynamic complexity'. The former involves identifying all the variables that could influence a problem. Even this would be enormously difficult for one person or a group to orchestrate. But detailed complexity is not reality. Dynamic complexity is the real territory of change: when 'cause and effect' are not close in time and space and obvious interventions do not produce expected outcomes because other 'unplanned' factors dynamically interfere... Complexity, dynamism, and unpredictability, in other words, are not merely things that get in the way. They are normal!'

Fullan, M (op. cit.)

A classic example of this 'complexity, dynamism and unpredictability' occurred in the early 1990s in a Scottish education authority which had just succeeded in persuading all of its secondary headteachers to commit their schools to development planning. One of the key attractions of this then relatively new approach to school management, it was claimed, was that schools could agree their priorities for the next year or two, allocate staff development time and other resources accordingly, and proceed to implement their plans with confidence in a climate of stability.

Imagine the uproar, then, when at the first headteachers' meeting of the new session the Assistant Director of Education cut right across the carefully laid school development plans by announcing that the authority would be requiring all management and guidance staff to undertake several days of authority-led training within the next three months. And the reason? A major national report on child abuse had prompted the government to require all local authorities to draw up Child Protection Guidelines and train the relevant staff within six months. In other words, the 'real world' had intervened in all its unpredictable, dynamic complexity - as it has an irritating habit of doing with monotonous regularity!

So there seem to be at least two good reasons for including a holistic element in development planning:

(i) It improves communications by enabling the more 'right-brained' thinkers amongst the staff to understand and participate more fully in planning and management processes. As another of the West Lothian Headteachers group reporters put it:

> 'We need to take on board the issues of different learning styles in our management of staff.'

(ii) By presenting staff with a 'big picture' it enables them to gain a better appreciation of the functional relationships between the major elements of the plan. As a result, the school should be better able to see external forces in context and so judge the kinds of internal responses which will best support and improve classroom learning. To paraphrase Ornstein and Holly & Southworth, it should enable the school to 'search the horizon' (Ornstein) and so 'learn its way forward' (Holly & Southworth) more effectively.

Nevertheless, we must still bear in mind Michael Fullan's warning about the unpredictably dynamic complexity of the world in which schools operate. In other words, not even a 'big picture' incorporated into the development plan is going to provide an adequate representation of the dynamic complexity of the forces with which a school has to cope. Peter Senge, for example, after many years of work with a wide variety of organizations, has concluded:

> 'Control at the top, as many reform-minded leaders have found, is an illusion. No-one can control complex organizations from the top... While traditional organizations require management systems that control people's behaviour, learning organizations invest in improving the quality of thinking, the capacity for reflection and team learning, and the ability to develop shared understandings of complex...issues. It is these capabilities that will allow learning organizations to be both more locally controlled and more well co-ordinated than their hierarchical predecessors.'

Quoted by Fullan, M in **Change Forces**

This is why 'quality of learning and teaching' should have a different status to the other key areas of a development plan*; why there needs to be a *permanent* focus on improving learning and teaching, with a particular emphasis on teachers' professional knowledge and skills. For in the unpredictably complex world in which schools operate, the only effective way to improve the quality of learning in classrooms is to support and empower classroom teachers in the ways described in Chapter 4.

* See page 141.

In other words *in learning schools it is classroom teachers, not senior managers, who make most of the important decisions; and most of these are reached through collaborative thinking with colleagues and pupils (e.g. peer coaching and self-evaluation).* As Fullan again observes:

> 'Mandates are important. Policymakers have an obligation to set policy, establish standards, and monitor performance. But to accomplish ..important educational goals you cannot mandate what matters, because what really matters for complex goals of change are skills, creative thinking, and committed action. Mandates are not sufficient and the more you try to specify them the more narrow the goals and means become. Teachers are not technicians...

> 'The acid test of productive change is whether individuals and groups develop skills and deep understandings in relation to new solutions... (Mandates) have no chance of accomplishing these substantial changes even for single policies let alone for the ...reality of dynamic complexity. When complex change is involved, people do not and cannot change by being told to do so. Effective change agents neither embrace nor ignore mandates. They use them as catalysts to re-examine what they are doing.'

Fullan, M (op. cit.)

Therefore, just as Ornstein's animal uses its right brain to scan the wider environment before making appropriate, specific decisions with its left brain, so should a holistic element in the development plan enable schools to react positively to unpredictable forces - both external and internal - by seeing more clearly how they can be used as catalysts for effective action in the classroom rather than reacting in a defensive, 'go away world' mode. This is well illustrated by the primary school example described in part 4 of this chapter.

So while there is no doubt that development planning has brought a number of significant benefits to school management, there seems equally little doubt that the current model needs to evolve into a more 'whole brained' approach if we are to pay more than lip service to the concept of the learning school. As Peter Senge points out:

> 'Learning disabilities are tragic in children, especially when they go undetected. They are no less tragic in organizations, where they also go largely undetected.'*

Senge, P (op. cit.)

* See also Professor MacBeath's quote re. organizational learning from Argyris & Schon in Chapter 5, page 122.

The question worth asking, then, is:

How did this 'left-brained' approach to management gain such high status, despite the fact that many senior managers presumably have right-brained thinking and learning preferences?

To answer this question it is helpful to review some of the main functions of the two halves of the brain:*

* See the section on 'Brain Laterality' in Chapter 1, page 27.

Left brain - sequencing; analysis; individual facts; logic; words; numbers.

Right brain - holistic; synthesis; relationships; patterns; rhythm; imagination; creativity.

* Maths and the sciences do not have to be taught in a left-brained way, of course. But they generally are. As one of Maggie Farrar's 'University of the First Age' students wrote in her Learning Log: 'I have seen the other side of Maths.'!

It is clear from this list that formal education generally values left-brained more than right-brained activities. Text books and worksheets are commonly written in a logical, sequential manner, often without the benefit of a 'big picture'; and most assessments are mediated verbally and measured numerically. 'Left-brain' subjects such as mathematics and the sciences* generally have a higher academic status than 'right-brain' subjects such as home economics and art. Indeed, the very notion of academic rigour seems to be synonymous with left-brain thinking. Why should this be, if the functions of the right brain are of equal importance in our general lives?

Peter Senge provides a significant clue when he points out that '...traditional organizations require management systems that control people's behaviour'*. For in hierarchical systems most organizational decisions are taken by line managers away from the 'chalkface'. This produces strong pressure to 'value what's measurable rather than measure what's valuable' - i.e. to rely on *quantitative, outcome data* (test results, attendance rates, discipline referrals, etc.) at the expense of *qualitative, process details* (peer relationships; the developing 'skills and dispositions' of pupils (see Chapter 3); the views of pupils about their learning needs; the views of teachers about their professional development and resource needs). And *quantitative outcome data, tabularised and used for comparative purposes, demand a 'left-brained' approach to management.*

* See the quotation on page 147.

As Black & Wiliam have shown (see Chapter 1, page 26) a greater reliance on detailed, qualitative information through formative, self-assessment is a particularly powerful way of improving the quality of children's learning. And research by John MacBeath's QIE team on school self-evaluation (see page 126) has demonstrated similar benefits for whole-school management. But such qualitative information can only be used effectively if classroom teachers are given more control over day-to-day management decisions; and such a move would run entirely counter to the current political imperative towards greater external accountability.

Paradoxically, therefore, it seems that the outcome to which society universally aspires is rendered more difficult to achieve by the very political imperative which is meant to secure it. Indeed, as Chris Dickinson pointed out at the West Lothian Headteachers Conference:

> 'The problem with a focus on outcome targets rather than the means to achieve them is that it can hamper the learning process by producing tension, stress and anxiety.'

(op.cit.)

In a recent article entitled 'Don't try to control everything', Matthew Taylor, Director of the Institute for Public Policy Research, wrote the following:

> 'Accepting the idea of target-setting is one thing; setting the right targets is another... (For example), the target for 50 percent of pupils to achieve five A-C grades in GCSE gives schools every incentive to concentrate on those of middling ability... The target thus becomes a measure not of school performance but of the head's ability to direct resources ruthlessly to a particular group...
>
> *'It is a characteristic of management by target that more and more measures have to be developed to correct the perverse incentives created by earlier ones,* rather as the judge in the film "What's Up Doc?" took so many pills to deal with the side-effects of others that he forgot what was originally wrong with him.'*

New Statesman, 15 January 1999 (Emphasis added. Reproduced with the permission of New Statesman 2000)

* cf. the use of 'behaviour management' programmes to deal with problems caused by inappropriate learning activities - see the Classroom Rules cartoon on page 60.

And an even more bizarre, real life example of the 'perverse incentives' created by quantitative, externally set targets also occurred early in 1999 when BBC radio news reported the following incident on the COMEX South-East rail service:

> 'A train driver who had been regularly criticised by his managers for the late arrival of his train finally managed to reach his destination on time today. There was only one problem. In his concern to achieve his target he had missed out five stations on the way!'

* See the list of 'Critical Skills and Fundamental Dispositions' on page 70 which were generated in answer to the question: 'What skills and dispositions are vitally important for students to have by the time they leave school in order to be successful in their lives?'

It is interesting to speculate on what those missing stations might be called, in educational terms:*

Fullan and Senge, too, have amply demonstrated that there is very little chance of achieving significant, long-term improvements to standards of achievement if teachers' day-to-day decision making is subject to too much central control.* Perhaps, then, the cause of the problem is philosophical rather than psychological?

* See page 147.

In 1960, for example, Douglas McGregor described two opposing philosophies of human behaviour in his 'Theory X' and 'Theory Y' models of management behaviour. These are contrasted in the following table.

Two Patterns of Management Behaviour

Theory X: The Traditional View of Direction and Control	Theory Y: The Integration of Individual and Organization Goals
● The average human being has an inherent dislike of work and will avoid it if he can.	● The average human does not inherently dislike work. Depending upon controllable conditions, work may be a source of satisfaction... or a source of punishment.
● Because of this human characteristic of dislike of work, most people must be coerced, controlled, directed, threatened with punishment to get them to put forth adequate effort toward the achievement of organisational objectives.	● External control and the threat of punishment are not the only means for bringing about effort toward organizational objectives. Man will exercise self-direction and self-control in the service of objectives to which he is committed.
● The average human being prefers to be directed, wishes to avoid responsibility, has relatively little ambition, wants security above all.	● The average human being learns, under proper conditions, not only to accept but to seek responsibility. Avoidance of responsibility, lack of ambition, and emphasis on security are generally consequences of experience, not inherent human characteristics.

Adapted from **The Human Side of Enterprise**, *MacGregor, D (McGraw-Hill 1960)*

No doubt there would be widespread agreement that 'Theory Y' embraces the characteristics to which we aspire for our pupils. Yet the hierarchical, 'left-brained' approach to development planning seems largely predicated on the characteristics of 'Theory X'.   And since two different value systems cannot operate effectively in the one organization, we cannot expect teachers to treat their pupils according to the values of Theory Y if they themselves are treated according to those of Theory X.* As more than one prominent politician has discovered to his cost in recent years, *values - like principles - are indivisible!*

* See also the comments about this phenomenon on page 127.

3. Introducing a Holistic Element to the Planning Process

The key principles of learning which relate to part 3 are:

Learning activities should -

- *encourage the use of whole brain learning.*

Teachers should -

- *continually update their professional knowledge about learning and teaching.*

This part of the chapter describes the proposed *holistic element* and considers how it might be combined with the current sequential approach to make the processes of *auditing* and *action planning* more relevant to the improvement of classroom learning and teaching.

(i) The holistic element.

A schematic outline of the proposed holistic element is shown overleaf. It is based on the 'key planning areas' listed on page 141.

Two key points need to be made first of all.

● This outline illustrates in general terms the relationships that should exist between the key planning areas in a learning school. By providing a 'big picture' of the internal and external environment in which a school has to operate it serves as a continual reminder of the need to focus management energies on supporting and improving what goes on in classrooms.

However, it does *not* provide a complete description of the complexity of interrelationships that a school must deal with in the 'real world'. As Senge and Fullan have made clear, any attempt to do this would be doomed to failure. Therefore, in practice, it will be necessary to focus on smaller parts of the big picture to indicate the functional relationships between different management activities at any one time. This process is described in part 4 and in *Appendix 2.*

The 'Secondary School Example' in *Appendix 2* describes how such an holistic element can be routinely and systematically used as an audit tool, i.e. to check that the necessary structures and processes are in place at each stage of a development initiative (see page 183).

DEVELOPMENT PLANNING IN A LEARNING SCHOOL
THE HOLISTIC ELEMENT

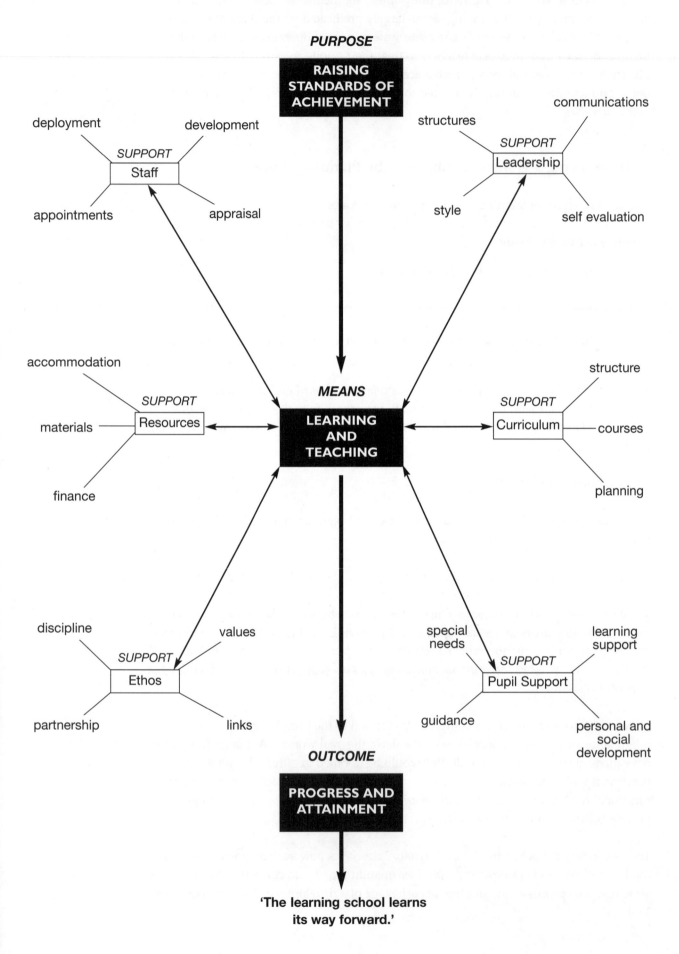

● This holistic element is intended to *supplement* rather than replace the current sequential approach outlined in the diagram on page 142. Clearly it will still be necessary for a learning school to make 'a series of precise decisions'* in carrying through its management priorities.

*See the quote from **The Right Mind** on page 143.

Therefore, the sequential approach to implementing action projects - with targets, success criteria, evaluation procedures etc. as shown on page 142 - will need to continue. But it is important to emphasise that *these targets, criteria and procedures should be set internally, as a result of collaborative self-evaluation.* Again, this process is described in some detail in the 'Secondary School Example' in *Appendix 2.*

The essential feature of the holistic element is that it represents visually the oft-repeated aspiration to put 'learning and teaching at the *heart* of the plan'. In so doing it shows the relationships that should exist between the key planning areas in a learning school. These may be categorised under the headings of *purpose; means; support;* and *outcome* as follows:

Purpose. A school's main purpose is to *raise standards of achievement* by passing 'generative knowledge'* from one generation to the next.

* See the quote from David Perkins on page 144.

Means. The means by which this purpose will be achieved is by *improving the quality of learning and teaching.*

Support. The role of most of the other key planning areas is to provide effective *support for the improvement of learning and teaching* so that standards of achievement are raised.

Outcome. The main outcome of these improvements to learning and teaching should be *improved pupil progress and attainment.*

(ii) Auditing and action planning in a learning school.

> 'Through the process of audit, schools should undertake a systematic evaluation of performance in key areas of their work...(but)...*the level of detail of the audit will have to be well judged to ensure that useful management information is produced without creating an unnecessarily complex or time-consuming exercise.*'

The Role of School Development Plans in Managing School Effectiveness*, HMI Inspectors of Schools (Scotland) Quality, Standards and Audit Division (HMSO 1994 - emphasis added)*

Clearly, the HMI's advice to 'well judge' the level of detail is based on widespread difficulties with this process in practice! Indeed, there is no doubt that teachers often find the audit part of the development planning cycle difficult and demotivating. Unfortunately, the Audit Division booklet gives little information about the criteria to be used in this 'well judging', which will indeed be a problem if the relevant criteria are not well understood. And as we have seen (pages 51 and 138), most of the relevant criteria for the improvement of learning and teaching are unlikely to be widely *or* well understood.

By contrast, the holistic representation shown opposite clearly indicates that these judgements should almost always come back to a key question which teachers should find relatively easy to answer, whatever the current level of their knowledge of learning:

* For example, in the primary school case study described in Chapter 5, the majority of teachers clearly felt that classroom learning and teaching would be most helped at that point in time by improvements to school and classroom ethos.

'At this point in time, what kind of support will best help me to improve my pupils' learning?' *

Of course, this layout can also stimulate a related and equally important question:

'How does each of our current development plan priority initiatives help us to improve our pupils' learning?'

This highlights the fact that *managers of learning schools are primarily accountable to their staff and pupils for ensuring that development planning initiatives will promote and support continuous improvements to classroom learning and teaching.*

So the suggestion is that this approach to auditing should be combined with a systematic focus on active and collaborative learning about the process of learning itself and the application of this knowledge to classroom practice. And this can be done very effectively through the aegis of a development group such as the 'cadre' described in Chapter 5. As a result, staff are likely to be clearer about the kinds of judgements to be made, and to have the knowledge and insights to make these judgements more relevant and productive.*

*See the Secondary Example in Appendix 2.

* See page 140.

This approach should also improve the process of action planning. For example, it is clear from Michael Fullan's comments on *ready, fire, aim**, that teachers will need to spend a considerable amount of time working actively and collaboratively to develop their knowledge of fundamental learning issues (*fire*) before they can be expected to produce a detailed action plan with valid criteria (*aim*). To quote Fullan again:

> '*Fire* is action and inquiry where skills, clarity and learning are fostered.'

So a detailed focus on project action planning will only represent a profitable use of time and energy *after* such 'action and inquiry' has produced a sufficient level of clarity and shared understandings. And as Fullan points out, these kinds of activities are also most likely to develop the shared visions that are essential for effective strategic planning. As already noted (page 140), the description of the 'Administrator's Challenge' in Gilboa-Conesville School (Chapter 5) exemplifies this process to a high degree.

4. Integrating the Holistic and Sequential Elements

The key principles of learning which relate to part 4 are:

Learning activities should -

- *encourage learners to perform their understandings;*
- *encourage the use of whole brain learning.*

Part 4 consists of a relatively brief description of the proposed integration process. *Appendix 2* illustrates in greater depth how this process is likely to proceed in practice, in response to the 'unpredictable, dynamic complexity' of both the internal and external environments of the school.

It is important to stress again that this 'whole brain' approach to planning is firmly predicated on the notion that life is unpredictable. To quote **Change Forces** again:

> 'There are fundamental reasons why the change process is uncontrollably complex, and in many circumstances 'unknowable'. The solution lies in better ways of thinking about, and dealing with, inherently unpredictable processes.'

Unexpected events such as the Child Protection Guidelines incident described on page 146 should therefore be treated as the norm, to be coped with by the school's 'learning system'*, rather than temporary but highly irritating disruptions to the (totally illusory!) smooth running of the school.

See the quote from Holly & Southworth at the beginning of this chapter.

It is also important to stress that whole brain planning, like whole brain learning, is about more than simply using both sides of the brain. Crucially, it is about using them in an *integrated, interactive* way. In other words, it is not just a question of outlining holistic and sequential elements but rather of developing the two elements together in an interactive manner. The way in which this can be done is outlined here by means of the two diagrams which relate to the primary school case study described in Chapter 5 . They show a holistic representation of the initial phase and a sequential representation of the final phase of the discipline policy development. For a more detailed description of the way in which these two elements would interact as a development initiative proceeds, see the 'Secondary School Example' in *Appendix 2* (page 180).

(i) The holistic element (see page 157) - illustrates the relationships between the initiatives that took place over the first few weeks and, in particular, their relevance to the improvement of classroom learning. The continuous lines indicate those areas which were being developed in this initial phase, while the numbers relate to the sequence of events, as described overleaf:

KEY PLANNING AREAS

Staff – *development*	**1.** The initial staff INSET workshop to raise staff's *knowledge of learning*.
Leadership - *style*	**2.** The headteacher's failed attempt to persuade the staff to move straight to specific learning and teaching issue(s), followed by her decision to reinforce her *collaborative leadership style* by suggesting a cross-hierarchical 'cadre' group to examine the whole issue.
Leadership - *structure*	**3.** Agreement of the staff and the setting up of the *cadre*.
Staff - *deployment*	**4.** Arrangement of *cover* for members of the cadre to attend an initial all-day meeting.
Leadership – *self-evaluation*	**5.** Reports from the nominated staff members of the cadre, confirming the general wish to look first at discipline issues. In effect, the teachers had responded to the headteacher's request to focus on 'learning and teaching' with an informal *audit*. As a result of this they judged that work on school and classroom ethos, leading to improved discipline, would be of most help to their teaching at that time.
Ethos - *discipline* *Resources* – *materials*	**6.** Several meetings of the cadre with the author to study discipline issues, in the context of both behaviourist and constructivist learning principles. The concepts of external vs. internal *locus of control*, and a *networking* support structure amongst staff figured prominently in these discussions, which culminated in preparations for a series of staff workshops.
Leadership - *communications*	**7.** A series of three staff *policy workshops* on discipline, culminating in a draft policy statement which was agreed by the staff.
Progress and Attainment	**8.** The learning school 'learns its way forward' (for the further developments see *Appendix 2*).

My role at this stage was to provide reference materials and other relevant information, often in the form of brief background papers on issues such as 'locus of control' and 'values in action'. The ultimate aim was that the members of the cadre would themselves develop sufficient knowledge of learning issues to be able to support their colleagues by organising a peer coaching programme as well as the workshops. In the event the network support structure agreed for the discipline policy proved to be an ideal base from which to develop peer coaching. Further details of this process are given in Chapter 5, page 133.

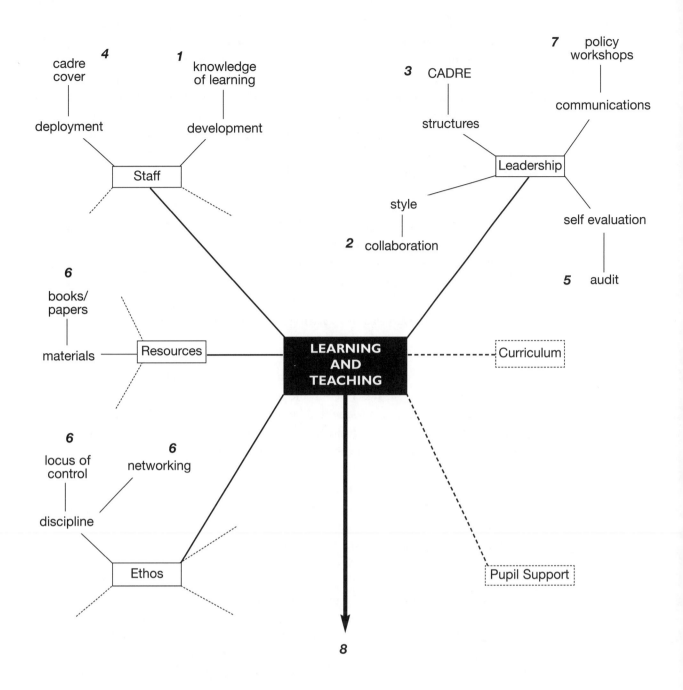

The staff workshops were run entirely by the staff nominees on the cadre. The author took no lead role, but did make occasional comments to keep the link between discipline and the provision of an appropriate learning environment at the forefront of the discussion. The aim here was to avoid producing, in Eric Jensen's terms, 'merely a model for teaching and controlling the learners'.

(ii) The sequential element (see page 159). The first point to emphasise here is that in a hierarchical organization the project action plan (i.e. the sequential element) would probably have been produced by one or more members of the line management team. Therefore it is highly unlikely that the kind of feedback provided by the staff nominees on the cadre would have occurred and so there would have been a real danger of exemplifying Argyris & Schon's observation that 'the organization cannot seem to learn what everybody knows' (see Chapter 5, page 122). As a result the action plan might well have been for a learning and teaching initiative for which the majority of staff were ill-prepared and unmotivated.

In this instance, however, the headteacher emphasised her collaborative leadership style by setting up the cadre. As a result of this and the subsequent decision to make learning and teaching the overall focus of planning activities, the school was able to ensure that the great majority of staff were more confident and committed when they came to tackle the original learning and teaching issues, albeit several months later than originally planned. It had been a longer journey, certainly, but the staff as a whole now knew a good deal more about some of the fundamental issues involved than when they had started. As T.S. Eliot put it:

> 'We shall not cease from exploration
> And the end of all our exploring
> Will be to arrive where we started
> And know the place for the first time.'

'Little Gidding' *from* **Four Quartets** *in* **The Complete Poems and Plays of T.S Eliot** *(Faber and Faber Ltd., 1969)*

The following page shows the sequential 'action plan' element at an advanced stage of the policy development, as described in the report extract in Chapter 5. But it is important to remember that a sequential layout made, say, at stage 5 of the holistic layout would have looked significantly different because the sequential and holistic elements interact with each other throughout such a development.

For example, the list of success criteria shown here includes aspects which only occurred to the staff as a result of cadre and workshop discussions about the relationship between discipline and learning, thus reinforcing Michael Fullan's telling observation about the change process being 'uncontrollably complex', and in many circumstances 'unknowable'.

It is also worth noting that, unlike the example shown on page 142, the evaluation criteria in this case focus on the *process* of improvement rather than its *outcomes*. Staff were involved in detailed discussions about the relationship between discipline and learning so that the emphasis was on identifying the kinds of procedures which would be most likely to improve classroom and school ethos and provide more supportive conditions for learning, rather than simply measuring whether or not such improvements had occurred.

The confident expectation, of course, is that such a focus – Fullan's *fire* ('action and inquiry where skills, clarity and learning are fostered') - will indeed lead to improved outcomes which can then be evaluated using official performance indicators. But performance indicators are essentially instruments of *summative evaluation* whereas, as we have seen, real improvements in learning and teaching are unlikely to come about unless all staff are able to engage in regular, *formative evaluation*.

Project: To develop an effective discipline policy.

Target:
'To produce a discipline policy which reflects the views and needs of every member of the teaching staff; reflects the professed values of the school; promotes self-esteem; and supports effective learning in the classroom.'

The criteria for success are:

i.   All teachers will have the opportunity to play a full part in the development of the overall policy.

ii. All non-teaching members of staff will have the opportunity to play a full part in the development of the non-classroom aspects of the policy.

iii. All pupils will have the opportunity to contribute to the development of classroom and playground charters.

iv. The School Board and parents will be fully informed about the progress of the policy and have the opportunity to contribute views on its application.

v.   Staff will feel more confident and secure in their relationships with children and each other.

vi. Pupils will feel more confident and secure in their relationships with staff and each other.

vii. Incidents of indiscipline will reduce.

viii. Staff, parents and pupils will feel that school and classroom ethos better reflects the school's professed values.

ix. Staff and pupils will feel that school and classroom ethos is more supportive of learning.

Implementation strategies:

i.   Children's learning needs discussed with external consultant at PAT session.

ii.   Cross-hierarchical development group (cadre) set up.

iii. Cadre conducts staff audit.

iv.   Cadre studies learning, teaching and discipline issues with consultant.

v.   Cadre members lead policy development workshops.

vi.   Cadre produces draft policy statement for staff discussion.

vii. Draft policy discussed with Pupil Council, PTA, School Board and non-teaching staff.

viii. Policy explained to all pupils at assembly, followed by Circle Time class discussions.

ix.   Policy introduced.

x.   Member of cadre monitors and evaluates progress of the policy.

Timescale:
2 terms to implementation. Initial evaluation after 1 term of operation.

Resources and staff development requirements:

People
i.   Cadre (development group).   ii. Whole staff.   iii. External consultant.
Time
i.   4 x 2 hour PAT sessions   ii. 1 x whole-day cadre meeting.   iii. 3 x 1½ hour after-school cadre meetings.
Materials
i.   paper/reprographics ii. flip chart for workshops.   iii. reference books.
Cost
i.   materials.   ii. consultant's fee. iii. cover for initial cadre meeting (2 x supply teachers).

Evaluation procedures:
One member of the cadre will evaluate progress from the staffs' perspective, as part of her M.Ed work. Another member will evaluate pupils' and parents' reactions.

The staff evaluation will include non-teaching staff and will deal with success criteria nos. (i), (ii), (v), (vii) and (ix). The pupils/parents evaluation will deal with success criteria nos. (iii), (iv), (vi), (vii), (viii) and (ix).

Staff evaluation will be by questionnaire and interview, to give quantitative and qualitative data respectively. At this stage the details of the pupil/parent evaluation have not been decided.

Developing a Discipline Policy to Support Effective Learning in the Classroom: The Sequential Element.

It is worth concluding this section by combining the final paragraph of the report on this project with the comments of the IQEA project team on the planning process:

> 'The openness and honesty of staff during this process has been marked. The level of sharing has increased and staff seem open to suggestion from one another.'

Primary School report (see page 132)

> 'In some ways, involvement in planning activity is more important than producing plans - it is through collective planning that goals emerge, differences can be resolved and a basis for action created. The 'plan' is really a by-product from this activity, and will almost always need to be revised, often several times. The benefits of the planning activity, however, will often outlast the currency of the plan.'

Hopkins, D, West, M & Ainscow, M (op.cit. - see page 133)

Conclusion

The contention throughout this book has been that the most effective way to raise standards of achievement is by creating and leading 'learning schools', in which leadership and management at all levels are firmly based on key principles of learning.

The development planning model described in this final chapter, while not in any sense definitive, has two features which seem to make it particularly worth considering as a learning school management tool:

1. There is a permanent, priority focus on improving learning and teaching in classrooms.

2. It represents a 'whole brain' approach which recognises and caters for the fact that in the real world the unexpected is always happening.* Or as Michael Fullan characteristically puts it:

* See the 'Secondary School Example' in Appendix 2 (page 186 - 'a key leader leaves'; page 187 - 'a conflict erupts') for a description of how this whole brain approach can help a school to deal more effectively with 'unexpected' events.

> 'Complexity, dynamism, and unpredictability...are not merely things that get in the way. They are normal!'

Change Forces, Fullan, M

In the knowledge-based society of the Twenty-First Century, where change is increasingly rapid, complex and unpredictable, the challenge of preparing young people for fulfilling and productive lives is ever more demanding. The contention throughout this book has been that schools can successfully meet this challenge by becoming true 'learning schools', in which key principles of learning are consciously and rigorously applied to the management of classroom learning, staff development, and whole-school development. In short -

principles are indivisible.

Appendix 1: A Selection of Learning Materials from the Critical Skills Programme

This selection of CSP materials has been chosen to illustrate how some of the key activities in the CSP Experiential Learning Cycle (see page 72) are carried out. It is worth stressing that this a very small selection from the full range of CSP materials. For each part of the learning cycle a large selection is available to suit different circumstances such as the age and maturity of the pupils and the experience of the teacher.

The following diagram shows where an experienced CSP teacher would use each of these examples in the learning cycle to promote effective long-term development of knowledge, understanding, skills and dispositions.

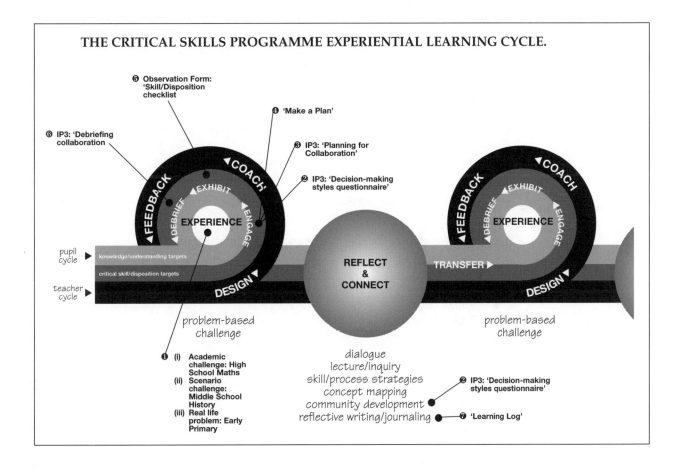

1. The Challenges

These are described in outline on page 74 and in more depth on pages 87-92. A typical example of each type of challenge is shown here. These have been selected from the **Leading EDGE 'Sampler' of Challenges** (1999) and relate to the New York State curriculum.

(i) Academic Challenges. These relate directly to the curriculum. They are designed to help pupils

- understand essential knowledge
- develop specifically targeted 'critical' skills and dispositions
- work co-operatively or collaboratively
- work towards clear standards of quality

Knowledge 'Standard' - use mathematical modelling... to provide a means of processing, interpreting, communicating and connecting mathematical information and relationships	**Academic Challenge** High School Regents Course II	**Skill/Disposition 'Standard'** - interpersonal and citizenship competence: teaches others; helps other to learn

Question/Issue | How do we determine dimensions of objects plotted on the co-ordinate plane?

Challenge: Using classroom and library resources, develop a manual from which the rest of the class will learn the following techniques:

- Calculating distances between points
- Calculating mid point of two points
- Finding area of various common geometric shapes

It is important to remember that a manual is a specific type of book. Always keep in mind the purpose of a manual and why people will be reading it.

Product Criteria Book
Rule criteria
- Includes at least one example of each of the three techniques

Form criteria
- Cover
- Author page
- Table of contents
- Index

Content Criteria
- Finding area of various common geometric shapes
- Calculating distances between points
- Calculating mid point between points
- Important vocabulary

Evidence of: | **Targeted Standard/Indicator(s):**

- **Knowledge** - Understands and applies targeted concept(s)
- Knowledge | <u>Look for/Listen</u> for - Student can successfully complete homework problems on
- Skill | the three calculations. Student can pass a quiz on the three calculations.
- Disposition |

- **Interpersonal/Citizenship Competencies** - Teaches others. Helps others learn
<u>Look for/listen</u> for - Student answers others' questions about something mathematical they don't understand. Student takes time to explain something new to someone else. Student creates an example to show someone something about mathematics.

(ii) Scenario Challenges. These increase the authenticity of the learning experience by asking pupils to role-play real life or imaginary situations. In addition to the knowledge, skills and dispositions developed by the Academic Challenges, they also help pupils to

- develop their imagination and creativity through role-playing

- relate their school work to more authentic out-of-school situations (the 'big picture').

<table>
<tr>
<td>

Knowledge 'Standard' - speak and write to transmit information. World History - use a variety of intellectual skills to demonstrate an understanding of major ideas, eras and themes.

</td>
<td>

Scenario Challenge
A Roman Dig

</td>
<td>

Skill/Disposition 'Standard' - Problem solving - constructing and employing problem solving strategies

</td>
</tr>
</table>

Middle School
ELA/Soc. Studies

The Setting

You are a team of highly trained archaeologists. You've recently made an amazing discovery and have 'uncovered' an ancient Roman town close to the city of Rome itself. Immediately upon discovering the site, you contacted your employer, the curators at the famous Delaware County museum located in Delhi, NY., and told them the good news via a satellite link.

Since your employers had been looking to expand their museum in order to promote more tourism in Delhi, they were very excited about your find.

Your sponsors requested that you make an excavation of the site and return home with artefacts and other knowledge about life in ancient Rome.

The Challenge

Your challenge is to present your findings to a panel from the museum. Your job is to clearly describe the culture of the time period you have excavated. Your sponsors want to know how people of this time period lived, and how their lives were similar or different from ours. Your sponsors know that visitors to museums are most interested in the topics listed below. If your sponsors are going to be at all interested in what you have, you should address all of these topics in your presentation.

- **home life**: roles of family members, what homes looked like, contents of a home, marriage customs, religious beliefs;
- **the military**: how it was run, weapons used, who conquered whom;
- **technology**: what inventions of the time helped make life easier or more comfortable for the people;
- **the land itself**: what land forms affected them (helped them or hurt them);
- **rulers or government**: how the people interacted with the rulers or government, how much did it affect the people's every day lives;
- **entertainment**: what did these people do for enjoyment.

As part of your presentation, please be sure to include:

- a 'blueprint' drawing of the town you've uncovered;
- at least two artefacts from each area of discovery;
- a 3-5 minute explanation of the findings from each of the areas. Please indicate what the artefacts are, what they were used for, and how people of today might see a connection to their own lives;
- a projection of funds needed to continue research for next year.

This presentation will determine whether grant money of $1,000,000 will be given to you. This money will be used not only to continue your research in Italy, but to oversee the building of a new wing at the museum where your artefacts will be displayed.

(iii) Real Life Problems - present pupils with real problems in need of real solutions. Depending upon the age, maturity and experience of the pupils, these challenges can relate to problems at class, school, community, regional, national or even international levels. In addition to the knowledge, skills and dispositions developed by the Academic Challenges they are also designed to help pupils

- solve real problems
- receive authentic feedback from people who have a vested interest in receiving a quality solution or product
- use a wide range of skills, knowledge and strategies such as those used by adults to tackle real problems in the real world.

REAL LIFE PROBLEM
(read to students)

Primary (K-2) 5 -7 years old

Dear Students

I am Miss Dottie from the Cackling Hen Nursery School. I care for small children who could really use the help of some bigger kids like you. I was speaking to your teacher, Ms Penney, and she tells me that you are a very caring class with many good ideas. I sure hope so because I have a problem that I would like you to help me solve.

In my nursery school I have 15 children who are only 3 or 4 years old. They need help in learning about our community. I want my students to learn something about the people in our community who have important jobs. We need to learn how these people help us to have better lives.

I know that I cannot take my children to see all those people in our community who have important jobs, and I can't think of any way to have all those people come to one place to meet my children.

 I do have one idea that might work. That is why I need your help. I would like to bring my children to your classroom for a visit. I would like each of you to find out about a person in our community who has an important job which makes our lives better. When my class and I come for our visit, I would like you to teach my children about the people and the jobs you have learned about.

Please remember that the children in my care are very young. They learn best when they can see, touch, smell, or taste things. If you could find a way to let them play with something that will teach them about the person and the job that you select, I am sure my kids will really enjoy themselves.

Will your class help me out?

Sincerely,

Ms. Dottie
Teacher, Cackling Hen Nursery School

---

2. IP3: Decision Making Styles Questionnaire

3. IP3: Planning for Collaboration

The IP3 'tool' is described on page 83. The samples shown here are an extract from the 'Decision Making Styles Profile Questionnaire' and the 'Planning for Collaboration' sheet, both of which were developed by Leading EDGE to support the original Critical Skills Programme, based at Antioch New England Graduate School. The questionnaire is actually used with adults, i.e. on teacher training programmes. Its language would be suitably modified for use with all but the oldest of pupils.

The questionnaire has been put alongside the 'Planning for Collaboration' sheet (page 166) because it relates closely to it. In practice it would probably be used as a community building exercise (see page 83), which is why it is shown twice in the Experiential Learning Cycle diagram on page 161.

**Decision Making Styles Profile
Questionnaire***

Directions:
Each item below has four answers that complete the statement. On the space in front of each statement, rank the answers on a scale of 1 to 4. The answer that is MOST like you should receive a 4; the answer that is least like you should receive a 1.

1. In my work, I tend to place the greatest value on

    a. people's feelings
    b. creative ideas
    c. final products
    d. effective planning

2. When I work with others on a difficult task, I tend to focus on

    a. organizing practical details
    b. getting the job done
    c. how the group gets along
    d. the potential for new approaches

3. In group settings, my best contribution is often my ability to

    a. work hard to do things right
    b. offer creative ideas
    c. communicate well with others
    d. use common sense

4. When people criticize me, they tend to say that I am too

    a. inconsistent
    b. sensitive
    c. impatient
    d. authoritarian

In order to find your Decision Making Style score, write the number value you attached to each of the letters for each item. Then, total the numbers in each column.

Item	Ideas	People	Product	Process
1	b=	a=	c=	d=
2	d=	c=	b=	a=
3	b=	c=	a=	d=
4	a=	b=	d=	c=

15	d=	b=	c=	a=
Totals				

* Note: This questionnaire was developed by Pete Fox, teacher of high school English Language Arts at Gilboa-Conesville CS, Gilboa, NY.

IP3
PLANNING
FOR COLLABORATION

IDEAS

What will you do to ensure that all ideas are heard/considered?

PEOPLE

What will you do to invite all group members to participate actively and feel valued?

PROCESS/PROCEDURES

What will you do to ensure that your group is well organized and that you use available resources efficiently?

PRODUCT

What will you do to ensure that your final product is of the highest quality possible given the resources available?

*Adapted from: Adizes, Ichak: **Mastering Change, The Power of Mutual Trust and Respect in Personal Life, Family Life, Business & Society**, (Ichak Adizes, 1991)*

4. **Make a Plan for Your Work**

5. **Skill / Disposition Checklist**

These are used to help pupils develop organizational skills. See, for example, the 'Whales' Challenge on page 75. The observations made with the help of the Checklist then feed into the 'debrief' process described on pages 95-97.

Make a Plan for Your Work

In what order?	What has to be done?	Who should do it?	When should it be finished?

Observation Form
Skill/Disposition "Checklist"

Class Period: _____   **Challenge Name:**   Date(s): _____

'WHALES'

Skill/Disposition: *Organization*

Targeted Indicator: *Employing organizational tools; reviewing & revising plan*

Specific Observable Behavior(s) to "Look for/Listen for"

Student Name	Project plan gives work schedule for each group member		Group discusses progress in relation to work schedule		COMMENT
	YES	NO	YES	NO	

6. IP3 Debriefing Sheet. This is a powerful way of encouraging metacognition by focusing pupils' attention on how well their collaborative work skills are developing.

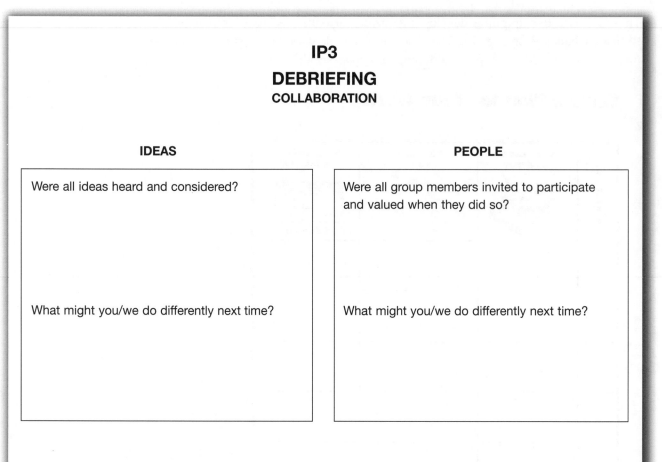

IP3

DEBRIEFING

COLLABORATION

IDEAS

Were all ideas heard and considered?

What might you/we do differently next time?

PEOPLE

Were all group members invited to participate and valued when they did so?

What might you/we do differently next time?

PROCESS/PROCEDURES

Was your group well organized and did it use available resources efficiently?

What might you/we do differently next time?

PRODUCT

Was your final product of the highest quality possible given the resources available?

What might you/we do differently next time?

7. Learning log. The value of learning logs in developing metacognitive skills is described on page 99. This particular example also encourages pupils to think about the kinds of future experiences that would best help them to develop important knowledge, skills and dispositions.

Learning Log

Name: _____ Class: _____ Date: _____

Please write your thoughts on at least 3 of the following questions

> What I learned was...
> What I found interesting about this work was...
> What surprised me was...
> I want to know more about...
> Right now I'm feeling...
> This experience might have been more valuable to me if...

Appendix 2: Two Worked Examples of Whole Brain Development Planning

It should be stressed that neither of these examples represent actual case studies of the proposed model. The Primary School example is heavily based on the case study of collaborative policy development in a Scottish primary school which was described in Chapter 5 (pages 130-133) and which actually stimulated the idea of developing a whole brain approach. But the model itself has been applied retrospectively to this case study, to show how the whole brain approach could improve the overall management of the process.

The Secondary School example is purely notional - albeit based on considerable personal experience of similar problems! It is intended to show how a complex initiative such as the introduction of new teaching methods to raise attainment could be managed more effectively by taking a whole brain approach to the planning process.

1. A Primary School Example

This is the complete version of the example which was used on pages 155-160 to illustrate the integration of the holistic and sequential elements in the proposed model of whole brain planning. For the sake of completeness and clarity this example starts and ends with extracts from those pages.

The description which follows refers to the case study described on pages 130-133. It will be much easier to follow if that study is reread first.

(i) Using the Holistic Element

Diagram 1 (opposite) - shows the complete holistic element, as previously described in Chapter 6 (page 152).

Diagrams 2-4 (pages 172, 174 and 176) - illustrate the relationships between the initiatives which took place in the school in question, and their relevance to the overall priority of *promoting continuous improvements in classroom learning and teaching*. The continuous lines in these diagrams indicate those areas which were subject to development at that time, while the numbers in bold italics show the sequence of the events at each stage of development.

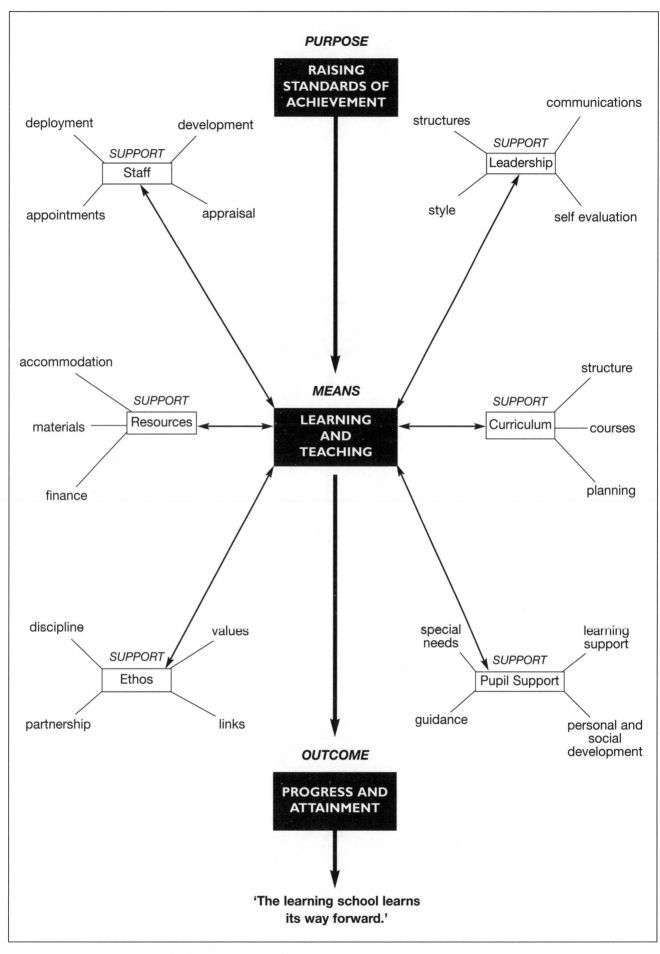

Diagram 1: The Basic Holistic Element

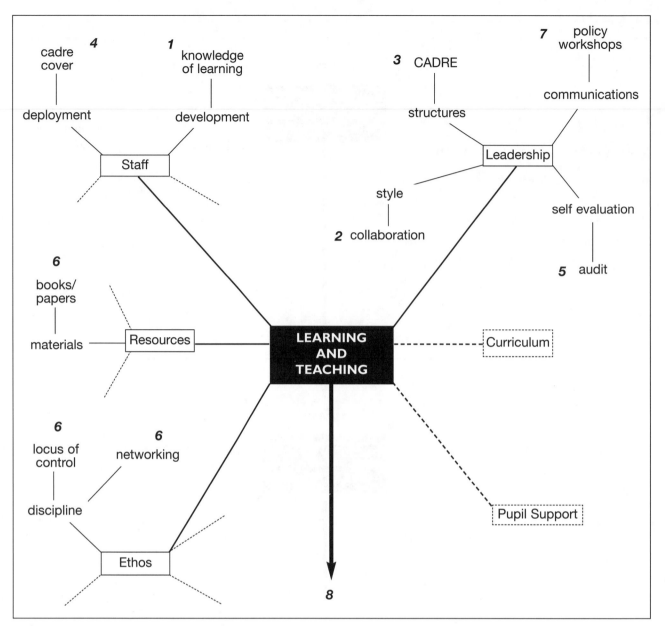

Diagram 2: Developing a Discipline Policy to Support Effective Learning in the Classroom: Stage 1

Diagram 2 - shows the initial sequence of events, as follows:

KEY PLANNING AREAS	**STAGE 1**
Staff - development	**1.** The initial INSET workshop to increase staff's *knowledge of learning.*
Leadership - style	**2.** The headteacher's failed attempt to persuade the staff to move straight to specific learning and teaching issues, followed by her decision to reinforce her *collaborative leadership style* by suggesting a cross-hierarchical 'cadre' group to examine the whole issue.
Leadership - structures	**3.** Agreement of the staff and the setting up of the *cadre.*
Staff - deployment	**4.** Arrangement of *cover* for members of the cadre to attend an initial all-day meeting.

Leadership - *self-evaluation*

5. Reports from the nominated staff members of the cadre, confirming the general wish to look first at discipline issues. In effect, the teachers had responded to the headteacher's request to focus on 'learning and teaching' with an informal *audit*. As a result of this they judged that work on school and classroom ethos, leading to improved discipline, would be of most help to their teaching at that time.

Ethos - *discipline*

6. Several meetings of the cadre with the author to study discipline issues, in the context of both behaviourist and constructivist learning principles. The concepts of external versus internal *locus of control*, and a *networking* support structure amongst staff figured prominently in these discussions, which culminated in preparations for a series of staff workshops.

Resources - *materials*

My role at this stage was to provide *reference materials* and other relevant information, often in the form of brief background papers on issues such as 'locus of control' and 'values in action'. The ultimate aim was that the members of the cadre would themselves develop sufficient knowledge of learning issues to be able to support their colleagues by organising a peer coaching programme as well as the workshops. In the event the network support structure agreed for the discipline policy proved to be an ideal base from which to develop peer coaching. Further details of this process are given in Chapter 5, pages 131-133.

Leadership - *communications*

7. A series of three staff *policy workshops* on discipline, culminating in a draft policy statement which was agreed by the staff. The staff workshops were run entirely by the staff nominees on the cadre. The author took no lead role, but did make occasional comments to keep the link between discipline and the provision of an appropriate learning environment at the forefront of the discussion. The aim here was to avoid producing, in Eric Jensen's terms, 'merely a model for teaching and controlling the learners' (see the quotation at the top of page 17).

For example, discussion of a Playground Charter produced the suggestion to paint a number of games on the playground surface, in conjunction with the Pupil Council and PTA. This provided the opportunity to mention Carla Hannaford's book **Smart Moves** (*1995*) which describes many ways in which learning can be enhanced through movement and also has an excellent section on 'Brain Gym ®'.* This caused sufficient interest for several teachers to move on after introducing the new discipline arrangements, to use Brain Gym ® activities in their classroom routines (see Diagram 4 on page 176).

*See Chapter 2, page 61.

Progress and Attainment

8. The learning school 'learns its way forward'.

It is now widely recognised that an external consultant can play an important facilitating role by helping staff to develop the knowledge base and support structures that are vital to the creation of a 'learning school'. The experience of this particular school would certainly support this conclusion.

Diagram 3 - shows what happened in Stage 2, i.e. after the draft discipline policy had been agreed by the teaching staff. The sequence of events is described opposite:

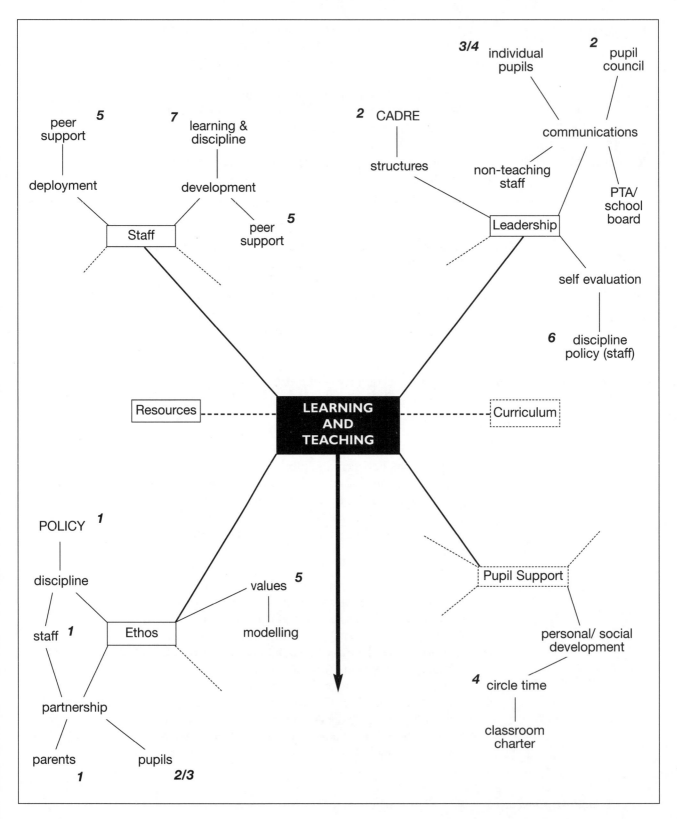

Diagram 3: Developing a Discipline Policy to Support Effective Learning in the Classroom: Stage 2

Ethos - *discipline & partnership*   **1.**   The *draft policy statement* was agreed by the teaching staff (see Diagram 2, stage 7).

Leadership - *communications*   **2.**   Members of the cadre discussed the draft policy with *non teaching staff, the PTA*, the *School Board* and

Ethos - *partnership*   the *Pupil Council.*

Ethos - *partnership*   **3.**   All *pupils* were informed about the new policy at assemblies.

Pupil Support - *personal & social development*   **4.**   Class teachers discussed individual *Classroom Charters* with their classes at 'Circle Time'.*

Staff - *development*   **5.**   The networking system provided *peer support* to teachers in dealing with discipline problems. It also

Staff - *deployment*   provided a means of *modelling the school's values*, as

Ethos - *values*   discussed below.

Leadership - *self-evaluation*   **6.**   One member of the cadre took responsibility for *monitoring and evaluating* the new policy (see pages 131/132).

Staff - *development*   **7.**   As part of the monitoring and evaluation programme, in-service time was used to provide *staff workshops* at which the effectiveness of the policy was discussed, particularly in the context of the staff's developing knowledge of the relationship between learning and discipline.

An early topic of discussion at these follow-up workshops was the way in which the networking support system could be used by teachers to model the school's professed values, by referring pupils to their network partners for *positive* behaviour and good work. In this way behaviourist principles of learning were applied to raise pupils' self-esteem and intrinsic motivation to learn ('internal locus of control').

By contrast, an emphasis on negative referrals - sometimes referred to as the 'zero tolerance' approach - would have signalled that the school was primarily interested in gaining the pupils' conformity to other people's values rather than helping them to develop self-knowledge and intrinsic motivation to learn. As a result, they would have been less likely to learn well and develop self-control.

* This highly effective programme for raising pupils' self-esteem is described in Jenny Mosley's book **Turn Your School Round** (see Appendix 3).

One significant feature of a learning school is that staff are encouraged and supported to formalise their learning and professional development by undertaking professional qualifications. Very often these can dovetail well with the school's priorities - which ought in any case to be closely linked to individual teachers' priorities.*

*See the section on 'promoting a shared vision', page 137.

This was exemplified well in the case of the development group member who took responsibility for monitoring and evaluating the discipline policy, which she linked to her M.Ed. studies (see the case study on pages 130-133).

Diagram 4 - shows some of the developments which occurred once the new discipline policy had been implemented. Again, the sequence of events is described opposite:

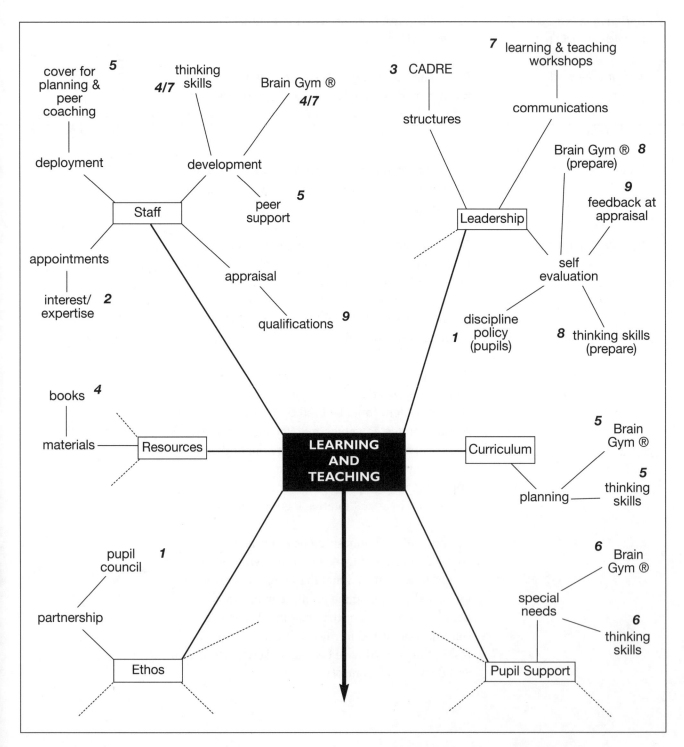

Diagram 4: Developing a Discipline Policy to Support Effective Learning in the Classroom: Stage 3

KEY PLANNING AREAS	STAGE 3

Leadership - self-evaluation

Ethos - partnership

1. The pupils' reactions to the new discipline policy were *monitored and evaluated* by a second member of the cadre, in conjunction with the *Pupil Council* (see page 132).

Staff - appointments

2. Interest and/or expertise in learning became an even more important criterion in the appointment of *new teachers*. A new senior teacher with a particular interest in *Philosophical Inquiry* (a thinking skills programme) and *Brain Gym* ® was appointed at this time.

Leadership - structures

3. The *cadre* member responsible for evaluating the discipline policy left the cadre to devote more time to her M.Ed studies, but retained responsibility for monitoring the discipline policy with staff. She was replaced on the cadre by the new senior teacher.

Staff - development

Resources - materials

4. A number of teachers expressed interest in taking forward specific learning and teaching programmes such as *Brain Gym* ® and *Philosophical Inquiry*. Relevant *books and other materials* were bought for them to study and use.

Staff - development

Curriculum - planning

Staff - deployment

5. *Cover* arrangements were made for interested staff to *plan* together how they would introduce one and/or other of these approaches into their classrooms. They then team-taught and *peer coached*.

Pupil Support - special needs

6. These new programmes were particularly suitable for pupils with *special needs*.

Staff - development

Leadership - communications

7. The cadre organized *INSET workshops* on learning and teaching which provided opportunities for teachers trying out these programmes to *inform and discuss* their work with their colleagues.

Leadership - self-evaluation

8. Preparations were made to *monitor and evaluate* the progress of these new teaching approaches.

Staff - appraisal

Leadership - self-evaluation

9. Meanwhile, the annual *appraisal* of the teacher who was evaluating the discipline policy provided valuable *feedback* for both teacher and school. This is a particularly important feature since it clearly addresses in a powerful way the limitations of hierarchical management described by Professors MacBeath and Brown (see pages 127 and 134).

(ii) Using the Sequential Element

It has already been pointed out (see page 157) that this element represents the standard 'project action plan' which in a hierarchical organization would probably have been produced by one or more members of the school management team. Therefore it is most unlikely that the kind of feedback provided by the staff nominees on the cadre would have occurred. Consequently, there would have been a real danger of exemplifying Argyris & Schon's observation that 'the organization cannot seem to learn what everybody knows' (see Chapter 5, page 122); and as a result the action plan might well have been for a learning and teaching initiative for which the majority of staff were ill-prepared and unmotivated.

In this instance, however, the headteacher emphasised her collaborative leadership style by setting up the 'cadre' development group. As a result of this and the subsequent decision to make learning and teaching the overall focus of planning activities, the school was able to ensure that the great majority of staff were more confident and committed when they came to tackle the original learning and teaching issues, albeit several months later than originally envisaged.

Diagram 5 (opposite) - shows how the sequential 'action plan' element would look at an advanced stage of the policy development, as described in the report extract in Chapter 5 (pages 131/132). But it is important to remember that a layout made, say, at stage **5** in **Diagram 2** would have looked significantly different because the sequential and holistic elements interact with each other throughout such a development. This kind of interaction is described in some detail in the Secondary School example which follows (page 180).

For example, the list of success criteria shown in Diagram 5 includes aspects which only occurred to the staff as a result of cadre and workshop discussions about the relationship between discipline and learning, thus reinforcing yet again Michael Fullan's telling observation about the change process being 'uncontrollably complex, and in many circumstances "unknowable"' (see page 155).

It is also worth noting that the evaluation criteria focus more on the *process* of improvement than its *outcomes*. Staff were involved in detailed discussions about the relationship between discipline and learning so that the emphasis was on identifying the kinds of *procedures* which would be most likely to improve classroom and school ethos and provide more supportive conditions for learning, rather than simply *measuring* whether or not such improvements had occurred.

The confident expectation, of course, is that such a focus - Fullan's *fire* ('action and inquiry where skills, clarity and learning are fostered') - will indeed lead to improved outcomes which can then be evaluated using official performance indicators. But performance indicators are essentially instruments of *summative evaluation* whereas, as we have seen, real improvements in learning and teaching are unlikely to come about unless all staff are able to engage in regular, *formative evaluation*.

Project: To develop an effective discipline policy.

Target:
'To produce a discipline policy which reflects the views and needs of every member of the teaching staff; reflects the professed values of the school; promotes self-esteem; and supports effective learning in the classroom.'

The criteria for success are:

i.   All teachers will have the opportunity to play a full part in the development of the overall policy.

ii.   All non-teaching members of staff will have the opportunity to play a full part in the development of the non-classroom aspects of the policy.

iii. All pupils will have the opportunity to contribute to the development of classroom and playground charters.

iv.   The School Board and parents will be fully informed about the progress of the policy and have the opportunity to contribute views on its application.

v.   Staff will feel more confident and secure in their relationships with children and each other.

vi.   Pupils will feel more confident and secure in their relationships with staff and each other.

vii. Incidents of indiscipline will reduce.

viii. Staff, parents and pupils will feel that school and classroom ethos better reflects the school's professed values.

ix.   Staff and pupils will feel that school and classroom ethos is more supportive of learning.

Implementation strategies:

i.   Children's learning needs discussed with external consultant at PAT session.

ii.   Cross-hierarchical development group (cadre) set up.

iii. Cadre conducts staff audit.

iv.   Cadre studies learning and teaching issues with consultant.

v.   Cadre members lead policy development workshops.

vi.   Cadre produces draft policy statement for staff discussion.

vii. Draft policy discussed with Pupil Council, PTA, School Board and non-teaching staff.

viii. Policy explained to all pupils at assembly, followed by Circle Time class discussions.

ix.   Policy introduced.

x.   Member of cadre monitors and evaluates progress of the policy.

Timescale:
2 terms to implementation. Initial evaluation after 1 term of operation.

Resources and staff development requirements:
People
i. Cadre (development group).   ii. Whole staff.   iii. External consultant.
Time
i.   4 x 2 hour PAT sessions   ii. 1 x whole-day cadre meeting.   iii. 3 x 1½ hour after-school cadre meetings.
Materials
i.   paper/reprographics ii. flip chart for workshops.   iii. reference books.
Cost
i.   materials.   ii. consultant's fee.   iii. cover for initial cadre meeting (2 x supply teachers).

Evaluation procedures:
One member of the cadre will evaluate progress from the staffs' perspective, as part of her M.Ed work. Another member will evaluate pupils' and parents' reactions.

The staff evaluation will include non-teaching staff and will deal with success criteria nos. (i), (ii), (v), (vii) and (ix). The pupils/parents evaluation will deal with success criteria nos. (iii), (iv), (vi), (vii), (viii) and (ix).

Staff evaluation will be by questionnaire and interview, to give quantitative and qualitative data respectively. At this stage* the details of the pupil/parent evaluation have not been decided.

*See Diagram 3, page 174.

Diagram 5: Developing a Discipline Policy to Support Effective Learning in the Classroom: The Sequential Element.

2. A Secondary School Example

It is important to stress at the outset that this notional example is not a comprehensive description of a development planning initiative. It is simply designed to show how the introduction of a 'holistic element' would simplify auditing, improve communications and increase the likelihood of creative, effective responses to developmental issues and problems.

The example describes how whole brain planning could be used to improve the effectiveness of a programme to raise standards of achievement in a medium to large sized secondary school. Let us assume that this has been stimulated by a local authority or OFSTED inspection which has identified a general need to raise attainment by improving the quality of teaching.

*See Chapter 6, page 138.

Following the inspection report the school's senior management team discusses ways of tackling the problem with authority advisory staff, who recommend an initial INSET session on learning and teaching for the whole teaching staff as a way of generating 'shared understandings'* through shared experience. This consists of an introductory workshop on the Critical Skills Programme (CSP - see Chapter 3), which raises considerable interest and enthusiasm amongst the staff, not least because it seems to cater well for two of their greatest concerns - *classroom discipline* and *covering the syllabus!*

The senior management team meets to discuss the outcome of the workshop. They agree that it has been well received and that they wish to introduce CSP materials and methodology into as many classrooms as possible, as soon as possible. The CSP trainer is engaged as a consultant to organize training for interested staff and to advise on appropriate follow-up support.

*See Chapter 5, page 129.

At the consultant's suggestion the headteacher first of all organizes the setting up of a core 'cadre' group,* consisting of the deputy head with responsibility for learning and teaching, two heads of department, and two unpromoted teachers. The senior management team gives considerable thought to the composition of the cadre since, although its members will be expected to take a lead role in teaching and promoting CSP, a group consisting exclusively of enthusiastic idealists is unlikely to communicate effectively with the more sceptical members of staff!

Ideally, there should be at least one 'sceptic' on the group - preferably a widely respected head of department with a successful, traditional teaching approach. (For example, Peter Fox at Gilboa - Conesville (see pages 69 and 116) was a widely respected and successful 'traditional' teacher who on his own admission was so sceptical about experiential learning that he nearly walked out of the Level 1 CSP training at mid-morning break on the first day! In the event he was persuaded to stay until the end of the day and went on to become an enthusiastic and highly successful exponent of CSP, with an outstandingly positive impact on the ethos and attainment of Gilboa.)

Because of the relatively large size and complex organization of a secondary school each member of the cadre is given a 'link' responsibility for communicating regularly with specified departments, including the one in which they teach. The deputy head is also responsible for ensuring that other members of the school's senior management team are kept fully informed and involved.

The first task of the cadre members is to conduct an unofficial 'audit' by means of informal discussions with teachers in their link departments to gauge their responses to the suggestion that CSP training might be an effective way of addressing the attainment issue. At their first meeting with the consultant the members of the cadre report a high level of interest in CSP and so they draft out a preliminary sequential 'action plan' with targets, criteria etc. The first four sections of this plan are shown in **Diagram 6**.

Project:

To improve the quality of classroom learning by implementing the materials and methods of the Critical Skills Programme.

Targets:
(i)   Organize Level 1 CSP training for interested staff
(ii)   Provide effective support to teachers who wish to implement CSP

The criteria for success are:
(i)   All interested staff receive at least Level 1, part A CSP training within 2 terms
(ii)   All CSP trained staff have designed and taught at least two Challenges within 1 term of their initial training
(iii) All CSP trained staff have successfully created a 'collaborative learning community' with at least one of their classes within 1 term of initial training

Implementation strategies:
(i)   Cadre members invite applications for training from staff in their link departments
(ii)   Issue discussed with Heads of Departments (HoDs)
(iii) Cadre organizes Level 1 CSP training for all interested staff
(iv)   Cadre organizes appropriate support for implementation of CSP in classrooms

Timescale:
(i)   Level 1 CSP training - 2 terms
(ii)   Challenges and 'collaborative learning community' by end of session

Diagram 6: The First Draft of the Sequential Element

Note that at this stage there is no attempt to produce a comprehensive action plan. It is sufficient to provide enough information to stimulate productive discussion when the cadre members next meet their link colleagues. Above all, it is important to avoid 'bogging down the process...before you know enough about dynamic reality', i.e. to move as quickly as possible from the 'ready' to the 'fire' phase of development by engaging a significant number of staff in 'educational thinking' about learning and teaching.*

*See the quotations from Michael Fullan (page 140) and Sally Brown (page 139).

CSP training will certainly stimulate much 'educational thinking', e.g. by challenging the widely held '*transmission*' model of learning and highlighting the importance of regular feedback through self and peer assessment. It will also stimulate in-depth discussion of key issues such as the need for effective post-training support, e.g. *peer coaching*.* In other words CSP training epitomises Fullan's description of the 'fire' phase of development planning:

*See Chapter 4, page 111.

> '**Fire** is action and inquiry where skills, clarity and learning are fostered.'

Change Forces, *Fullan, M (see page 140)*

Therefore, after staff have been through a period of 'fire' via CSP training and practice they will be in a better position to produce a more detailed and insightful action plan - i.e. to take 'aim' with considerably more accuracy than when they started the initiative:

*e.g. changing from the 'transmission' to the 'transformation' mental model of learning.

> '**Aim** is crystallising new beliefs,* formulating mission and vision statements and focusing on strategic planning. Vision and strategic planning come later.'

Fullan, M (see page 140)

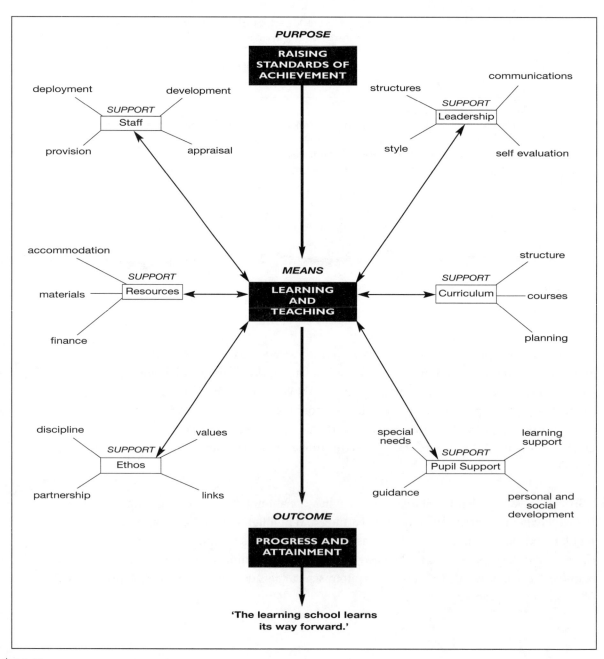

Diagram 7: The Basic Holistic Element*

* First shown on page 152.

Leading the Learning School

The consultant then introduces the basic holistic element (**Diagram 7**) and suggests that they use this as a means of translating their provisional sequential layout (**Diagram 6**) into a holistic layout (**Diagram 8**). As they do so, the consultant encourages them to scan Diagram 7 systematically to check that the main structures and processes to support this first phase of the development have been identified. In effect, they are using the 'right brain' planning element to 'scan the horizon' (Ornstein - see pages 143/144) and identify which of the key 'support' areas should be addressed at this first stage.

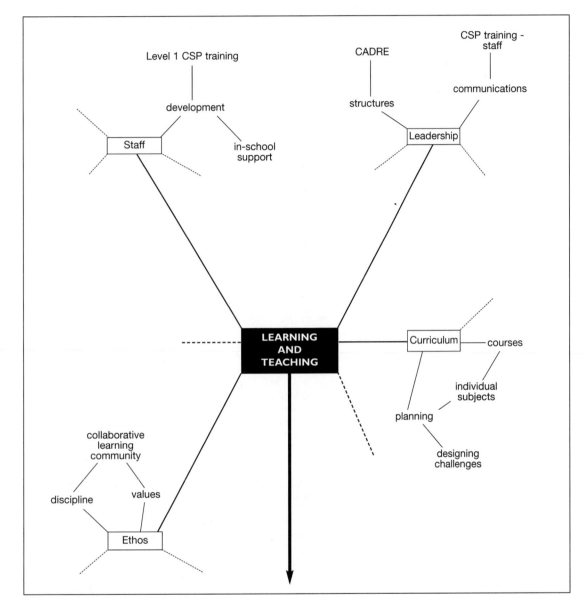

Diagram 8: The first draft of the Basic Holistic Element

For example, when they look at the **Leadership** area in **Diagram 7** they realise that they will need to consider what *communications* systems might be helpful. This leads to a general discussion about the importance of explaining CSP effectively to parents and governors, many of whom are likely to be sceptical about 'new-fangled' courses and to argue for a more 'back to basics' approach to raising standards. So they agree that the school should invite the Board of Governors and the PTA to an evening workshop with the CSP trainer/consultant. They also agree that they will need to ensure continued backing from the LEA advisers by keeping them fully informed and involved in the project.

One of the main issues of concern at their first meeting had been the need to ensure that the 'collaborative' role of the cadre was not perceived to be devaluing the status of line managers in the existing hierarchical structure. Therefore they had readily agreed that the two heads of department would ask their colleagues if a standing item on the monthly Head of Department meetings could be a report from them on the progress of the project, with an opportunity for questions and discussion.

All of these items are then added to the *sequential element* (see the additional targets, criteria etc. shown in italics in **Diagram 9**); and the *holistic element* (see *Leadership - communications* and *Ethos - partnership* and *links* in **Diagram 10**).

Project:

To improve the quality of classroom learning by implementing the materials and methods of the Critical Skills Programme.

Targets:
(i)   Organize Level 1 CSP training for interested staff
(ii)   Provide effective support to teachers who wish to implement CSP
(iii)   Ensure effective communications with all staff, pupils, parents and governors
(iv)   Keep LEA advisers/inspectors fully informed and involved in the development of the project

The criteria for success are:
(i)   All interested staff receive at least Level 1, part A CSP training within 2 terms
(ii)   All CSP trained staff have designed and taught at least two Challenges within 1 term of their initial training
(iii)   All CSP trained staff have successfully created a 'collaborative learning community' with at least one of their classes within 1 term of initial training
(iv)   Staff, pupils, parents, governors and advisers are given regular (at least monthly) written information on the progress of the project
(v)   Heads of department are given monthly written and verbal information on the progress of the project
(vi)   Parents and governors are invited to an Introductory Workshop on CSP within 1 term
(vii)   There is general support for the project from parents and governors
(viii) LEA advisors visit the relevant CSP classrooms at least once in the first term following training

Implementation strategies:
(i)   Cadre members invite applications for training from staff in their link departments
(ii)   Issue discussed with Heads of Department (HoDs)
(iii)   Cadre organizes Level 1 CSP training for all interested staff
(iv)   Cadre organizes appropriate support for implementation of CSP in classrooms
(v)   (Named member of the cadre) provides regular written progress reports in the School Newsletter
(vi)   (Named member of the cadre) provides regular written and verbal progress reports to the HoD meeting
(vii)   (Named member of the cadre) organizes an evening workshop by (date)
(viii) Views of parents and governors are sought through - a) evaluation sheets; b) individual discussions with members of the cadre, senior management team and other CSP trainees; c) raising the issue at PTA and Board of Governors meetings
(ix)   Cadre members arrange for relevant advisers to visit CSP trainees at their link groups

Timescale:
(i)   Level 1 CSP training - 2 terms
(ii)   Challenges and 'collaborative learning community' - by end of session
(iii)   Information via School Newsletter - at least monthly
(iv)   Introductory Workshop for parents and governors - by (date)
(v)   Evaluation of parents' and governors' responses - by (date)
(vi)   Advisers visits to CSP teachers - by (date)

Diagram 9: The Second Draft of the Sequential Element

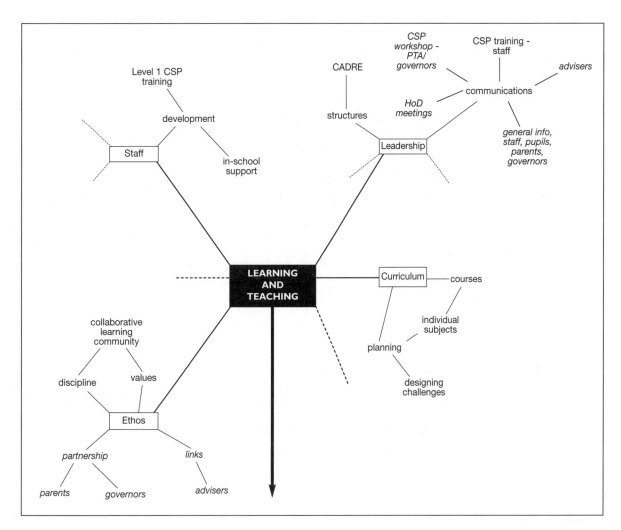

Diagram 10: The Second Draft of the Holistic Element

Scanning the basic holistic element (Diagram 7, page 182) also reminds them that the issue of *Progress and Attainment* of pupils will need to be monitored (via *Leadership - self-evaluation*) - including the vexed question of a timescale for the improvement of examination results. It is agreed that the identification of both qualitative and quantitative measures of progress will need to wait until the first group of teachers have undergone Level 1 CSP training and identified the classes with which they will pilot the programme.*

The cadre then considers how best to organize the training. The basic holistic layout (Diagram 7) reminds them that they will need to consider the issues of class cover (*Staff - deployment*) and the cost of cover, training, and materials for training and piloting CSP (*Resources - finance and materials*) all of which will be limiting factors on both the timing and uptake for this initial round of training. Again, this information is added to the developing elements (shown in italics in **Diagrams 11** and **12**, overleaf) which by now are becoming sufficiently detailed for the programme to get under way.

* For the sake of clarity only two changes are considered here. In practice it is likely that several more additions and/or alterations will be made to the initial layouts of both elements at this point.

Project:

To improve the quality of classroom learning by implementing the materials and methods of the Critical Skills Programme.

Targets:
(i)   Organize Level 1 CSP training for interested staff
(ii)   Provide effective support to teachers who wish to implement CSP
(iii)   Ensure effective communications with all staff, pupils, parents and governors
(iv)   Keep LEA advisers/inspectors fully informed and involved in the development of the project

The criteria for success are:
(i)   All interested staff receive at least Level 1, part A CSP training within 2 terms
(ii)   All CSP trained staff have designed and taught at least two Challenges within 1 term of their initial training

(ix) *Teachers and pupils agree that the quality of pupils' learning experiences and work has improved*
(x)   *Test and examination results improve*

Implementation strategies:
(i)   Cadre members invite applications for training from staff in their link departments
(ii)   Issue discussed with Heads of Department (HoDs)

(x)   *Criteria for judging the quality of learning experiences and pupils' work will be thoroughly discussed either during or soon after the initial CSP training*
(xi) *A timescale for test and examination improvements will be agreed once initial training is over and pilot classes have been identified*

Timescale:
(i)   Level 1 CSP training - 2 terms
(ii)   Challenges and 'collaborative learning community' by end of session

(vii) *Setting criteria for evaluating the quality of CSP learning and its outcomes - 1 month from initial training*
(viii) *Assessing impact on test and examination results - see **(x)** above*

Diagram 11: The Third Draft of the Sequential Element

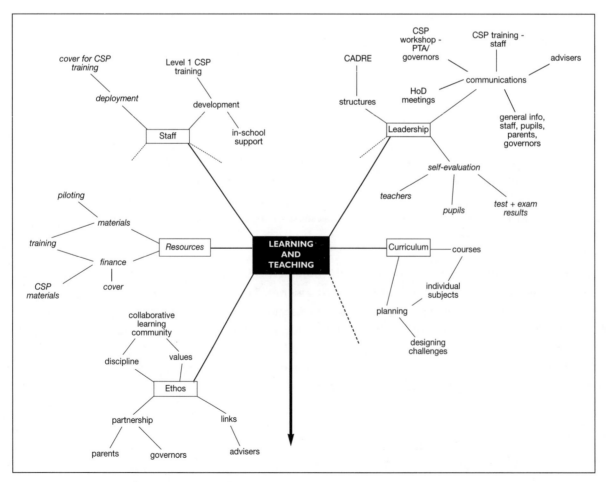

Diagram 12: The Third Draft of the Holistic Element

Note that many important details have only emerged and been added to the action plan as a result of discussions stimulated by the regular transfer of information between the sequential ('left brain') and holistic ('right brain') elements. Therefore, although the initiative is still in its early stages we can already see the potential value of integrating a holistic element into the planning process. By focusing attention on the 'big picture' it constantly reminds staff about the relationships between the developmental activities. Regular, systematic review of this element can provide an effective means of auditing progress and identifying future needs, as well as stimulating creative thinking and helping 'right brain' thinkers to follow the planning process more easily.

The whole brain approach can also help a school deal more effectively with those unexpected events which occur with such irritating regularity! Take, for example, two of Michael Fullan's 'inevitable, unplanned factors' – *'key leaders leave'*; and *'a conflict erupts.'*[*]

* See page 146.

'A key leader leaves.' Suppose that one of the key members of the cadre, an enthusiastic and highly effective head of department, is promoted to deputy head in another school. There are many examples of such a move effectively killing off a promising initiative. In this case, however, the holistic element provides a constant reminder that the permanent priority is on improving classroom learning. Therefore a major criterion in selecting her successor should be relevant experience in learning and teaching innovation - preferably including CSP training - so as to maintain the considerable momentum generated in her department. This is then added to both elements as shown in italics in **Diagrams 13** ('Implementation Strategies': *(xiii)*) and **14** (*Staff - appointments*).

Project:

To improve the quality of classroom learning by implementing the materials and methods of the Critical Skills Programme.

Targets:
(i)   Organize Level 1 CSP training for interested staff
(ii)   Provide effective support to teachers who wish to implement CSP
(iii)   Ensure effective communications with all staff, pupils, parents and governors.
(iv)   Keep LEA advisers/inspectors fully informed and involved in the development of the project.

The criteria for success are:
(i)   All interested staff receive at least Level 1, part A CSP training within 2 terms
(ii)   All CSP trained staff have designed and taught at least two Challenges within 1 term of their initial training

(xi)   At least 70% of the Level 1 teachers go on to Level 2 training within 2 years
(xii)   At least 15% of the Level 1 teachers achieve CSP Practitioner status within 3 years
(xiii) At least 2 teachers achieve CSP Leadership status within 5 years
(xiv)   The school is recognised as a 'Centre of Excellence in Learning' within 4 years

Implementation strategies:
(i)   Cadre members invite applications for training from staff in their link departments
(ii)   Issue discussed with Heads of Department (HoDs)

(xii)   CSP teachers and their pupils organize a workshop evening for the governors, PTA, local politicians and business people
(xiii) Every effort is made to ensure that new teachers in 'CSP' departments are willing and able to undertake CSP training

Timescale:

Diagram 13: A More Advanced Stage of the Sequential Element

---

*Note that the early identification of this partnership as an important communication issue was helped by the process of systematically scanning the basic holistic element at the initial planning meeting.

'A conflict erupts.' Then suppose that the Chair of the School Governors - a high-flying businesswoman who has become strongly supportive of the school's 'Critical Skills' initiative - is also promoted away from the area and is replaced by an abrasive local businessman who is strongly opposed to 'wishy washy liberal ideas about child-centred education'! In this case the initial emphasis which the cadre placed on developing an effective partnership with parents and governors is of considerable value.* They respond to the new challenge by mounting another evening workshop on CSP for parents and governors (**Diagram 13** - 'Implementation Strategies': *(xii)*), to which they also invite local politicians and business people. This time the workshop is run by some of the newly trained teachers and their pupils. The response is so positive that the new governor agrees to give the initiative time to prove its value.

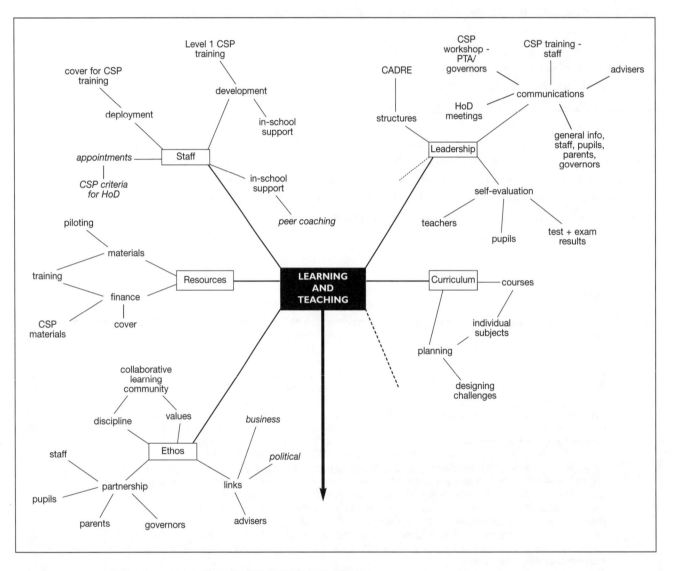

Diagram 14: A More Advanced Stage of the Holistic Element

Diagrams 13 and **14** show what the initiative might look like after several months of development. The important point to note here is that there is no way of predicting all of these details at the beginning of the programme. They will only emerge as a result of the CSP training and subsequent 'action and inquiry where skills, clarity and learning are fostered'. In other words, in a learning school 'vision and strategic planning come later'.

Finally, it must be emphasised again that this example is *not* intended to provide a comprehensive description of a development planning initiative. It has been deliberately simplified in order to highlight the important role that a holistic element can play in development planning in a learning school, by simplifying the audit process, improving communications and encouraging participation and creativity. Therefore in many ways the whole brain approach described here epitomises the observation of Hopkins et. al. that:

'In some ways, involvement in planning activity is more important than producing plans - it is through collective planning that goals emerge, differences can be resolved and a basis for action created. The "plan" is really a by-product from this activity, and will almost always need to be revised, often several times. The benefits of the planning activity, however, will often outlast the currency of the plan.'

Improving the Quality of Education for All, *Hopkins, D, West, M & Ainscow.*
(David Fulton, 1996 - see also page 160)

Appendix 3: References, Recommended Reading and Useful Addresses

References

Argyris, C & Schon, D (1978) *Organizational Learning* Addison Wesley

Barnes, D (1992) *From Communication to Curriculum* (Second Edition) Boynton-Cook

Bennett, N (1992) *Managing Learning in the Primary Classroom* Trentham Books Ltd.

Black, P & Wiliam, D (1998) *Inside the Black Box* King's College London School of Education

Bonney, B (ed) (2000) *A Sampler of Critical Skills Challenges* Leading EDGE, New York

Boyd, B (1997) West Lothian Education Seminar No. 3: *Raising Achievement: Mixed Ability or Setting - Does it Matter?* West Lothian Council

Brown, S (1997) West Lothian Education Seminar No. 1: *School Effectiveness* West Lothian Council

Brown, S (1992) *Raising Standards: Factors Influencing the Effectiveness of Innovations* Scottish Council for Research in Education

Buzan, B & Buzan, T (1995) *The Mind Map Book : Radiant Thinking* BBC Books

Covey, S (1989) *The 7 Habits of Highly Effective People* Simon & Schuster Inc.

Dalin, P & Rolff, H (1993) *Changing the School Culture* Continuum International Publishing Group Ltd.

D'Arcangelo, M (ed) (1998) *The Brain and Learning* (Video Programme) Association for Supervision and Curriculum Development (ASCD)

Dennison, P & Dennison, G (1994) *Brain Gym ®: Revised Teacher's Edition* Edu-Kinesthetics Inc.

DePorter, B & Hernacki, M (1992) *Quantum Learning* Judy Piatkus (Publishers) Ltd.

Dickinson, C (1996) *Effective Learning Activities* Network Educational Press

Dickinson, C (1998) West Lothian Headteachers Conference: *Raising Standards by Improving the Quality of Learning and Teaching: Session 4: 'Issues Arising...'* West Lothian Council

Dillon, J (1994) *Using Discussion in Classrooms* Open University Press

Dillon, J (1988) *Questioning and Teaching: A Manual of Practice* Routledge

Donaldson, M (1978) *Children's Minds* HarperCollins Publishers Ltd.

Farrar, M (1998) West Lothian Headteachers Conference: *Raising Standards by Improving the Quality of Learning and Teaching: Session 2: Creating and Leading a Brain-Based Organization* West Lothian Council

Forbess - Greene, S (1983) *Encyclopedia of Icebreakers* Jossey Bass Inc.

Fullan, M (1993) *Change Forces* Falmer Press

Fullan, M (1991) *The New Meaning of Educational Change* Continuum International Publishing Group Ltd.

Gardner, H (1993) *Frames of Mind* (Second Edition) HarperCollins Publishers Ltd.

Gardner, H (1991) *The Unschooled Mind* HarperCollins Publishers Ltd.

Gould, S (1995) *The Mismeasure of Man* (Revised Edition) Penguin Books Ltd.

Greenfield, S (1997) *The Human Brain* Weidenfeld & Nicolson

Hannaford, C (1995) *Smart Moves* Great Ocean

H M Inspectors of Schools (Scotland) Quality, Standards and Audit Division (1996) *How good is our school? : Self-evaluation using performance indicators* HMSO

H M Inspectors of Schools (Scotland) Quality, Standards and Audit Division (1994) *The Role of School Development Plans in Managing School Effectiveness* HMSO

Holly, P & Southworth, G (1989) *The Developing School* Falmer Press

Hopkins, D, West, M & Ainscow, M (1996) *Improving the Quality of Education for All* David Fulton

Jensen, E (1998) *'How Julie's Brain Learns', Educational Leadership* (Nov.) Association for Supervision and Curriculum Development (ASCD)

Jensen, E (1996) *Completing the Puzzle : A Brain-Based Approach to Learning* The Brain Store

Jensen, E (1995) *Super Teaching* The Brain Store

Joyce, B & Showers, B (1995) *Student Achievement Through Staff Development* (Second Edition) Longman USA

Kolb, D (1984) *Experiential Learning : Experience as the Source of Learning and Development* Prentice-Hall, Inc.

Lincoln, P (1987) *The Learning School* British Library

MacBeath, J (1998) West Lothian Headteachers Conference: *Raising Standards by Improving the Quality of Learning and Teaching: Session 3: Leadership for the Learning School* West Lothian Council

MacBeath, J (1997) West Lothian Education Seminar No. 7: *Raising Standards for All* West Lothian Council

MacGregor, D (1960) *The Human Side of Enterprise* McGraw-Hill

Mobilia, W, et. al. (2000) *The Critical Skills Programme Level 1 Training Manual* Antioch New England Graduate School/Network Educational Press

Mosley, J (1993) *Turn Your School Round* LDA

Murphy , J (1992) *Landscape of Leadership Preparation* Sage

Ornstein, R (1996) *The Right Mind* Harcourt, Brace and Co.

Perkins, D (1995) *Outsmarting IQ* The Free Press

Perkins, D (1992) *Smart Schools* The Free Press

Perkins, D (1998) West Lothian Headteachers Conference: *Raising Standards by Improving the Quality of Learning and Teaching: Session 1: Teaching and Learning for Understanding* West Lothian Council.

Postman, N & Weingartner, C (1969) *Teaching as a Subversive Activity* Pearson Education

Relf, P et.al. (1998) *Best Behaviour* Network Educational Press

Scottish Office Education Department (1999) *Targeting Excellence: Modernising Scotland's Schools* HMSO

Senge, P (1990) *The Fifth Discipline : The Art and Practice of the Learning Organization* Hutchinson

South Gloucestershire Council Advisory Service (1999) *A Guide to School Strategic Planning* South Gloucestershire Council

Smith, A (1996) *Accelerated Learning in the Classroom* Network Educational Press

Sparks, D & Hirsh, S (1997) *A New Vision for Staff Development* Association for Supervision and Curriculum Development (ASCD)

Stigler, J & Hiebert, J (1999) *The Teaching Gap* The Free Press

Sylwester, R (1995) *A Celebration of Neurons: An Educator's Guide to the Human Brain* Association for Supervision and Curriculum Development (ASCD)

Sylwester, R (1998) *'Art for the Brain's Sake', Educational Leadership* (Nov.) Association for Supervision and Curriculum Development (ASCD)

Taylor, M (1999) *Don't Try to Control Everything* New Statesman (15.01.99)

Wiske, M (ed) (1998) *Teaching for Understanding* Jossey Bass Inc.

Recommended Reading

Books with practical ideas for everyday classroom use

Bennett, N (1992) *Managing Learning in the Primary Classroom* ASPE/Trentham, £3.95
30 page booklet which starts with a particularly clear and succinct outline of modern views on the nature of learning for understanding, and then relates these to primary classroom practice.

DePorter, B (1992) *Quantum Learning* Piatkus, £10.99
Contains a number of excercises for identifying styles of learning and thinking, as well as techniques for improving memory, note-taking, reading etc.

Dickinson, C (1996) *Effective Learning Activities* Network Educational Press, £8.95

Relf, P, Hirst, R, Richardson, J & Youndell, G (1998) *Best Behaviour* Network Educational Press, £12.95

Smith, A (1996) *Accelerated Learning in the Classroom* Network Educational Press, £15.95

Smith, A (1998) *Accelerated Learning in Practice* Network Educational Press, £19.95

Smith, A & Call, N (1999) *The Alps Approach* Network Educational Press, £17.95
All the Network books are full of practical ideas for applying sound, up-to-date research on learning and behaviour to classroom practice.

Jensen, E (1995) *SuperTeaching* Turning Point, £21.00

Jensen, E (1996) *Completing the Puzzle* Turning Point, £17.00
Eric Jensen is by some way the most prolific writer on brain-based learning, with a number of best-sellers of which these are probably the most directly helpful to classroom practice. He focuses sharply on the implications of brain research for practice in relation to both learning and behaviour. His books contain lots of ideas for practical classroom action.

Books about specific programmes/techniques

Buzan, T (1995) *The Mind Map Book* BBC Books, £14.99
This is the definitive book on Buzan's mind mapping techniques. Mind Mapping epitomises the whole brain approach to learning and planning advocated in this book. Information on other books and training courses on Mind Mapping is available from Buzan Centres Ltd (see 'Useful Addresses').

Dennison, P & Dennison, G (1994) *Brain Gym ®: Revised Teacher's Edition* Edu-Kinesthetics Inc., £12.99
Contains about 30 different Brain Gym ® exercises with suggestions for their general use in the classroom. There is also a section which identifies specific combinations of activities to help develop reading, writing, spelling, maths, and self-awareness skills. Several other Brain Gym ® publications are available from the Educational Kinesiology Foundation (see 'Useful Addresses').

Mobilia, W et. al. (2000) *The Critical Skills Programme Level 1 Training Manual* Antioch New England Graduate School/Network Educational Press
See Chapter 3 and Appendix 1 for details of this comprehensive, practical and immensely impressive teaching programme. Introductory workshops and training courses are now available in the UK through Network Educational Press (see 'Useful Addresses').

Mosley, J (1993) *Turn Your School Round* LDA , £19.95
The book which describes Circle Time, an effective and extremely popular approach to the whole school development of self esteem (see the margin note on page 132).

Books with more general information - useful for M.Ed study, for example.

Barnes, D (1992) *From Communication to Curriculum* (Second Edition) Heinemann, £18.95
Originally written in 1978 and based on extensive observations of secondary school classroom practice, this is still a powerfully persuasive introduction to the concepts which underpin constructivist learning theory. Now out of print in the UK, this is the American edition which can be obtained through the Anglo American Book Company (see 'Useful Addresses').

Black, P & Wiliam, D (1998) *Inside the Black Box* King's College London School of Education, £2.00
A clear, succinct (20 page) summary of a comprehensive survey of modern research into the relationship between assessment and learning. The authors reach some challenging conclusions in relation to classroom practice, particularly on the role of self- and peer-assessment in promoting learning for understanding.

Diamond, M & Hopson, J (1999) *Magic Trees of the Mind: How to nurture Your Child's Intelligence, Creativity and Healthy Emotions from Birth Through Adolescence* Plume, £11.99
Marian Diamond carried out the original research on cortical development in rats' brains that led to the concept of 'plasticity', i.e. the development of more neural links and networks in stimulating than in impoverished learning environments. This is therefore an authoritative and well written book with a very comprehensive 'Resource Guide' to books, games and other experiences designed to stimulate intellectual and emotional development through all the stages of childhood and adolescence.

Donaldson, M (1978) *Children's Minds* Fontana, £6.99
Published in the same year as Barnes' book, it provides an equally clear and beautifully written account of constuctivist learning theory, focusing on early childhood. Like Barnes, Donaldson's argument is heavily based on Lev Vygotsky's developmental psychology but there is also a particularly clear and concise account of Jean Piaget's Theory of Intellectual Development.

Fullan, M (1993) *Change Forces* Falmer Press, £12.95
Michael Fullan is one of the leading international authorities on school leadership and improvement with a number of best-selling books to his name, of which this is probably the most readable and insightful. It tackles head-on the chaotic nature of the forces of change at all levels of society, and shows why we need a new mind-set for contending with the complexity of dynamic and continuous change. Highly recommended for all senior education managers.

Gardner, H (1993) *Frames of Mind* (Second Edition) Fontana, £8.99
The book in which Howard Gardner originally described his Theory of Multiple Intelligences.

Goleman, D (1996) *Emotional Intelligence* Bloomsbury, £7.99
An engagingly written exploration of the crucial role that emotions play in effective learning.

Greenfield, S (1997) *The Human Brain* Wiedenfeld & Nicolson, £11.99
A highly authoritative account of the most recent ideas on the workings of the brain.

Hannaford, C (1995) *Smart Moves* Great Ocean, £13.50
Relates brain theory to practice very clearly and also has an excellent section on the application of Brain Gym ® techniques in both mainstream and special education. Very highly recommended.

Sylwester, R (1995) *A Celebration of Neurons* Association for Supervision and Curriculum Development (ASCD), £19.00 (£16.00 to members of ASCD - see 'Useful Addresses')
A succinct, highly readable account of the most recent knowledge of the structure and functioning of the brain and its implications for school organization and classroom practice. Sylwester is particularly informative about the role of the emotions in learning.

Useful Addresses

Anglo-American Book Company, The Accelerated Learning Centre, Crown Buildings, Bancyfelin, Carmarthen, SA33 5ND Tel: 01267 211886
Website: www.anglo-american.co.uk E-mail: books@anglo-american.co.uk
Will send regular catalogues of the most up-to-date literature on learning from both sides of the Atlantic. Most of the above titles are obtainable by telephone/post from this source.

Association for Supervision and Curriculum Development (ASCD), 1703 North Beauregard Street, Alexandria, Virginia 22311-1714, USA. Tel: (001) 703 578 9600
Website: www.ascd.org E-mail: member@ascd.org
An annual subsricption of $54 provides for monthly copies of Educational Leadership and various other newsletters as well as regular brochures on their many books, video and audio cassette programmes by respected North American educationists.

Buzan Centres Ltd., 54 Parkstone Road, Poole, Dorset, BH15 2PX Tel: 01202 674676
E-mail: 101737.1141@compuserve.com
For publications and training programmes on Mind Mapping.

Critical Skills Program, Antioch New England Graduate School, 40 Avon Street, Keene, New Hampshire 03431, USA. Tel: (001) 603 357 3122
Website: www.edbydesign.org E-mail: edbydesign@antiochne.edu
Developers and publishers of the Education By Design materials and training courses, now available in the UK as the Critical Skills Programme through Network Educational Press (see below).

Educational Kinesiology (UK) Foundation, 12 Golders Rise, Hendon, London NW4 2HR
Tel: 020 8202 3141 E-mail: ekukf@mccarrol.dircon.co.uk
Supplier of all Brain Gym ® publications in the UK. Organizes conferences and workshops and sends out biannual newsletters. Provides information on local Brain Gym ® trainers throughout the UK.
Educational Kinesiology (US) Foundation, 1575 Spinnaker Drive, Suite 204B, Ventura, CA 93001.

Network Educational Press Ltd., PO Box 635, Stafford, ST16 1BF Tel: 01785 225515
Website: www.networkpress.co.uk
E-mail: enquiries@networkpress.co.uk
UK agent for Critical Skills Programme training and publications. Publishes the School Effectiveness series of books and runs numerous high quality presentations and workshops on learning and teaching issues.

INDEX

Leading the Learning School *is book 15 of The School Effectiveness Series, which focuses on practical and useful ideas for individual schools and teachers. The series addresses the issues of whole school improvement along with new knowledge about teaching and learning, and offers straightforward solutions that teachers can use to make life more rewarding for themselves and those they teach.*

Book 1: *Accelerated Learning in the Classroom* by Alistair Smith
ISBN: 1855390345

- The first book in the UK to apply new knowledge about the brain to classroom practice
- Contains practical methods so teachers can apply accelerated learning theories to their own classrooms
- Aims to increase the pace of learning and deepen understanding
- Includes advice on how to create the ideal environment for learning and how to help learners fulfil their potential
- Full of lively illustrations, diagrams and plans
- Offers practical solutions on improving performance, motivation and understanding
- Contains a checklist of action points for the classroom – 21 ways to improve learning

Book 2: *Effective Learning Activities* by Chris Dickinson
ISBN: 1855390353

- An essential teaching guide which focuses on practical activities to improve learning
- Aims to improve results through effective learning, which will raise achievement, deepen understanding, promote self-esteem and improve motivation
- Includes activities which are designed to promote differentiation and understanding
- Offers advice on how to maximise the use of available – and limited – resources
- Includes activities suitable for GCSE, National Curriculum, Highers, GSVQ and GNVQ
- From the author of the highly acclaimed 'Differentiation: A Practical Handbook of Classroom Strategies'

Book 3: *Effective Heads of Department* by Phil Jones & Nick Sparks
ISBN: 1855390361

- An ideal support for Heads of Department looking to develop necessary management skills
- Contains a range of practical systems and approaches; each of the eight sections ends with a 'checklist for action'
- Designed to develop practice in line with OFSTED expectations and DfEE thinking by monitoring and improving quality
- Addresses issues such as managing resources, leadership, learning, departmental planning and making assessment valuable
- Includes useful information for Senior Managers in schools who are looking to enhance the effectiveness of their Heads of Department

Book 4: *Lessons are for Learning* by Mike Hughes
ISBN: 1855390388

- Brings together the theory of learning with the realities of the classroom environment
- Encourages teachers to reflect on their own classroom practice and challenges them to think about why they teach in the way they do
- Develops a clear picture of what constitutes effective classroom practice
- Offers practical suggestions for activities that bridge the gap between recent developments in the theory of learning and the constraints of classroom teaching
- Ideal for stimulating thought and generating discussion
- Written by a practising teacher who has also worked as a teaching advisor, a PGCE co-ordinator and an OFSTED inspector

Book 5: *Effective Learning in Science* by Paul Denley and Keith Bishop
ISBN: 1855390395

- Looks at planning for effective learning within the context of science
- Encourages discussion about the aims and purposes in teaching science and the role of subject knowledge in effective teaching
- Tackles issues such as planning for effective learning, the use of resources and other relevant management issues
- Offers help in the development of a departmental plan to revise schemes of work, resources and classroom strategies, in order to make learning and teaching more effective
- Ideal for any science department aiming to increase performance and improve results

Book 6: *Raising Boys' Achievement* by Jon Pickering
ISBN: 185539040X

- Addresses the causes of boys' underachievement and offers possible solutions
- Focuses the search for causes and solutions on teachers working in the classrooms
- Looks at examples of good practice in schools to help guide the planning and implementation of strategies to raise achievement
- Offers practical, 'real' solutions along with tried and tested training suggestions
- Ideal as a basis for INSET or as a guide to practical activities for classroom teachers

Book 7: *Effective Provision for Able & Talented Children* by Barry Teare
ISBN: 1-85539-041-8

- Basic theory, necessary procedures and turning theory into practice
- Main methods of identifying the able and talented
- Concerns about achievement and appropriate strategies to raise achievement
- The role of the classroom teacher, monitoring and evaluation techniques
- Practical enrichment activities and appropriate resources

Book 8: *Effective Careers Education & Guidance* by Andrew Edwards and Anthony Barnes
ISBN: 1-85539-045-0

- Strategic planning of the careers programme as part of the wider curriculum
- Practical consideration of managing careers education and guidance
- Practical activities for reflection and personal learning, and case studies where such activities have been used
- Aspects of guidance and counselling involved in helping students to understand their own capabilities and form career plans
- Strategies for reviewing and developing existing practice

Book 9: *Best behaviour and Best behaviour FIRST AID* by
Peter Relf, Rod Hirst, Jan Richardson and Georgina Youdell
ISBN: 1-85539-046-9

- Provides support for those who seek starting points for effective behaviour management, for individual teachers and for middle and senior managers
- Focuses on practical and useful ideas for individual schools and teachers

Best behaviour FIRST AID
ISBN: 1-85539-047-7   (pack of 5 booklets)

- Provides strategies to cope with aggression, defiance and disturbance
- Straightforward action points for self-esteem

Book 10: *The Effective School Governor* by David Marriott
ISBN 1-85539-042-6   (including free audio tape)

- Straightforward guidance on how to fulfil a governor's role and responsibilities
- Develops your personal effectiveness as an individual governor
- Practical support on how to be an effective member of the governing team
- Audio tape for use in car or at home

Book 11: *Improving Personal Effectiveness for Managers in Schools* by James Johnson
ISBN 1-85539-049-3

- An invaluable resource for new and experienced teachers in both primary and secondary schools
- Contains practical strategies for improving leadership and management skills
- Focuses on self-management skills, managing difficult situations, working under pressure, developing confidence, creating a team ethos and communicating effectively

Book 12: *Making Pupil Data Powerful* by Maggie Pringle and Tony Cobb
ISBN 1-85539-052-3

- Shows teachers in primary, middle and secondary schools how to interpret pupils' performance data and how to use it to enhance teaching and learning
- Provides practical advice on analysing performance and learning behaviours, measuring progress, predicting future attainment, setting targets and ensuring continuity and progression
- Explains how to interpret national initiatives on data-analysis, benchmarking and target-setting, and to ensure that these have value in the classroom

Book 13: *Closing the Learning Gap* by Mike Hughes
ISBN 1-85539-051-5

- Helps teachers, departments and schools to close the Learning Gap between what we know about effective learning and what actually goes on in the classroom.
- Encourages teachers to reflect on the ways in which they teach, and to identify and implement strategies for improving their practice.
- Helps teachers to apply recent research findings about the brain and learning.
- Full of practical advice and real, tested strategies for improvement.
- Written by a teacher, for teachers, to stimulate thought and interest 'at a glance'.

Book 14: *Getting Started* by Henry Leibling
ISBN 1-85539-054-X

- Provides invaluable advice for Newly Qualified Teachers (NQTs) during the three-term induction period that comprises their first year of teaching.
- Advice includes strategies on how to get to know the school and the new pupils, how to work with induction tutors, and when to ask for help.

ACCELERATED LEARNING SERIES

General Editor: **Alistair Smith**

Accelerated Learning in Practice by Alistair Smith
ISBN 1-85539-048-5

- The author's second book, which takes Nobel Prize winning brain research into the classroom.
- Structured to help readers access and retain the information necessary to begin to accelerate their own learning and that of the students they teach.
- Contains over 100 learning tools, case studies from 36 schools and an up-to-the-minute resource section
- Includes nine principles of learning based on brain research and the author's seven-stage Accelerated Learning Cycle.

The ALPS Approach: Accelerated Learning in Primary Schools
by Alistair Smith and Nicola Call
ISBN 1-85539-056-6

- Shows how research on how we learn, collected by Alistair Smith, can be used to great effect in the primary classroom.
- Provides practical and accessible examples of strategies used by highly experienced primary teacher Nicola Call, at a school where the SATs results shot up as a consequence.
- Professional, practical and exhilarating resource that gives readers the opportunity to develop the ALPS approach for themselves and for the children in their care.
- The ALPS approach includes: Exceeding expectation, 'Can-do' learning, Positive performance, Target-setting that works, Using review for recall, Preparing for tests ... and much more.

MapWise by Oliver Caviglioli and Ian Harris
ISBN 1-85539-059-0

- Provides informed access to the most powerful accelerated learning technique around – Model Mapping.
- Shows how mapping can be used to address National Curriculum thinking skills requirements for students of any preferred learning style by infusing thinking into subject teaching.
- Describes how mapping can be used to measure and develop intelligence.
- Explains how mapping supports teacher explanation and student understanding.
- Demonstrates how mapping makes planning, teaching and reviewing easier and more effective.
- Written and illustrated to be lively and engaging, practical and supportive.

EDUCATION PERSONNEL MANAGEMENT SERIES

These new Education Personnel Management handbooks will help headteachers, senior managers and governors to manage a broad range of personnel issues.

The Well Teacher – management strategies for beating stress, promoting staff health and reducing absence by Maureen Cooper
ISBN 1-85539-058-2

- Provides straightforward, practical advice on how to deal strategically with staff absenteeism, which can be so expensive in terms of sick pay and supply cover, through proactively promoting staff health.
- Includes suggestions for reducing stress levels in schools.
- Outlines ways in which to deal with individual cases of staff absence.

Managing Challenging People – dealing with staff conduct by Bev Curtis and Maureen Cooper
ISBN 1-85539-057-4

- Deals with managing staff whose conduct gives cause for concern.
- Summarises the employment relationship in schools, as well as those areas of education and employment law relevant to staff discipline.
- Looks at the differences between conduct and capability, and between misconduct and gross misconduct.
- Describes disciplinary and dismissal procedures relating to teaching and non-teaching staff, including headteachers.
- Describes case studies and model procedures, and provides pro-forma letters to help schools with these difficult issues.

Managing Poor Performance – handling staff capability issues
by Bev Curtis and Maureen Cooper
ISBN 1-85539-062-0

- Explains clearly why capability is important in providing an effective and high quality education for pupils.
- Gives advice on how to identify staff with poor performance, and how to help them improve.
- Outlines the legal position and the role of governors in dealing with the difficult issues surrounding poor performance.
- Details the various stages of formal capability procedures and dismissal hearings.
- Describes case studies and model procedures, and provides pro-forma letters.

Managing Allegations Against Staff – personnel and child protection issues in schools
by Maureen Cooper
ISBN 1-85539-069-8

- Provides invaluable advice to headteachers, senior managers and personnel staff on how to deal with the difficult issues arising from accusations made against school employees.
- Shows what schools can do to protect students, while safeguarding employees from the potentially devastating consequences of false allegations.
- Describes real-life case studies.
- Provides a clear outline of the legal background plus a moral code of conduct for staff.

VISIONS OF EDUCATION SERIES

The Unfinished Revolution by John Abbott and Terry Ryan
ISBN 1-85539-064-7

- Draws on evidence from the past to show how shifting attitudes in society and politics have shaped Western education systems.
- Argues that what is now needed is a completely fresh approach, designed around evidence about how children actually learn.
- Describes a vision of an education system based on current research into how our brains work, and designed to encourage the autonomous and inventive thinkers and learners that the 21st century demands.
- Essential reading for anyone involved in education and policy making.

OTHER TITLES FROM NEP

Effective Resources for Able and Talented Children by Barry Teare
ISBN 1-85539-050-7

- A practical sequel to Barry Teare's Effective Provision for Able and Talented Children (see above), which can nevertheless be used entirely independently.
- Contains a wealth of photocopiable resources for able and talented pupils in both the primary and secondary sectors.
- Provides activities designed to inspire, motivate, challenge and stretch able children, encouraging them to enjoy their true potential.
- Resources are organised into National Curriculum areas, such as Literacy, Science and Humanities, each preceded by a commentary outlining key principles and giving general guidance for teachers.

Imagine That... by Stephen Bowkett
ISBN 1-85539-043-4

- Hands-on, user-friendly manual for stimulating creative thinking, talking and writing in the classroom.
- Provides over 100 practical and immediately useable classroom activities and games that can be used in isolation, or in combination, to help meet the requirements and standards of the National Curriculum.
- Explores the nature of creative thinking and how this can be effectively driven through an ethos of positive encouragement, mutual support and celebration of success and achievement.
- Empowers children to learn how to learn.

Self-Intelligence by Stephen Bowkett
ISBN 1-85539-055-8

- Helps explore and develop emotional resourcefulness in teachers and their pupils.
- Aims to help teachers and pupils develop the high-esteem that underpins success in education.

Helping With Reading by Anne Butterworth and Angela White
ISBN 1-85539-044-2

- Includes sections on 'Hearing Children Read', Word Recognition' and 'Phonics'.
- Provides precisely focused, easily implemented follow-up activities for pupils who need extra reinforcement of basic reading skills.
- Provides clear, practical and easily implemented activities that directly relate to the National Curriculum and 'Literacy Hour' group work. Ideas and activities can also be incorporated into Individual Education Plans.
- Aims to address current concerns about reading standards and to provide support for classroom assistants and parents helping with the teaching of reading.

Class Talk by Rosemary Sage
ISBN 1-85539-061-2

- Looks at teacher–student communication and reflects on what is happening in the classroom.
- Looks at how students talk in different classroom situations and evaluates this information in terms of planning children's learning.
- Considers the problems of transmitting meaning to others.
- Discusses and reflects on practical strategies to improve the quality of talking, teaching and learning.

Copyright acknowledgements